As Jew, and non-Jew, sharing a story of hope and resilience in the darkest moments, we dedicate this book to our grandchildren. May they use the lessons of the past to build a better future.

Miracle

www.penguin.co.uk

Miracle

The Boys Who Escaped the
Gas Chamber in Auschwitz

MICHAEL CALVIN

WITH

NAFTALI SCHIFF

bantam

TRANSWORLD PUBLISHERS

UK | USA | Canada | Ireland | Australia
India | New Zealand | South Africa

Transworld is part of the Penguin Random House group of companies
whose addresses can be found at global.penguinrandomhouse.com.

Penguin Random House UK, One Embassy Gardens,
8 Viaduct Gardens, London SW11 7BW

penguin.co.uk

Penguin
Random House
UK

First published in Great Britain in 2026 by Bantam
an imprint of Transworld Publishers

001

Typeset in 12/15.5pt Minion Pro by Six Red Marbles UK, Thetford, Norfolk
Printed and bound in Great Britain by Clays Ltd, Elcograf S.p.A.

The authorized representative in the EEA is Penguin Random House Ireland,
Morrison Chambers, 32 Nassau Street, Dublin D02 YH68.

A CIP catalogue record for this book is available from the British Library.

ISBNS:
9780857507891 (cased)
9780857507907 (tpb)

'There's no survivor who didn't experience
absolute miracles.'

YAAKOV YOSEF WEISS

Contents

Map   x

Introduction: The Sanctity of Memory   xiii

Prologue: Death Foretold   1

  1 The Way They Were   15
  2 The Great Betrayal   30
  3 Journeys to Hell   46
  4 The Valley of Tears   60
  5 The Art of Survival   77
  6 Sixty Years On   90
  7 The First Cut   108
  8 The Football-Pitch Selection   120
  9 Revolt   132
 10 Miracle   143
 11 March or Die   157
 12 Free   171
 13 Second Chances   185
 14 The Banality of Evil   199
 15 Reflections   212

Afterword: The Things We Carry   227

Acknowledgements   235
Picture Acknowledgements   239

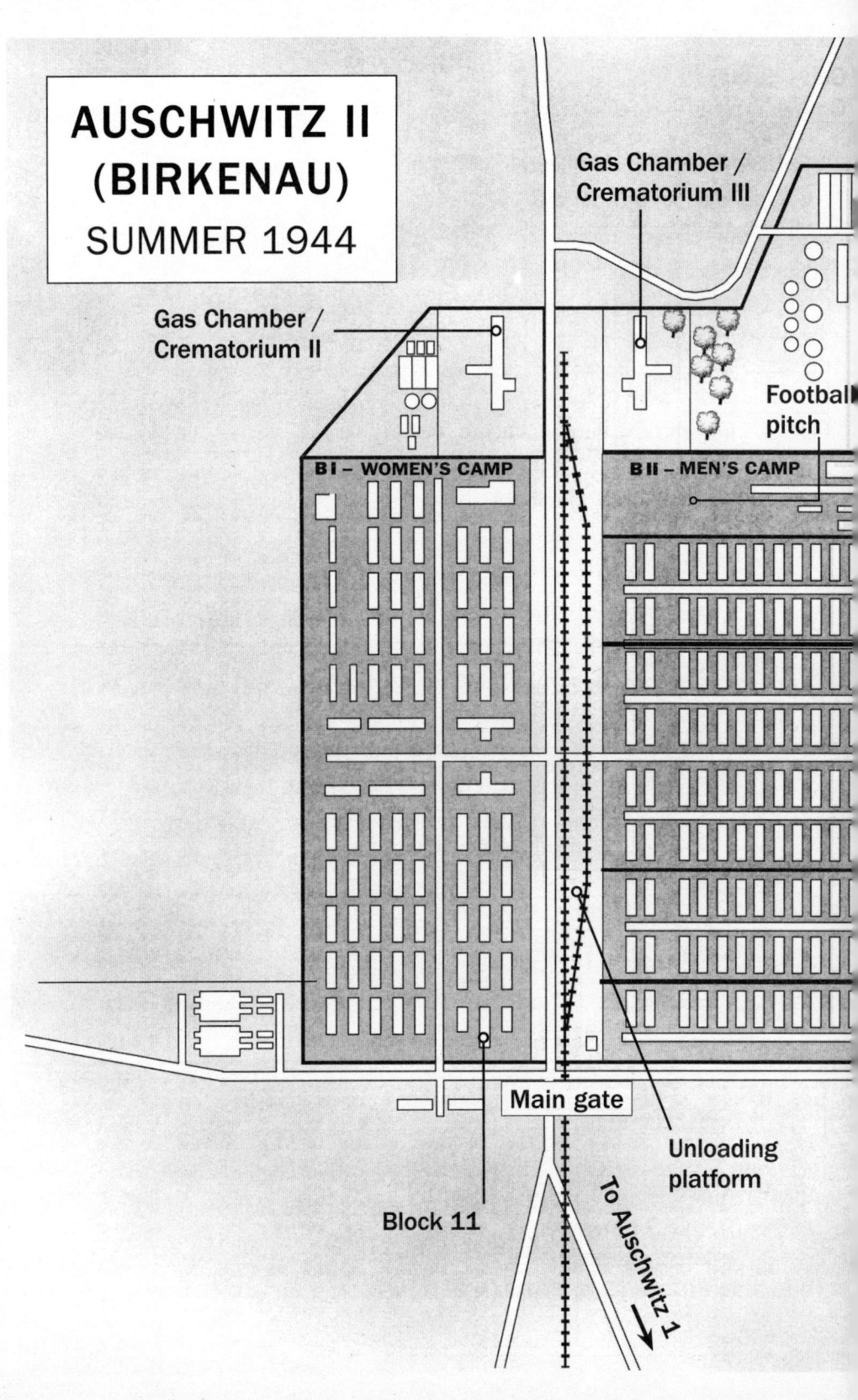

AUSCHWITZ II (BIRKENAU)
SUMMER 1944

Gas Chamber / Crematorium III

Gas Chamber / Crematorium II

Football pitch

B I – WOMEN'S CAMP

B II – MEN'S CAMP

Main gate

Block 11

Unloading platform

To Auschwitz 1

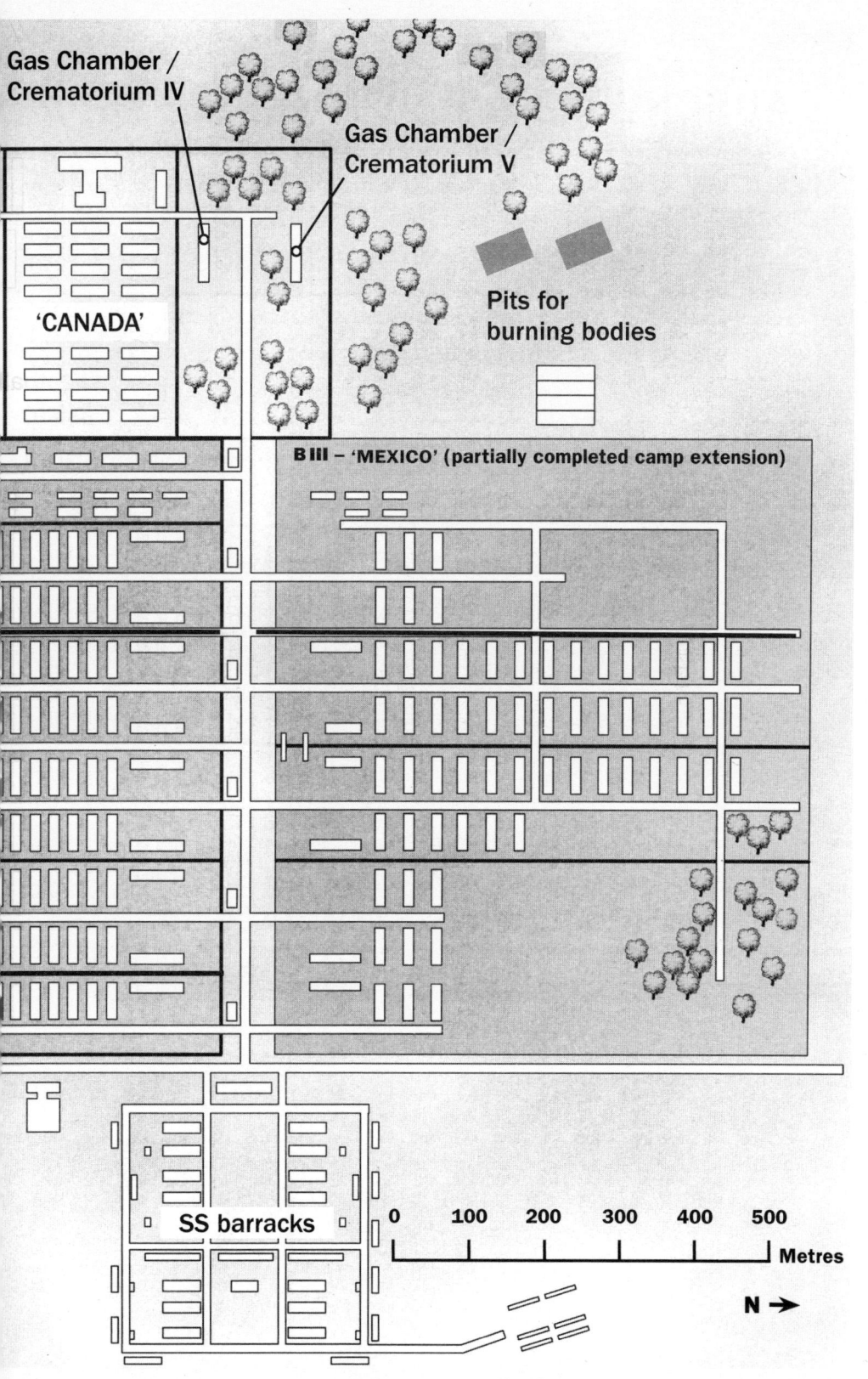

Gas Chamber /
Crematorium IV

Gas Chamber /
Crematorium V

'CANADA'

Pits for
burning bodies

B III – 'MEXICO' (partially completed camp extension)

SS barracks

0   100   200   300   400   500

Metres

N →

INTRODUCTION

The Sanctity of Memory

A BLIND MAN SITS, SUPPORTED by grey cushions, in a bay window on the top floor of his London home, marking time with his left foot as he sings songs of remembrance. Hershel Herskovic is approaching his ninety-eighth birthday, but when he throws his head back, and his face softens into a full-toothed smile, he exudes the spirit of the rebellious, mischievous child he once was.

Naftali Schiff, one of the world's leading collators of Holocaust testimony, leans forward towards him, as if in the old man's gravitational pull. I am to their right, perched on the edge of a two-seater settee, feeding in questions that are answered in a mixture of Yiddish and English, joy and sorrow, reflection and urgency.

On this hot June afternoon in 2024, when the sun, filtered through net curtains, dapples a patterned mustard carpet, and the sound of children at play rises from the street below, we are both aware we are touching history. It has taken Naftali nearly twenty years to reach this point in confirming details of the Holocaust's last great untold story.

He believes Hershel is the only living survivor among fifty-one boys reprieved from the gas chamber at Auschwitz-Birkenau on Simchat Torah, one of the most festive days of the Jewish calendar, which fell on 10 October in 1944. That something so life-affirming, so miraculous, can happen amidst such monumental evil is simultaneously sobering and inspiring. Hershel regards it as providential.

Hungary was the Final Solution's final frontier. Hitler was forced to wait a year before his plans for an extermination campaign there were put into operation between May and July 1944. The Second World War was being lost, yet some 424,000 Hungarian Jews were deported in those months to Auschwitz-Birkenau. A further 140,000 were murdered later in the year. In Budapest thousands were shot on the banks of the Danube and their bodies thrown into the river.

Heinrich Himmler, the principal architect of the Holocaust, set the Auschwitz command structure a minimum target of 5,000 deaths a day, but, though precise figures are hard to come by, it is thought four times that many were killed when the annihilation programme was at its height. Four crematoria operated ceaselessly, and additional bodies were burned in open-air pits.

Eighty years later, in that top-floor room in London, lined with leather-bound books of scriptures, written in braille, Hershel Herskovic would reflect, with a crushing weight of desolation, that 'the Germans were determined that no Jews would be left alive'.

He was one of 800 Hungarian Jews, largely aged between thirteen and seventeen, who were marched to Crematorium 5 by twenty-five bayonet-wielding SS men. They were forced to strip, then herded into the so-called bathhouse in a killing field where around a million Jews, and another 120,000 'undesirables', spent their final moments in unimaginable agony.

Victims simply do not walk off the gallows when the noose is around their neck, yet for the fifty-one boys who would re-emerge this was its equivalent. The *Sonderkommando*, Jewish prisoners who postponed their own execution by disposing of corpses, crushing bones and spreading ashes, had closed the

vents. Dr Josef Mengele, the Angel of Death, was primed to oversee the release of Zyklon B hydrogen-cyanide gas pellets into the
chamber.

The heavy front doors were being closed when three German
officers, including another infamous SS doctor, Heinz Thilo, arrived
on motorbikes, and ordered the evacuation of the chamber. They
selected fifty boys to unload and plant a consignment of potatoes,
which had arrived in the camp's railway sidings from Greece.

They were lined up in rows of five in such haste that the guards
did not notice an additional boy, who had hidden in a pile of discarded clothing before sneaking into the line. They were ordered
to dress quickly; Hershel did so in such a hurry that he selected
two right-footed shoes.

Their doomed companions were driven back into the chamber, to meet their fate. The last words they heard were uttered by
SS-Obersturmführer Johann Schwarzhuber, the officer who oversaw the gassing programme and would later be executed for his
war crimes. One of the reprieved boys, Yaakov Yosef Weiss, never
forgot the venom in his voice: 'Werfen sie in den Ofen' – 'Throw
them into the oven.' One boy chose suicide and threw himself at
the electric fence.

This is a story of contrasts and contradictions, of hope and
horror, of faith, fate and fortitude. It features inhumane cruelty
and human kindness, and begs the question what we, in a subsequent generation, would do with a second chance at life. In an
age of denial and disinformation, the story emphasizes the sanctity of memory.

It is a cross between a morality play and a detective story, and
has, as its centrepiece, the only recorded instance of a group of
Jewish prisoners being removed from a gas chamber and given
the chance to live. Even for someone as well versed in the folklore
of the Holocaust as Naftali, its drama 'hit me full in the face'.

He had initially heard of the legend of the fifty-one in the late 1990s, through one of his earliest contacts among the survivors, Eva 'Bobby' Neumann. She had settled in Manchester and continues to provide a thought-provoking perspective on her experiences in Auschwitz-Birkenau. Nevertheless, Naftali was not specifically seeking to tell their tale.

As a Rabbi, community leader and educator, his principal motivation in taking the testimonies of hundreds of survivors was to provide a link to a younger generation. He sought to influence through the insight of those who had faced the ultimate evil, and who posed a profound question that has renewed relevance in an era of increasing antisemitism.

'It's complicated to be a Jew,' he reasoned. 'The post-Holocaust generation saw that. In the drive for prosperity in the latter half of the twentieth century, many Jews felt they had earned the right to raise a generation in comfort and pleasure, so it was no wonder they lost their religion. They asked, "Where was God in Auschwitz?" I was fascinated to understand why some people who were there, who saw their family and friends murdered, would want to return to their faith, or even to live lives of moral virtue.'

The question is sociological as well as theological. It touches on the essence of humanity, and the importance of heritage. Time is a tyrant; gradually, the voices of the Holocaust are being stilled. It is imperative that they are captured, for future generations, before they are silenced completely.

As a non-Jew, I feel a special sense of responsibility to protect the authenticity of memory. When you sit with these men and women in their twilight years, they have nothing to hide. If they like you, they will tell you. If they feel you are impertinent, or superficial, they will not camouflage their feelings.

I first came across Naftali when he introduced me to Josef Lewkowicz, a survivor of six camps who subsequently hunted down one of the Second World War's great monsters, Amon Göth, commandant of the Płaszów concentration camp. Collaborating on Josef's Holocaust memoir remains one of the most rewarding personal and professional experiences of my life.

I identify with Naftali when he characterizes survivors as the greatest teachers, because of their extreme humanity. They have looked death in the face, and escaped its grasp. They have no fear in living life, and of passing on that freedom to their children, grandchildren and great-grandchildren.

Speaking of whom, the extended families of survivors whose first-hand accounts of endurance are woven through this book total more than 1,000 people. All owe their existence to fate; if those three SS men had arrived on their motorcycles a minute later, they would not exist.

The fifty-one boys were products of an ultra-Orthodox upbringing, and shaped by the inherited disciplines of their faith. We will follow them from childhood, through incarceration and tragedy, to rebirth, adulthood, old age and death. Their lives, long and successful, are elevated from whispers and myths by the diligence of Naftali's research, and his affinity with his subject.

He runs a network of charities from two office blocks in North London. In one, he organizes educational programmes for sixty-five schools and twenty-three universities, including visits to concentration camps by youth groups and trainee leaders. In the other, he oversees outreach work and a study centre.

When I last visited, on a grey late-spring day in 2025, the ground floor was given over to a foodbank that fed 1,700 members of the local community. The first floor was set aside for the study of Jewish texts; while writing this book I often summoned the memory of two young men, their heads inches apart across a small desk as they earnestly discussed the significance and integral meaning of the texts spread out before them.

They were pulling at the threads of their faith, just as we pull at the threads of history. Naftali recentres himself by praying three times a day, but his devotion is neither introspective nor arcane. The values he promotes within his organization – Aspiration, Authenticity, Balance, Care, Humility, Passion, Relevance, Responsibility, Trust and Unity – are universal.

Four of the first six surviving boys he found from the fifty-one – Yaakov Yosef Weiss, Chaim Schwimmer, Wolf Greenwald and David 'Dugo' Leitner – have passed away. Their legacy is a unique series of filmed interviews, detailing their experiences in Auschwitz-Birkenau, and their subsequent life lessons.

Their recollections are augmented by the eyewitness accounts of two more Hungarian Jewish boys who made it out alive, Avigdor Neumann and Yisroel Abelesz, and by the first-hand reflections of Yosef Zalman Kleinman, the youngest of 110 witnesses at the trial of Adolf Eichmann in Jerusalem in 1961.

Kleinman's memories are acute, emotional without being overwrought. He embodied a survivor's innate resilience during the Covid epidemic, when he posed for photographs in the narrow doorway of his apartment in Jerusalem, wearing a prison cap and a striped jacket with his Auschwitz number, 114968, above his heart.

In some instances, he held a photograph of his extended family, to symbolize the promise of the future. In others, he sought to address contemporary concerns with a note that read: 'We will get through this.' Naftali interviewed Kleinman in Israel in August 2020; he passed away, aged ninety-one, in May 2021.

Gathering testimony is not an exact science, since reminiscences are inevitably individualized. When old men tell their tales, recall can be selective, and beauty is invariably in the eye of the beholder. Yet there is a golden thread of authenticity to their reflections, which cannot be denied.

Yaakov Yosef Weiss, who was from Szilágysomlyó, which became known as Șimleu Silvaniei after it passed from Hungarian to Romanian control in 1944, was the first of the fifty-one to be tracked down by Naftali, at his home in Manchester two days before Yom Kippur, the Day of Atonement, in late September 2007.

'Who are you?' a gruff disembodied voice thundered across the intercom, in response to the ringing of his doorbell. 'What do you want?' Naftali, an honours student in the art of thinking fast on his feet, replied that his Rabbi had sent him to seek Weiss out 'because anyone who has a number [an Auschwitz tattoo] and got out of that place with his faith has the power to bestow blessing'.

A tall, imposing figure emerged, framed by the doorway. Yaakov might have been intrigued by the younger man's audacity, but it was not until July 2011 that he agreed to submit to a filmed interview. He had an agile brain and an encyclopaedic knowledge of the scriptures that aided philosophical debate, but he had little fondness for personal projection.

Weiss carried himself with a natural dignity, radiated an indomitable faith, and spoke with convincing clarity in measured, even tones, but it was his physical presence that left a lasting impression. He answered to the nickname of 'Tarzan' and had an unmistakable aura of authority.

A Rabbi, hugely respected in his community, he had a survivor's self-sufficiency, and a painfully acquired perspective. 'In the camp you see who has good character, and who is rotten,' he reflected. 'I have seen millionaires crawling for a piece of bread, and I've seen clever people being diminished to stupidities.'

He passed away, aged eighty-two, on 30 October 2013. It was not until November the following year, in the Jewish communities of New York, that two more of the fifty-one, Wolf Greenwald and Chaim Schwimmer, were discovered, living four blocks from one another in the Borough Park district of Brooklyn.

Despite the profundity of their shared experience, the pair were not especially close. Wolf never attended the annual Seudat Hodoya, a so-called gratitude meal, hosted by Chaim at the Satmar Synagogue on 52nd Street for almost sixty years on the anniversary of their reprieve from the gas chamber. No slight was intended; Wolf's life simply had different priorities.

Wolf had just celebrated his fourteenth birthday when he was transported to Auschwitz-Birkenau from Hajuduhadhaz, a town on Hungary's Northern Great Plain. After liberation, he made it his life's work to nurture future generations. He was revered for his commitment to his community, and spent fifty-five years as an administrator at a religious school in Borough Park.

Many of his twelve children became teachers, ensuring the family's educational legacy. Like most of the fifty-one, he had been driven to honour the values instilled in him by his mother, from whom he was separated on their arrival in Auschwitz. He insisted: 'The best way to teach is by example.'

'My mother would have given the poor the clothes off her back. We were not a rich home, but she would spot a poor man, invite him in, and give him two slices of bread and butter. I never got the chance to say goodbye to her. So many people had their souls marched to the crematorium. It was such a lonely place.'

For Naftali, the dominoes began to fall when Chaim mentioned that his London-based cousin, Hershel Herskovic, was another of the fifty-one. Together with Hershel's younger brother Yisroel, who escaped from the holding pen the night before their intended execution, they came from Munkacs, a commercial crossroads in the Transcarpathian region that typified the turbulence of the times.

The town was part of the Austro-Hungarian Empire until the

end of the First World War, and was subsumed into Czechoslovakia in 1920. The Nazi annexation of the Sudetenland in 1938 led to fascist Hungarians seizing control of Munkacs until 1945, when, as Mukacevo, it became part of western Ukraine.

Perhaps unsurprisingly, the Jewish community was deep rooted and self-supportive. Until Yisroel made his break for freedom, leaping from the roof of their barracks before finding refuge with some Russian prisoners of war, the three boys had been inseparable in the camp. Chaim and Hershel entered the gas chamber together, determined to be as close in death as they were in life.

Hershel subsequently saved Chaim's life on two occasions. Chaim would not have survived an initial death march, following the evacuation of Auschwitz-Birkenau in January 1945, without his cousin placing Chaim's hands into the pockets of his own jacket, and dragging him behind him. Both knew that to stumble would be fatal.

Their ordeal was far from over when they reached Mauthausen concentration camp, where, in freezing temperatures, they lived in tents for two months from the start of February. Chaim was barely clinging to life following a second, gruelling, 60-kilometre march to Gunskirchen, on which around a quarter of the 20,000 prisoners died.

Hershel vividly remembers the pity in the eyes of their American liberators, who arrived in early May: 'Chaim looked so ill. He could no longer walk, and his eyes were bulging. I was so exhausted I couldn't think. They saw us and shook their heads. They obviously didn't think there was any way we could live.'

Chaim takes up the story: 'I got typhus and laid unconscious on the floor of an old hut in the woods for five days when we were liberated. My cousin thought I was about to die and begged the Americans to take me to hospital. They agreed, and nuns looked after me. I was full of lice, which they brushed off with steel rods. After they washed me, I slept for two days. When I woke up, I was a new person. It was a kind of divine intervention.'

Following brief spells in France and England on an orphans' relocation programme immediately after the war, Chaim moved to Montreal. The owner of a successful paper-products company, he spent twenty-nine years in Canada before settling in New York. He had five sons, fifty-three grandchildren and around 200 great-grandchildren when he died, aged ninety-four, in Brooklyn in May 2024.

Survivors tend to be complex, multidimensional characters, because they are products of a complex, multidimensional age. In emotional terms they are often like icebergs; a powerful presence with a hint of the unknown, since much lies beneath the surface.

Hershel is officially known by his mother's family name, Herskovic, but in an interview for Steven Spielberg's Survivors of the Shoah Visual History Foundation, conducted in London in July 1997, he referred to himself as Solomon Taub, his father's family name, which was taken by his younger brother Yisroel.

Such idiosyncrasy was common, in the shifting social, cultural and geopolitical climate in areas like Munkacs. Hershel's parents were married in a religious ceremony, but their union was not officially recognized by the state, because of his father's Galician origins. In such circumstances, families often used the mother's family name.

It would also have been a prudent response to the plight of his father, who was in hiding at the time, because of the dangers of deportation to Poland. Yisroel felt able to take his father's name, Taub, in the brief interlude of optimism in the early phase of the Second World War, when Munkacs moved from Czech to Hungarian control.

For the purposes of this book, we will continue to refer to him as Hershel Herskovic. The twists and turns of the project were borne out soon after I met him when, by chance, I read an article on the Jewish Telegraphic Agency, from October 2011, which led to the discovery that he was not the only living survivor among the fifty-one.

The 'Seeking Kin' column, by Hillell Kuttler, related the story of Mordechai Eldar, who was living in Herzliya, in the central coast area of Israel. He was looking for fellow beneficiaries of the Simchat Torah reprieve, and had made contact with one, Mordechai Linder, just before Linder's death in the summer of 2011.

Eldar met up with another survivor, David 'Dugo' Leitner, but it was not until a follow-up article was published in 2016 that a breakthrough was made. Eldar received two emails in a week; the first was from Isaac Schwimmer, Chaim's grandson, who also mentioned Wolf Greenwald, the grandfather of his wife's brother-in-law.

The second was from Harry Ullman in London. He was a friend of Hershel Herskovic and had also known Yaakov Yosef Weiss. Chaim, Hershel and Wolf all admitted they did not know Eldar, and were unaware of his search, but his recollections, of what he arrestingly called an 'exciting' shared experience, because 'exciting is the only word to describe it', were clear and authentic.

Eldar, too, endured the second death march to Gunskirchen, where, weakened chronically by typhus, he was helped to a refugee camp by his American liberators. He returned briefly to his home town of Campulung La Tisa in Transylvania, where the only survivors of an extended family of fifty were his sisters, Ita and Sarah, and an aunt. He was reunited with his brother, Yehuda, in Germany in January 1946.

The four surviving siblings settled in the new state of Israel. Mordechai, a fervent Zionist, served in the Israel Defence Forces

(IDF) for thirty years, suffering a serious head wound in battle before retiring as a lieutenant general. He subsequently worked in construction and logistics management, and recently had his first great-grandchild.

When I passed on the two relevant articles inspired by his search to Naftali, he checked through his archives and found, to his great surprise, that he had forgotten a filmed interview he had conducted with Eldar in August 2023. It was a relatively simple task to confirm he was still alive, and playing a prominent role in Holocaust education.

His great friend Dugo Leitner, whom Naftali interviewed in Israel in August 2020, was a magnetic individual with a sharp sense of humour and a telling sense of optimism. He was established as a national treasure when he passed away, aged ninety-three, on Tisha Be'Av, the saddest day of the Jewish calendar, in July 2023.

The fondness towards Leitner owed much to his annual ritual of eating falafels on 18 January, the day he set off westwards on the death march from Auschwitz in early 1945. He ate them because they reminded him of the *bilkelach*, the golden-brown dough balls made by his mother, who was gassed within hours of the family's arrival at the camp.

Such was the impact of Leitner's simple act of homage that, by the time of his death, more than 100,000 people around the world, including Israel's President Isaac Herzog, made a point of eating falafels on that day, in his and her honour.

Hope, he was fond of saying, is the greatest gift.

PROLOGUE

Death Foretold

JOSEF MENGELE, THE ANGEL of Death, entered Block 11 in the Auschwitz-Birkenau extermination camp on a cold, wet afternoon in October 1944. He had no need to be there, other than habitual devotion to the minutiae of his murderous task, and a perverted pride in his impact on those he had already condemned.

Eight hundred or so Hungarian boys were crammed into that bare, wooden barracks, which measured 116 by 36 feet. The bunks had been removed following an outbreak of scarlet fever that sent the previous occupants to the gas chambers. The boys were seized by a combination of sheer terror and morbid fascination.

They had not eaten for nearly two days. Many wept or prayed with desperate intensity; some appeared awestruck. In a place of brutally imposed servitude, everything about Mengele, from his haughty demeanour to his black leather overcoat, pristine white gloves and highly polished boots, was designed to intimidate and impress. His presence sucked the air out of the room.

David 'Dugo' Leitner, a fourteen-year-old boy from Nyíregyháza in north-eastern Hungary, thought of him as 'spotless', a handsome man with the aura of a film star. Yisroel Abelesz, another fourteen-year-old boy, from Kapuvar, a small Hungarian town known for its thermal waters, was similarly mesmerized by the sharpness of his uniform, and the arrogance of his demeanour.

As Wolf Greenwald, who was approaching his sixteenth birthday, watched him instruct an underling to perform a headcount, he remembered stumbling off the cattle car at the railhead, and being ordered by an SS officer to take notice of Mengele's fingers.

They moved from the knuckles upwards in a contemptuous flicking motion. The doomed were directed to the left; those reserved for hard labour before they were sent to meet their Maker were pushed to the right. The ritual was hypnotic, theatrical, dehumanizing and deadly.

Given quasi-scientific backing by the Kaiser Wilhelm Institute of Anthropology, Genetics and Eugenics in Berlin, Mengele used these selections to seek out raw material for his research into racial purity. Block 11, the first on the left after the entrance to the camp, had more recently been used as an infirmary but was his original laboratory.

A new numeration system was introduced in the latter half of 1944. Twins, girls aged from two to sixteen, and boys aged seven and eight, were placed in Block 1; their mothers remained in Block 22. Older boys, adult men, the disabled and dwarfs were imprisoned in Block 15.

Pairs of twins, dwarfs and others with ethnically defined or inherited medical conditions were initially examined and photographed. Their toeprints and fingerprints were taken, and plaster casts were made of their mouths, teeth and jaws. They were then killed, with phenol injections in the heart, so autopsies and analysis of internal organs could begin. Mengele personally administered deadly injections of phenol, petrol, chloroform or air.

Block 11 was now being used as a holding pen for those boys about to be taken to the crematoria. For the infamous doctor, who had returned from the Russian front with an Iron Cross and the rank of *SS-Hauptsturmführer*, the boys were a means to an end, in fulfilling a quota of a minimum of 5,000 deaths a day.

They were literally numbers in a ledger, the remnants of between 3,000 and 4,000 Jewish boys who had been transported to Auschwitz-Birkenau from Hungary between 19 May and 9 July that year. The camp, which contained more than 100,000 slave labourers, was full to bursting point.

Chaim Schwimmer captured the mood:

Each time we saw a German we were terrified. You have no idea what fear we lived. We could see that just a few boys were left, they had burned all the rest. By then we were all in Block 23. When we were called for *appel*, we knew the devastation that awaited.

The selection was horrendous. Mengele selected entire rows. He barely glanced at anyone, saying, 'Go, go, go.' As my row was selected to go to the crematorium, darkness fell upon my eyes and I could not see a thing. I had to grab hold of someone else so that I didn't fall down. I knew I was going to die and I no longer stood a chance of survival. It took about ten minutes till I calmed down and we were then driven into the holding block.

Yaakov Yosef Weiss had yet to celebrate his fourteenth birthday, but, having lost his father at the age of nine, he had a maturity beyond his years. Physically strong, despite his youth, he was a thoughtful, observant boy who knew his own mind. Even in such circumstances, those around him recognized the indefinable quality of a natural leader.

He had been one of the first of the boys to realize their fate, typically taking the initiative when Mengele ordered his *Schreiber*, his clerk, to process each inmate's camp identity card before they were incarcerated in Block 11. 'Ich bin Weiss,' he said, with as much defiance as he could muster when he approached the table.

He stared hard at the functionary and could not believe the evidence of his own eyes. The card was perfunctorily stamped with a single German word, *gestorben*. Weiss recoiled in recognition. He knew the essence of the language because Yiddish is derived from it.

It meant died, or dead.

Weiss, like everyone herded into Block 11, was a living ghost. He paid particular attention to the headcount, peering into the long, thin book that contained details of each block's human cargo. Once the numbers had been calculated, the functionary took a pen and drew a line across the page detailing the boys' barracks.

In the bureaucracy of mass murder, the occupants had ceased to exist.

'We are finished, now,' Weiss thought to himself. 'We have been crossed off the list of the living.' To reiterate the point, they were being denied even the basics of bread and water. The date of their execution, the following day, Tuesday, 10 October 1944, had been set.

***

Their deaths would be an everyday obscenity, obscured by the scale and strategic priorities of the Second World War, which was being fought on several different levels. On that day, 10 October, British Prime Minister Winston Churchill was in Moscow, confirming the Soviet Union's entry into the war against Japan, and dividing up the Balkans with Joseph Stalin. Canadian troops were engaged in bloody fighting as part of the Battle of the Scheldt, which eventually opened up the port of Antwerp. This was critical to the Allied advance into Germany the following year.

In Amsterdam the Nazi occupiers, fearful of the Allied advance and their own creeping lack of civic control following a strike of 30,000 railway workers in September, which was designed to disrupt German troop movements, cut off the electricity. In Auschwitz, the days were measured in what the prisoners grimly called the Goebbels calendar, after Joseph Goebbels, the Nazis' chief propagandist.

In an attempt to break their spirit, and underline the Nazis' contempt for a cultural and religious bond built up over generations, the biggest, most symbolic, mass exterminations were deliberately set for Jewish high days and holidays. Around 1,200 of the Hungarian boys were sent to the gas chambers on Rosh Hashanah, the Jewish New Year; a similar number were slaughtered ten days later on Yom Kippur, the Day of Atonement.

Simchat Torah, a traditional time of joy, renewal and resilience, fell on 10 October that year. It marks the end of an annual cycle of readings from the Torah, a combination of the first five books of the Hebrew Bible, and is celebrated by dancing in circles and a collective reinvigoration of faith.

***

The boys came from religious backgrounds, and relied upon a bush telegraph of fellow believers to follow the Jewish calendar. Some traded precious pieces of bread for stolen prayer books, which were hidden in the barracks, or even sewn into the seams of their striped uniform.

These prayer books had been acquired from inmates who sifted through belongings discarded on disembarkation, or in the disrobing room that led to the death trap of a communal shower area, where the doors were locked, and the Zyklon B pellets were usually dropped through the roof. On contact with air, hydrogen-cyanide gas was released, suffocating the occupants.

The boys lived within the daily restraints of their mortality. Time meant little in Auschwitz, but also meant everything because they assumed it was borrowed. Realities had been reshaped the moment they were separated from grandparents, parents and siblings in the tragic chaos of the railway ramp, and watched them melt into the crowds being herded towards the killing zone.

Mengele oversaw at least seventy-four of those selections, and made an indelible impression. It was understandable, then, that his departure from the barracks, that afternoon, prompted a frenzied response. The boys' terror, suppressed in his presence, was unleashed. Wailing gathered in volume and force.

In the maelstrom of emotion, some boys sought refuge in the rituals of their religion. They tearfully made *Vidui*, a confessional prayer said by the dying. This is a form of spiritual accounting, of the soul being returned to God. It was the most profound recognition that an individual's life or death was in God's hands. Others did laps of the inside of the barracks as if they were performing *Hakafot*, the traditional circular dance. Chaim Schwimmer recalled: 'We all knew we would be killed and we discussed meeting our mothers and fathers again. I started praying in anguish. You could have collected five glasses of my tears.'

Chaim summoned his father's words, first heard at the start of the war, when he was ten years old: 'Believe in the Shepherd and nothing evil will affect you.' Despite his despair, he was, however, among those unwilling to meekly accept their fate.

Together with Hershel Herskovic, his cousin, and Yisroel Taub, Hershel's younger brother, they joined a group plotting to escape through an air vent. A Transylvanian boy, Sruli Salmanovitch, volunteered to be the first to scale a central strut, and managed to open the vent and scramble out on to the roof.

Several boys joined him and negotiated the twenty-foot drop before running into the shadows on a dark night with low, scudding clouds. Hershel and Chaim followed, but were immediately recaptured because troops from the nearby guardhouse raised the alarm.

For the Nazis, this had unintended consequences, because as troops rushed into Block 11 to impose order, another group of boys surged past them and fled out of the back door. These opportunists included 'Dugo' Leitner, Nachum Hoch and Mordechai Eldar, a resourceful boy who had survived the Rosh Hashanah and Yom Kippur selections by escaping through a window and hiding in the latrines.

Leitner was quickly pounced upon by three guards as he dived under the wooden block. 'The three of them gripped me, as if with pincers,' he recounted later. 'They were big and strong and I was just a boy who hadn't eaten in a long time. I went wild. We were hunted down like rats.'

At first light, Hoch, a boy from an Orthodox Jewish family in Borsa, Transylvania, and Eldar were discovered, and bullied back into the barracks that acted as a holding cell. In such a febrile atmosphere, created by the *Sonderkommando* revolt that led to crematoria being destroyed two days earlier, they could just as easily have been summarily executed.

Yisroel Taub and Yisroel Abelesz were among a handful of the boys who managed to remain as fugitives until the danger had passed. Max Steinmetz, another sixteen-year-old from Transylvania, was 'gripped by horror and scared to death' at the sight of Mengele, whom he described as 'an evil man who was not satisfied with the blood of the holy Jews he shed each day'.

He carried with him the terrible image of his first meeting with Mengele at Auschwitz, after a ninety-hour journey by cattle car, in which half of those travelling had died. The doctor was wielding a two-metre-long leather switch and had the hint of a smile while SS guards prevented Max from saying goodbye to his

parents, Ilona and Louis, and his sister Esther, who were immediately sent to the gas chamber.

Max was tall for his age, a little over six feet in height, and agile.
He gambled his life on fleeing to the barracks containing the
Sonderkommando, the legion of the damned who did the worst
jobs in the crematoria. The barracks was not normally searched,
so he climbed on to a bunk, and covered himself with a blanket
while the guards were distracted by a Ukrainian kapo chasing a
poor unfortunate who had stolen a potato from the kitchen.

Avigdor Neumann, a thirteen-year-old from Nagyszőlős,
which is now in western Ukraine, was another to take advantage of the chaos. Unlike Dugo, he hid successfully beneath and
between buildings until morning roll call, where he was able
to secrete himself in a group of around 200 Hungarian boys in
Block 13. It was only on joining them that he learned that his new
companions had been slated for a second wave of executions later
that day. He was trapped.

It had been a long, terrible night. Chaim Schwimmer cried
himself into a fitful sleep but by 8 a.m. he was weeping again,
while praying loudly and passionately, as if consumed by the cruelty of his fate. He was not alone; Yaakov Yosef Weiss struggled to
find words to describe the desolation of the scene.

Despite his youth, Yaakov showed immense self-control, and
awareness of the human dramas being played out around him.
Having been brought up with a strong sense of morality, duty and
practicality, he found himself challenging the few adult inmates
in Block 11, who were preoccupied with shaving before being sent
to the gas chamber.

For someone as self-possessed and devout as Yaakov, this was
a perplexing sense of priority. 'Are you mad?' he exclaimed. 'You
are going to be gassed. What do you want to shave for? You must
be completely out of your minds. We do not have the facilities,

in any case. Say *Vidui*, make your peace. At least before you die admit that you are dying like a true Jew.'

He accepted he had put himself in an exposed position. The best explanation he could find for his premature maturity lay in the Hebrew word *tzoris*, which directly translated means hardship, trouble and distress. It speaks to the educational aspects of struggle and worry.

Yaakov had been shaped by the disciplines of his childhood, and the founding principles of his religion. He was driven by a higher purpose, in serving God's will 'from the depth of your heart'. He took strength from the truths he had been taught, and consciously worked on his *middot*, his character traits, values and virtues.

He felt fortunate that, unlike in the two previous mass executions of the Hungarian boys, they had not been roused in the middle of the night and taken to their deaths in a fleet of lorries. It was only a short journey to the crematoria, a matter of a couple of hundred metres, but in those cases the Nazis took the precaution of operating under the cover of darkness.

A strange mood settled on Block 11 that morning. More of the boys retreated into themselves, leaning against the walls and praying quietly rather than vocally succumbing to despair. Others began to sing familiar religious verses, such as that which asked God to 'purify our hearts to worship You in truth'. It was as if resignation had bred renewed defiance.

This was tested to the full when guards arrived with what was intended to be a reassuring gesture, a last meal of potatoes. The boys were ravenous, not having eaten for more than forty-eight hours, but threw the potatoes on the floor to demonstrate their contempt for their captors. It was only when the Nazis had left that they fell on the food.

Everyone was waiting for the summons that finally came at noon, when SS men burst in screaming, 'Raus, raus', an order amplified by indiscriminate use of whips and sticks. Before the boys could be bundled out of the barracks, and positioned between two lines of around twenty-five armed SS men and their dogs, there was time for one final rebellious act.

Aware they would never return, the boys quickly discarded anything that could be of use to those they left behind. Spoons, forks and small knives, invaluable commodities to surviving inmates, were dropped on to the floor or the walkway between the barracks. As Yaakov Yosef Weiss rationalized to himself: 'What need would I have of such things in the gas chamber?'

The rain was torrential and the noise was infernal, but to Yaakov's surprise he found that he had not entirely given up hope. As the boys paused for several minutes before the main gate, while the column was bullied into some sort of marching order, he realized they had reached another moment of truth.

He thought he had prepared himself for the inevitable left turn that would take them along the thirteen-foot-high electrified perimeter fence, down a pathway between camps, and into the crematoria, where the square, stark smokestack belched its ceaseless contents, burned human flesh.

Yet just for a moment he looked out, towards the right of the gate, and fantasized about salvation. That way led to the original Auschwitz camp, where gangs of slave labourers were sent to work. What if the SS had had a change of heart, a gap they needed to fill, or a job, however filthy or degrading, they needed done? Maybe, just maybe, they would turn right and be reprieved . . .

The column turned left.

Max Steinmetz heard the commotion and looked out through a crack in the wooden wall of his refuge in the *Sonderkommando* quarters. When the column had passed, he emerged from his hiding place, and walked around the camp in a daze before he met another boy, who had managed to stay safe.

Max survived the war. He was transported from Auschwitz-Birkenau to Dachau, and then on to the sub-camps of Kaufering and Landsberg, where he was forced to build roads and work in a Messerschmitt aircraft factory. However, his brother Henry, his constant companion, died of starvation in Landsberg on 4 February 1945.

Max was himself skeletal, weighing barely eighty pounds when, ten days before liberation, he was marched into the Tyrolean Alps to dig fortification trenches. Though sick, and suffering hallucinations, he managed to escape, and threw himself on the mercy of the wife of an SS officer, who took him into a sequestered farmhouse, fed him, and gave him his first bath in three years.

Freed by American soldiers on 2 May, he spent four years in a Displaced Persons camp before successfully applying for a US visa. He worked in the ship's kitchen to pay for his transatlantic passage, and found a labouring job in New York that paid twenty-four cents an hour. He moved to Birmingham, Alabama, in 1955 and became a shoe salesman.

He had three children and six grandchildren, and was ninety-six when he passed away 'peacefully, after a brief illness' on 4 March 2021. It took him fifty years to decide to tell his story, and he would never forget the searing sight of the boys being swept towards their fate.

He recorded the moment for posterity: 'I looked outside to see what was happening. A dreadful, terrible sight appeared before my eyes. The wretched boys were being led on foot under heavy guard. This time the evildoers didn't bother bringing a truck. They led them to their death like sheep to the slaughter. May God avenge their blood. Life was as hard and bitter as wormwood.'

The image of the boys, soaked scraps of humanity, had a profound impact on even someone as hardened to death and depravity as Dayan Leib Langfuss, a member of the *Sonderkom-mando* whose hidden diary, unearthed by leading Israeli historian Esther Farbstein, recorded his feelings:

> The Jewish boys dressed in long striped uniforms, light and torn. They wore shoes or wooden clogs on their feet. The children were so beautiful, well-formed and seeming to shine in their rags. Their soft and pure voices became bitter and heavy from moment to moment.
>
> The loud crying began to echo into the distance; everyone was stunned and carried away by this desperate mourning. With a satisfied smile, with no trace of mercy, and with victorious pride, the SS rushed the children into the bunker with cruel blows until they had taken control of the situation. They were unimaginably happy. Were none of them ever fathers of children?

The boys were forced into the disrobing room to the right of the ground-floor entrance to Crematorium 5, which resembled a bathhouse. They were ordered to hang their clothes on nails in the wall; each had a serial number which the guards insisted they remember so they could find them again following a shower.

Contemptuous of such an obvious ruse, the boys refused to undress, only doing so when SS troops entered and started firing at the ceiling. The boys threw their clothes in the middle of the room, and waited for several hours, naked, to be taken to the gas chamber across the hall. As they did so, they were approached by a member of the *Sonderkommando,* a small Polish Jew who had somehow survived for nearly four years. 'Sing, fellows, sing,' he murmured. 'Don't show them that you are afraid.'

Some were too petrified to even speak, but small groups of boys began to gather in dancing circles, singing the songs they learned in the synagogue. A good number of voices were unbroken: 'The Master of the Universe is with us. Let us dance with him.' This so outraged *SS-Obersturmführer* Johann Schwarzhuber, the officer with overall responsibility for the gassing programme, that he threatened to take them to a place of torture, where they would die an even slower death.

It was a transparently empty threat, but in those terrible moments each boy was making peace with himself. Yaakov Yosef Weiss stood next to someone he barely knew, but started talking to him about his father's stories of God saving the Jews at the last minute. 'We still have hope,' he told him. 'He can help. We can be saved.'

His companion, an older boy of about sixteen, looked at him sourly and said: 'Don't you know where you are?' Yaakov remained calm, but moved away: 'I know I am going to die,' he said. 'But God does what He wants. I am in His hands.'

Mordechai Eldar lost his faith in Auschwitz. He refused to pray to a God he felt had deserted him. Instead, he began to weep wildly, and speak to his dead mother. That meant more to him than any prayer. He saw his mother's soft face in his imagination. On the second time she appeared she had tears running down her cheeks.

'I'm on my way to you,' he exclaimed. Seeing his companions stare, Mordechai felt embarrassed, but he had reached the point of surrender. He was more scared of additional beatings than imminent death, so he pushed open the door to the gas chamber, and peered into the darkness.

Even then, there was one more formality to observe. Each boy had to salute at the entrance to the chamber, which they entered in lines of five. Yaakob Yosef Weiss worked his way forward to ensure he was in the first line. He thought of the Rabbi who preached 'let me not see the death of my friend', a reference to a principle first established during the persecution of Jews by the Romans, and wanted to die with a clear conscience, with his beliefs intact.

Hershel Herskovic entered the chamber with his cousin Chaim Schwimmer. He had a strange surge of adrenaline, and, drawing sudden strength, continued to shout the Talmudic diktat: 'Even when the sharp sword of death is on your throat, you should not despair of mercy. Never give up hope.'

Outside, well-rehearsed execution routines were underway. According to Charles Bendel, a Romanian doctor responsible for the medical care of staff in the killing zone, the cylindrical tins of Zyklon B, around fifty centimetres tall and thirty centimetres in circumference, arrived in a truck with deceptive Red Cross markings five minutes after the boys entered the disrobing room.

One tin was enough to kill the 800 or so boys in the gas chamber, which measured six metres by three metres and was only 1.5 metres in height, within three to five minutes. Unlike other, older crematoria, where the blue-grey pellets were pushed in through vents in the roof, the poison was pushed through small windows set in the wall.

It was just another day in the life of Josef Mengele, who oversaw the extermination programmes in Crematoria 4 and 5. The boys would soon be off his hands. Preparations were complete, and the heavy front doors of the gas chamber began to close, snuffing out the last of the light.

Eternal darkness was about to descend.

ONE

The Way They Were

THE BOYS LIVED AND DIED in the crucible of history. In a region continually reshaped by prejudice, political expedience, military ambition and nationalist fervour, their home towns and villages were ruled by a succession of nations and regimes. Cherished cultural traditions, developed over hundreds of years, were eroded and destroyed in a matter of months.

Hungarian land, coveted by the Romanians, Czechs, Austrians, Serbs, Croats and Italians, had been regarded as the spoils of war ever since the Treaty of Trianon in June 1920. This ceded 71 per cent of Hungary's territory, resulting in the loss of a similar percentage of the population.

Resentment, allied to opportunism, led the Hungarian government to establish an alliance with Nazi Germany. Once Austria and Czechoslovakia had been annexed in 1938, the Hungarians regained land lost after the First World War. The rise of localized fascism resulted in them joining the Axis Alliance in November 1940.

People across Europe under German occupation faced stark choices between resistance, acquiescence or collaboration. The Nazis had swept across Southern and Western Europe by 1941, and portentously, set up an eastern front through the invasion of the Soviet Union that summer.

***

The momentum of the war had shifted irreversibly by 1943, leaving the Hungarian boys and their families dangerously exposed. Their way of life was under existential threat, as never before, despite the strategic importance of towns like Munkacs, which had enviable transport links via rail, road and river.

Chaim Schwimmer's father had moved there as a young man from Adorf, a picturesque municipality in the Elster Mountains on the German-Czech border that became part of East Germany in 1949 until reunification in 1990. A deeply religious man, he became a prominent figure in a Jewish community that followed Hasidic customs and practices.

He passed on the value of education, and his devotion to the literal translation of the Torah, to his four daughters and two sons. He took pride in Munkacs having the region's largest Jewish population in 1941, some 13,488 people, nearly 43 per cent of the town's residents. The first Jewish settlers had arrived in the latter half of the seventeenth century, and obtained government leases to sell meat, candles and soap. In addition, they transported wood to the port of Danzig.

In 1741 the town's first synagogue was built to meet the spiritual needs of a settlement of some eighty Jews. A charitable Jewish hospital was established in 1846, and, despite the objections of some of the more fundamentalist rabbis, a Jewish school offering general education in three classrooms was set up in 1866.

The following year Jews were granted equal rights, a concession immediately weakened by official efforts to restrict business permits. Fuelled by prejudice, envy and mistrust, this would be a portent of things to come. In the eyes of the authorities, some Jews, usually the most wealthy, were more equal than others; in 1900 only 550 of them, less than 10 per cent of the Jewish population in Munkacs, were permitted to vote.

Economic disparities defined an increasingly impoverished community, which took to selling seats in the synagogue and the *mikavot,* the ritual baths, to raise funds. Voluntary organizations, both religious and secular, came to the fore in the 1930s, providing healthcare and helping to counter widespread hunger. The Budapest elite scorned Munkacs as an insignificant backwater.

Despite high unemployment, an obvious contributor to poverty in the region, the Jews were still a convenient scapegoat. Chaim Kugel, director of a local Jewish high school, the Hebrew Gymnasium, who became a delegate to the Czechoslovak parliament, brought the prejudice to national attention during a debate in 1935.

'It is completely impossible to adequately describe the poverty in the area,' he said. 'The Jews are affected equally along with the rest. I strongly wish to protest any attempt to blame the poverty of the peasantry on them.' His defiance fell on deaf ears; the authorities routinely denied Jews good jobs in the civil service, and imposed high taxes.

The Schwimmer family were better off than most. Chaim's father owned a successful textile store, supplied principally by his eldest daughter, who made weekly visits to her contacts in textile mills in Budapest to source the best cloth and the latest designs. Competition was fierce, and the family often had to deal with petty thieves, who ran off with the goods after making the pretence of studying the fabric in the daylight.

As a man who adhered to strict moral standards, the father detested such dishonesty. He refused to lie and insisted that his wife, Chaim's mother Yachet, did not take the short cuts common to other outlets, such as increasing the profit margin by subtly stretching the material as it was being prepared for sale.

The Sabbath, signalled by Yachet lighting candles, was scrupulously observed. She too was devout; her name, based on that of Jochebed, the mother of Moses, was uncommon and its derivation was linked to prayer and spiritual purity. She would prepare fish specialities and *cholent*, a savoury slow-cooked stew consisting of meat, potatoes and beans.

All stores in the area were closed on the Sabbath. The streets were initially quiet, but after services had been completed they came alive with the processional traditions of the holy day. In a time-honoured scene, men wore *streimels*, Hasidic fur hats, and had *tallesim*, prayer shawls, draped across their shoulders. Women wore their best dresses, and freshly scrubbed children wore special outfits.

It was a day for song, dance and storytelling. Chaim was entranced by his father's tales of Dovid Hamelech, the shepherd boy who became the second king of Israel after slaying Goliath, the Philistine giant, with a rock and a slingshot. He was the all-action hero that all boys love, the warrior who conquered Jerusalem.

In the context of a world careering towards another global conflict, the lessons of his character were driven home. The Schwimmer children were brought up on Tehillim, the Psalms, the first book in the section of the Hebrew Bible known as Writings. This contains 150 poems attributed to King David, together with songs of praise to the Almighty, and reflections about personal and collective hardship and hope.

King David, or Dovid as he is also known, is a towering historical figure who has come to symbolize Jewish resilience and moral certainty. Chaim's father used the story of his advocacy, in seeking justice for a helpless widow in the biblical court of Shaul

Hamelech, to pass on the importance of taking responsibility for others, and fighting for truth.

He believed in rigorous study and regular reading. The largest local *batei midrash*, a traditional study hall, contained around 6,000 books, and displayed newspapers, written in Yiddish, which featured town politics and the latest developments in Mandatory Palestine. Stories of the persecution that marked the Nazis' rise to power in Germany had an ominous relevance.

Chaim's cousin Hershel Herskovic, the third of eleven children, was taken to the synagogue as soon as he could walk. His father owned a water-driven flour mill, around eight kilometres from Munkacs, returning home every second night. Friday-night meals were long, languid affairs; Hershel described the atmosphere as 'intimate, which gave us joy'.

Despite darkening clouds politically, the summers were long and gentle. Boys played in and around the Latorica river, a wide, gently meandering watershed of the Danube. They picked apples, legally and illegally. This suited perfectly Hershel's rebellious, rumbustious character.

He took childish delight in the jeopardy of invading a neighbour's garden, to steal nuts from their walnut tree. They began lying in wait for him, but Hershel was so agile and quick-witted that he would make his escape by leaping over a boundary fence. Unsurprisingly, he grew up as a free-spirited soul and developed a distaste for the status quo.

This was to manifest itself in Auschwitz-Birkenau, where Hershel was one of the rare boys not terrified of Josef Mengele. His rash refusal to be intimidated by the SS doctor's murderous reputation led him to accept a bet from another inmate, Mordechai Rimer, for a scrap of bread, that he would not have the nerve to approach Mengele with a complaint that a Polish kapo had stolen food from prisoners, and given it to his compatriots.

When he did so, airing his grievance in rudimentary German, Mengele sensed his tension. 'Was zagen Sie?' he asked ('What are you afraid of?'), but he was clearly disinterested. He promised politely to look into it, but with such lack of conviction that Hershel looked back on that as the moment he realized they were all going to die.

More immediately he was certain the kapo would take violent revenge. Hershel had, after all, seen him in a frenzy, kicking an inmate to death. He was not afraid of dying, and reasoned that whatever happiness he had experienced until that point of inevitability would have to come from within. Remarkably, the Pole kept his distance. It seemed he was more scared of Mengele than angry with the boy who had attempted to turn him in.

Dugo Leitner was a similarly free-spirited boy, one of six children of a Hasidic family from Nyíregyháza, in north-eastern Hungary. He was bright, and had an inquisitive mind, but chafed against the conventions of his *chader*, the elementary Jewish school in which children, from the age of five, were taught Hebrew.

Pupils were expected to read aloud from the Torah and other such books as the Mishnah and Talmud, learning passages by heart. Dugo lacked concentration, a fault that tended to be answered by a flick of the teacher's cane. 'Why do I have to go every day?' he would complain to his mother.

The logic of her reply – 'Well, Dugo, it's the same as eating every day. You have to do that, don't you?' – was inescapable, but it failed to keep him out of trouble. One day, at the age of nine, he was supposed to be studying a collection of rabbinical debates. Instead he was idly thinking of his mother's cooking.

A male teacher stole up behind him, heard him mumbling about watching her in the kitchen, grinding dried peppers to form paprika, one of his favourite spices, and lunged at him, intending to administer a beating. Dugo had his eyes closed, but was alerted by the sudden rush of movement.

He was agile enough to evade the teacher's grasp and ran around the wooden benches in the first-floor classroom, where the forty other boys, grateful for the respite from their academic chores and equally afraid of regular beatings, were captivated by the subsequent chase. The teacher interrupted his pursuit by taking the precaution of locking the door, closing off Dugo's main escape route.

'David,' he shouted. 'Those who do not learn will end up in Hell.' No one, least of all the teacher, reckoned on the boy's response – a sudden leap through the window. Dugo fell around fifteen feet, but was sufficiently nimble to avoid significant injury, other than scuffed knees. He ran away, to the warmth and certainty of his home.

He was a cheeky boy, capable of turning on the charm in an instant. He answered his parents' disapproval with a disarming smile, defusing tensions by offering to do household chores. He was happy learning at home; his father Meir, who preached the virtues of charity, recognized that the impulsive sprite had a kind heart, particularly in the way he approached those less fortunate than himself.

Feudal landowners in their town of Nyíregyháza, situated some 240 kilometres east of Budapest on the northern edge of the Great Hungarian Plain, did not allow Jews to settle within the town limits until 1840. The Jewish population grew from sixty in 1850 to 4,993 in 1941, a fraction under 10 per cent of the general population.

It was fertile agricultural country, known for its fruit trees, but suffered from the fallout from the First World War. Nyíregyháza remained under Romanian occupation for ten months during the subsequent war with Hungary, which lasted from November 1918 to August 1919.

The Orthodox Jewish community was self-contained and ben-efited, initially at least, from a fragile attitude of toleration. They contributed to the economic success of the region in the 1930s, when merchants joined an emerging middle class, but cultural and political ties were loose and perplexing.

Mordechai Eldar was born on 29 October 1929, into one of eighty-four Jewish families who lived in Campulung La Tisa. The village lay on the left bank of the River Tisza, on the border between Transylvania and Ukraine, some 15 kilometres north-west of the largest city in the region, Sighet. Only two of the families were secular Jews; one of them, the Kleins, ran the local factory.

His father Moses had served in the Austro-Hungarian Army during the First World War, and ate only bread and potatoes so that he would remain kosher. He married Tova, a local girl who was only sixteen and a half, on his return; they had their first daughter less than a year later. She would survive the Holocaust, and settle in Israel.

Tova was ten years younger than her husband, and went on to have six children. They adored her caring nature and particularly looked forward to the yellow and black pancakes she made at Passover. Though she was not particularly religious, Mordechai and his siblings enjoyed the weekly ritual of hugging and kissing her after the ceremonial lighting of the candles.

The prayers would become more intense, and their mother's crying more bitter, as the first signs of orchestrated antisemitism became apparent in the first half of the 1930s. But, by and large, Campulung La Tisa was a relative haven. Unlike in the majority of other local villages, around half of the local Jewish community were well off.

Moses was in the merchant class, working in the fruit-and-vegetable business. Like similar shop owners, he made what was considered to be a comfortable living. Other Jews were wealthy landowners; several families, the Mermelsteins, Hilmans and Banus, leased a large sawmill, which employed members of the Orthodox community.

Mordechai dutifully studied the Torah under his father's supervision on the Sabbath when he would much rather have been out playing football. He was at ease in the tree-lined local streets; he loved the fragrant, woody blooms of the nut trees, and collected walnuts for the family table.

The area had been a centre of Hungarian nationalism in the fourteenth century; monuments to local soldiers, who fell in the Hungarian War of Independence in 1848–9, were tended lovingly as symbols of national identity. Jews were allowed to settle in the area following the severe winter of 1850.

One pioneer, Mendel Zelig Festinger, who originated from Galicia, the region that today covers south-eastern Poland and western Ukraine, bought tracts of land, which he sold to fellow believers. This formed the bedrock of a flourishing community, which was served by a wooden synagogue. A cemetery was established near the original settlement.

This led to the creation of *Chevra Kadisha*, a burial society in which the dead were prepared for burial by an anonymous group of people who considered it as a high calling and were respected for their piety. They were involved prominently when the community mourned the loss of its elderly shochet, a ritual slaughterer of cattle and poultry who had served householders for decades, in 1928. This job might have been grisly, but it was hugely respected for its skill and cultural significance.

He was replaced as the village's slaughterer by Chaim Hillel, one of many accomplished religious scholars in the area. He formed a small rabbinical college in his home, but failed to survive the Holocaust. Elsewhere in Campulung La Tisa study groups proved popular, and one teacher, Reb Itzik, had been, by repute, a wealthy man who had fallen on hard times.

Moses Eldar was consumed by his faith. He hired a private Torah teacher and constantly read chapters from the Psalms, devouring other religious tracts as he sat on a bench outside his house after prayers and dinner. When the time came, he put his core values into practice.

He looked after a local family who lost their breadwinners when their sons were taken as slave labourers, through a concession to Hitler by Miklós Horthy, a former admiral in the Austro-Hungarian Navy who acted as Hungary's Regent. Though Moses was not a politically active man, his growing unease reflected the moral dilemma of the times, because he helped to supply fruit and vegetables to the German market.

***

Detached from the desperate moral challenges of the time, it is difficult to pass judgement on the fact that a small group of Zionists in Germany came to an arrangement with the Nazis in August 1933. The so-called Ha'avara Agreement allowed wealthy German Jews to emigrate to Palestine in exchange for the purchase of German goods, and a pledge to lobby the global Jewish community to end the boycott that accompanied Hitler's rise to power.

Moses had heard the whispers, and recognized the peril his community was in, especially after the events of May 1938, when the newly empowered Hungarian authorities introduced new laws, framed by a legal definition of a Jew, based on so-called racial and religious criteria.

Jews were denied free access to professions such as medicine, publishing, acting and state administration. Their democratic rights were restricted. In an ironic illustration of unintended consequences, the right-wing Hungarian Prime Minister, Béla Imrédy, was forced to resign in February 1939 because he could not disprove allegations by political opponents that his great-grandfather was Jewish.

Imrédy went on to found the fiercely antisemitic Hungarian Renewal Party. The Nazis failed in their attempts to reinstate him as Prime Minister in 1944, and, found guilty of war crimes and collaboration two years later, he was executed by firing squad in the courtyard of a jail in Budapest.

Mordechai was barely ten years old when war broke out, but his father realized the boy had to grow up fast. He shared stories of growing global distress; Mordechai was particularly struck by the ordeal of the 937 passengers on the German ocean liner *St Louis* when it sailed from Hamburg to Havana in May 1939.

Although thirty passengers were accepted, the Cuban authorities revoked the landing permits issued to the rest of the Jewish refugees, and refused to allow them to disembark. The US and Canadian authorities also turned them away. Great Britain eventually took in 288 passengers, Belgium 214. France offered temporary refuge to 224 refugees and the Netherlands accepted 181. Ultimately 254 of them, trapped in continental Europe, died in the Holocaust.

Refugees from Poland flooded into Nyíregyháza at the outbreak of war. Despite relatively meagre means, a communal committee, made up of Jewish residents, co-ordinated plans for their welfare. Their social conscience extended to a similar programme designed to help refugee children from Slovakia.

Any lingering optimism that the Hungarian authorities would look after their own quickly evaporated. Jews were subjected to

physical abuse, extortion and robbery. Zionist groups were harassed and increasing numbers of what was termed the 'politically
unreliable' were pressed into the *Munkaszolgálat*, the enforced
labour service.

The climate of fear deepened in the summer of 1941, when a
decree of deportation was suddenly issued against Jews of Polish
and Russian descent in the region. Freight cars were organized, and plans drawn up to deliver the passengers into German
hands. No one ever understood why the decree was suddenly
annulled.

Some 18,000 less fortunate Jews were expelled, often in family
groups, and occasionally, as part of entire communities. Many
had failed to provide documentary proof of their Hungarian citizenship. They were unloaded at Korosmezo, near the pre-war
border with Poland, and handed over to the Nazis.

They were then forced to march 16 kilometres to Kamenets-
Podolsk, a city in western Ukraine that was occupied by German
forces during the invasion of the Soviet Union in June 1941. It
was here that, between 26 and 28 August, they were ordered to
undress before being murdered by *Einsatzgruppen*, mobile para-
military death squads, and by SS troops commanded by General
Friedrich Jeckeln.

A line had been crossed; though the Nazis had killed up to
7,000 Jews in Białystok in late June and early July, burning the
Great Synagogue on 27 June with around 800 Jews inside, this
was the most concerted mass killing in the name of the Final
Solution undertaken up to that point.

The macabre jigsaw of the Holocaust was completed on 3 September when Soviet and Polish prisoners became the first victims
of a concerted gassing campaign in Block 11 of the original Auschwitz camp. This had been converted from a Polish army barracks
into a prison compound for political detainees, who were beaten,

tortured and executed for trivial matters by pardoned German criminals who acted as guards.

Construction of Auschwitz-Birkenau, the main death camp, where the Hungarian boys were taken in 1944, began the following month. Ten thousand Soviet POWs were used as slave labour, living in fenced-off blocks in the original camp before being marched daily to the building site in the village of Brzezinka. Residents had been expelled, and their houses demolished, earlier in the year.

Two farmhouses remained, next to the construction site. These were adapted as provisional gas chambers, known as Bunkers 1 and 2, and went into use from early 1942. It would not be long before the name Auschwitz would become synonymous with the mass-extermination programme.

***

Wolf Greenwald's father, Menachem Gershon Greenwald, was an outstanding religious scholar and Ashkenazi Jew, and worked as the only ritual slaughterer of cattle and poultry in his home village, Hajduhadhaz. Wolf's mother Zisel, the oldest from a family of ten children, had eight children of her own.

Wolf was the eldest, since two siblings had died in infancy. He was a diligent boy, and was sent away to study in deference to the traditions established by his father. Theirs was another tightly knit community with deep roots; the earliest settlement had been established there in 1312.

Hajduhadhaz veered from being officially designated as a village to a city before reverting to the status of a village in 1935, when, in keeping with other communities in the region, long-established freedoms began to be curtailed. By 1941 residents were convulsed by the trauma of seeing sixty local young men conscripted for enforced labour in the Hungarian Army. Subsequently sent to Ukraine on the Eastern front, the majority died there.

It was at about this time, on the festival of Yom Tov, that the reputation of Auschwitz acquired a terrifying authenticity. Menachem Greenwald took the considerable risk of offering sanctuary to two former slave labourers, who were on the run from the camp.

Wolf noticed how bravely they bore the scars of their beatings. One could barely walk, but had to keep moving for fear of recapture, and certain death. Menachem utilized his faith to rationalize the danger he faced; he told the men he was unafraid since, in helping them, he was following the principles of Hachnasat Orchim.

This Talmudic passage reinforces the doctrine that giving is the greatest form of spiritual expression. Menachem recoiled from the men's vivid insights into the horrors of Auschwitz, but reassured the fugitives he was following the example of Abraham, who emulated God by welcoming guests into his home.

***

Meanwhile, in Campulung La Tisa, events began to stretch even the most devoted believers. Enforced conscription of Hungarian men into labour battalions intensified. Poorly fed and sparsely clothed, they were subjected to severe cruelty and abuse by fellow countrymen, the policemen and soldiers who guarded them.

These sadists were drawn from the fascistic, relentlessly antisemitic Arrow Cross Party, and were allowed to feel they had immunity from their crimes, however despicable. Though the slave labourers were initially assigned to punishing building projects in Hungary, the threat to them grew exponentially when they were sent to mine quarries. There, in a disturbing echo of what was to come in certain concentration camps later in the war, they were murdered, thrown to their deaths off man-made cliffs.

***

Little wonder then, that as slave units were sent in great numbers to the Eastern front, fathers feared for their sons, and for themselves. Meir Leitner, Dugo's father, had those fears realized in the middle of the night, one early summer Saturday in 1942. The military police gave him precious little time to say his goodbyes.

'You are coming with us.'

TWO

The Great Betrayal

MEIR LEITNER DID NOT SEE his home or family for more than a year, but, in his absence, he saw too much. Deployed on the Eastern front, he was diminished by witnessing death and depravity on a mass scale. His faith survived, but his belief in his fellow man deserted him. He was haunted by terrible images, and a sense of foreboding.

On being sent to Kyiv, he was immediately confronted by first-hand accounts of one of the largest massacres of the war, in a ravine called Babyn Yar on the outskirts of the city. A total of 33,771 Jews had been shot there, in small groups, over two days, 29 and 30 September 1941.

It was a sin without shame, committed in plain sight.

Meir was told how the doomed were marched through the streets to the killing ground before dying within earshot of local residents. He could not avoid evidence of other smaller but similar atrocities. By the time Soviet troops reclaimed the city in 1943 the Nazis had murdered 100,000 supposed 'undesirables' there, including prisoners of war, Ukrainian citizens and Roma.

In addition, escapees from Poland brought vivid eyewitness testimony from the Warsaw ghetto. The numbers of victims, more than a quarter of a million Jews transported to their deaths in the Treblinka extermination camp in the summer of 1942, were almost too big to comprehend.

***

For such a moral man as Meir Leitner, there was a deep unease that, because of his Hungarian heritage, he found himself on the wrong side in the war. Others with troubled consciences, like second-term Prime Minister Pál Teleki, were unable to live with themselves.

Like Moses Eldar, Mordechai's father, Teleki had served on the front line in the First World War. His first spell as Prime Minister covered the febrile period of 1920 and 1921, but he then took a six-year break from politics, devoting himself to academic research teaching geography at several Budapest universities.

He also became Hungary's Chief Scout, before being drawn back into the newly established Upper House of Parliament. It was not until 1938 that he was elected to the House of Representatives, in the ruling faction, the Party of National Unity. Once Béla Imrédy resigned, because of supposed Jewish associations, Miklós Horthy, the Regent, persuaded Teleki to return as Prime Minister.

Sworn in on 16 February 1939, he committed himself to regaining territories lost in the aftermath of the First World War, renamed his party Hungarian Life, and hardened anti-Jewish laws to such an extent that Dr Bela Fabian, a prominent member of Budapest's Jewish community, warned that his people were 'condemned to a slow but sure death'.

The first legal definition of a Jew was contained in the 1935 Nuremberg Laws, more specifically in the 'Reich Citizenship Law and its supplementary decrees'. This marked out anyone with three or more Jewish grandparents; those with only two were

considered mixed race unless they practised Judaism or were
married to a Jew.

Teleki's so-called Second Jewish Law followed suit in 1939.
Individuals with between two and four Jewish-born grandparents were declared Jewish. This set the tone for subsequent edicts,
which banned sexual intercourse with non-Jews and forbade
Jews from owning land.

Private companies were given strict quotas to follow. Since no
more than 12 per cent of their workforces could consist of Jews,
more than a quarter of a million people lost their jobs overnight.
The majority also lost their right to vote.

Yet, when Germany invaded Poland on 1 September 1939, Teleki
refused to join forces with the Nazis, and denied Wehrmacht
troops access to supply routes. His administration provided
refuge for Polish refugees and soldiers, including many Jews.
However, he made a fateful, fatal miscalculation in 1940, when
he accepted German help in regaining Northern Transylvania.

Photographs of the time, which depict a tired-looking man,
with a moustache, deep-set eyes and a high, lined forehead,
hinted at the pressure he was under from increasingly strident
Nazi advocates within his own party, and the militant malignancy
of the fascist Arrow Cross Party. He ultimately signed more than
fifty anti-Jewish decrees without being given respite by his political enemies.

In December 1940 he signed a Treaty of Eternal Friendship
with Yugoslavia. When that pro-Nazi government was ousted in
a coup on 27 March 1941, Hitler demanded Hungarian assistance
in restoring it to power. The British, meanwhile, warned that they
would declare war on Hungary if they agreed to assist the Nazi
invasion.

Hopelessly compromised, and feeling a debt of honour to the
Yugoslavs, Teleki shot himself on 3 April. His suicide note read:

'We broke our word, out of cowardice. The nation feels it, and we have thrown away its honour. We have allied ourselves with scoundrels. We will become body snatchers. A nation of trash. I did not hold you back. I am guilty.'

The Great Betrayal was well underway. Teleki was succeeded by the pliable László Bárdossy, who, sensing an opportunity to reclaim land lost in the Treaty of Trianon, threw Yugoslavia to the wolves by initially allowing the Nazis to invade through Hungarian territory. He quickly sanctioned the involvement of the Hungarian Army on the pretext that, since a puppet state of Croatia had been established, Yugoslavia had effectively ceased to exist. The episode resulted in a far-reaching five-week delay to Germany's invasion of the Soviet Union, Operation Barbarossa, until 22 June. A wet summer and vicious early Russian winter that year was to have calamitous consequences.

Hungarian officials responded to Nazi aggression by sending forced-labour units into Ukraine. They were treated barbarically, being forced to dig graves on increasingly frozen ground and being marched into minefields to clear a path for regular troops. Some units were wiped out; only 20 per cent of the slave labourers made it back to Hungary.

Meir Leitner was caught up in the mobilization of Hungary's Second Army, which contained 190,000 troops, supported by 17,000 slave labourers. It lacked air support, suitable clothing, armaments and ammunition. When the Russians attacked from the direction of Stalingrad on 12 January 1943 they outnumbered the Hungarians by nearly three to one.

The disparity in firepower was emphasized by the Russians' possession of five times more artillery. The subsequent rout took barely two days and the Hungarian retreat lasted two months. Ultimately the campaign cost the lives of an estimated 150,000 Hungarians, either in battle or in Soviet prisoner-of-war camps.

Hórthy forced Gustav Jany, the Hungarian commander, to apologize for calling his troops cowards, but his weaknesses were manifest. Content to take his time before taking vengeance, Hitler diverted blame for the ruinous Axis defeat, following the surrender of the German Sixth Army in Stalingrad on 2 February 1943, towards his Hungarian allies.

***

Despite his youth, Mordechai Eldar gathered enough from the adults around him to feel his nation's shock, shame and anger at the human cost of the defeat. He had been stripped of a child's innocence. Doubts were starting to form in his mind. If there was a God, he reasoned, He was not a merciful God.

In such a tightly knit community as Munkacs, it was inevitable that Chaim Schwimmer knew, if only by sight, some of the young men whose lives were cruelly and needlessly wasted on the Eastern front. He celebrated what he regarded as decisive divine intervention.

His boyish assessment of the war reflected a firmer faith than Mordechai's. 'In Stalingrad, God started to fight with Hitler,' he reasoned. 'He didn't need guns or bullets or tanks. He just brought down the winter to end all winters. It was 40 below zero. It was His will that thousands and thousands of German soldiers were frozen to death.'

Religion was still an intrinsic part of Yaakov Yosef Weiss's life, despite the increasing deprivations of the summer of 1943. He lived in Szilágysomlyó, one of the towns in Northern Transylvania included in the deal Teleki made with the Nazis. It was subsequently named Simleu Silvaniei when the Romanians regained control in 1944.

Yaakov was the only boy; an elder brother died before he was born. He had three surviving younger sisters; another died from diphtheria in 1940. He loved the clean air, and walks along the Crasna river, where he watched for glimpses of local wildlife, but his religious studies, undertaken from the age of six, dictated the rhythm of his life.

His Rabbi, who handed out sweets to obedient children and made special versions of the breastplates and aprons worn by the High Priest for them, would board the same cattle truck to Auschwitz as the Weiss family in 1944. A private teacher, Shlomo Heimlech, hosted a study group in the backyard.

Each week, on the Sabbath, Yaakov would be tested on the scriptures by his father, a devout member of the Satmar sect, an ultra-conservative Hasidic dynasty that rejected modern culture. His father was outraged by a local chemist who opened on the Sabbath. This was regarded as *melacha*, forbidden work.

His parents were known as *balei chesed*, people who did kind deeds. They routinely hosted up to ten neighbours or friends for dinner, which was well stocked because of his father's role as the community's ritual slaughterer. Yaakov was fascinated by his father's instruction on how to remove fats, kidneys and the lobe of the liver, and struck by his mother's generosity of spirit. Their faith was practical, rather than theoretical.

His father woke Yaakov each morning, and gave him breakfast before school. On winter days, when the snow was deep and temperatures were perishing, he gave the boy a shot of schnapps. His death, when Yaakov was nine and a half, devastated the family, and plunged them into poverty.

His mother rented out the bedroom she once shared with her husband; the family lived in the other room, and the kitchen. She was devoted to her children, and used contacts in the Satmar community in the city of Szatmárnémeti, renamed Satu Mare when it came under Romanian control, to find a teacher to continue their religious education, free of charge.

Yaakov, who answered to the nickname Yankel, slept in his grandfather's house, without having the necessary permit to do so, but the old man could not afford to give him food. Once again, the community rallied around. During the week, he ate at a different house every night. Supper usually consisted of bread and jam. This defiance worked well until one morning he overslept.

Police arrived at his grandfather's door at 8 a.m., demanded the boy's papers, and took him to the local jail, where the police chief beat Yaakov before throwing him into a communal cell with drunks and petty criminals. He left him there all day before putting him on a train to Szilágysomlyó with dire warnings about future transgressions. Yaakov was only twelve, but that was the age from which boys were considered for military training.

His mother's devotion, and determination that he should grow up as an honest, upright citizen, made a lasting impression on him. Yaakov was steered through his bar mitzvah that autumn by his kindly tutor. His devotion 'went into the bones'. He heard the words of his late father: 'If you want, God will still help you. The wanting should be from the depth of your heart, and your truth. You should know that the purpose of your living is to be devoted to a higher calling.'

***

As 1943 drew to a close, people were afraid. Yaakov's religious school was shut down. Numerous decrees closed down businesses and threatened many with destitution. Hungary's Jews could not reconcile their plight with the external assumption that the tide of the war had changed.

The national leadership was flawed. Admiral Horthy was, paradoxically, a supporter of Hitler but appalled by the extremes of Nazism. He had successfully argued against what the Führer referred to as 'resettlement' of the Hungarian Jews in April 1943, warning that 'the Jews cannot be exterminated or beaten to death'.

Yet Horthy knew he was attempting to delay the inevitable. He gave tacit approval for his latest Prime Minister, Miklós Kállay, to attempt to negotiate with the Western Allies, through the diplomat László Veress, who on 9 September 1943 signed an unauthorized secret agreement to surrender.

British and American intelligence agents became involved, and, at the request of the British Special Operations Executive, which had been specifically set up to spread subversion and sabotage in enemy-held territory, Horthy even agreed to secretly install radio communications equipment in his castle in Buda.

The Nazis, however, were of course wise to the ways of espionage. Though the nature of his work was, by definition, opaque, it is widely believed that Wilhelm Hoettl, an Austrian SS member who served in the *Sicherheitsdienst*, the Security Service, informed Hitler of Hungary's attempted betrayal.

By early 1944, Hoettl was acting head of intelligence and counter-espionage in central and south-eastern Europe. True to his trade, he had few, if any, moral scruples. The following year, as German defeat was all but assured, he began selling fake passports to SS officers and their families in return for illicit gold.

While based in Budapest, he offered himself to American officials in Switzerland. He surrendered to them in Austria in May 1945, and testified against Nazi officers in the Nuremberg war-crimes trials before going on to work for US counter-intelligence. Despite his machinations, he became a respected school director, historian and author in Austria before his own death, aged eighty-four, in 1999.

Forewarned and forearmed, Hitler summoned Horthy to his headquarters, Schloss Klessheim in Austria, on 16 March 1944, under the pretence of supplying troops for a Balkan offensive. He knew, as well as anyone, the Hungarians barely had an army worthy of the name, but was playing for time.

Horthy protested that his nation had already paid too high a price in blood: 'Those men we have left have but few arms with which to fight. We cannot help you one bit more. We are through. We are doing our best to stave off the Bolshevik menace and we won't be able to spare a single man for the Balkans.'

Hitler kept him in essentially meaningless negotiations for two days, while German ground troops launched Operation Marga-rethe, a rapid, bloodless invasion of Hungary. By 19 March the nation had been overrun; its Jewish population of 825,000, the biggest in Europe at the time, now faced a new and deadly peril.

Horthy was allowed to remain as a largely futile figurehead, but Kallay was dismissed, and replaced as Prime Minister by the fanatically pro-Nazi General Dome Sztojay. Horthy naively believed that as a soldier, whose principal loyalty was to his nation, Sztojay would do his best to resist the Germans' most extreme demands.

He could not have been more wrong. Sztojay legalized the fas-cist Arrow Cross Party, jailed political opponents and banned labour unions. He committed the remnants of the Hungarian Army to assist Germany's war effort, and played a key role in preparations for the deportation of Hungarian Jews.

Edmund Veesenmayer, whose promotion to Reich plenipoten-tiary in Hungary followed his prominent role in the liquidation of Jews in Croatia and Serbia, had Hitler's support in rejecting Horthy's demand that Sztojay be sacked. By the time the general was replaced as Prime Minister in August 1944, Hungary's Jews were doomed.

Sztojay fled in the face of the Red Army's advance, but was captured by American troops and extradited to Hungary in October 1945. Tried by a People's Tribunal in Budapest, he was found guilty of war crimes, and of crimes against the Hungarian people. He was executed by firing squad in 1946.

The mass transportation of Hungarian Jews to Auschwitz-Birkenau was overseen by *SS-Obersturmbannführer* Adolf Eichmann, who operated from the Majestic Hotel in Budapest. He quickly summoned Jewish community leaders, and promised that, in return for what he called 'light labour' and 'minor concessions', compliant Jews would have nothing to fear.

Assured of complete support from the Hungarian authorities, his initial plan envisaged four trains a day, containing forty-five cattle cars. This, his team calculated, would transport 12,000 Jews a day from mid-May 1944. It proved to be an underestimation; at its height between ten and eighteen trains, pulling up to eighty cattle cars, arrived at the extermination camp each day.

A total of 147 trains were needed to deport 434,000 Jews, 80 per cent of whom were killed within hours. The operation was called *Aktion Höss* after Rudolf Höss, the first commandant of Auschwitz, who returned to the camp on 8 May to supervise the extermination process. His first act was to order the renovation of Bunker 2, the former farmhouse used as a gas chamber, and the digging of pits, in which bodies could be burned.

The vice closed with chilling precision. More than 100 edicts were issued by late March, and enforced days later. Jews had to wear yellow stars from 5 April; two days later they were prohibited from travelling, and banned from owning radios. New financial regulations prevented Jews from withdrawing cash from their bank accounts; all valuables had to be registered. More shops and businesses were confiscated.

By the middle of April, Eichmann's plan, to establish a network of around 180 ghettos and transit camps, in disused factories or closed-off street sections, was ready to be put into operation. Its timing, during severely restricted but devoutly observed Passover festivities, was deliberately insulting.

✳ ✳ ✳

Unlike other boys, Dugo Leitner in Nyíregyháza lacked the maturity to appreciate the gravity of the situation. He regarded the evasion of German guards and their Hungarian accomplices, as he surreptitiously collected *matzha*, the unleavened bread used in Passover meals, for the family, as a game, a great adventure.

Jews from surrounding villages had already been driven into a newly established ghetto based in two brick factories at the southern and northern edges of Nyíregyháza. Despite the family's financial problems, Meir Leitner helped to smuggle food into them. He would come to regret declining an offer from non-Jewish neighbours to hide his daughters Rachel and Esther.

Golda, Dugo's mother, had taken the precaution of hiding her best Passover tableware in the backyard, but was unprepared for the ordeal that awaited her when six local gendarmes burst into the house, demanding that she hand over all the family's valuables.

'Put silver and gold on the table?' she said scornfully. 'What money and what gold? We had no income when my husband was in Ukraine. We sold hardly anything in our store. Our consecrated cups for Passover are glass, not silver. We have nothing to give you.'

One of the policemen gestured towards her wedding ring: 'Take it off, or I will cut it off your finger.' Golda screamed, setting off Dugo, his brother Shmuel and his sisters, but Meir, sensing the danger posed by armed, officially sanctioned thugs, calmed the situation. 'Golda,' he said gently. 'Don't cry about it. I won't divorce you . . .'

The Leitners piled their few permitted packages, containing food, two sets of clothing for each family member, blankets and a camp bed, on to a horse-drawn cart, which took them to a ghetto in the centre of Nyíregyháza. There they lived with strangers, fifteen to a room, without adequate food or sanitation, for the next six weeks. There was a predictable outbreak of typhus in one section of the ghetto within three days.

Conditions rapidly deteriorated, but at least they had a roof over their heads. In several other cities Jews were forced to live outdoors, without shelter. Though it was a relatively mild spring, the nights were cold, and water supplies were sparse. Medical care was non-existent and corrupt policemen conducted protection rackets with impunity.

Wolf Greenwald and his family were sent from Hajduduhadhaz, together with the inhabitants of eight other small communities, to a ghetto in the Serly brickyards in Nyíregyháza. There 13,000 Jews were stripped of their few remaining valuables and left to fend for themselves as best they could before their deportation.

Chaim Schwimmer and his cousin Hershel Herskovic moved a short distance, with their families, to a ghetto in Latorica Street, a traditionally Jewish area of Munkacs. Three hundred or so young men were ordered to build a wall around it, using wooden fences that had once surrounded local houses.

They had lived in a climate of fear from 20 March 1944, when German soldiers occupied the town. The soldiers extorted money and possessions from families and forced observant Jews, identified by their beards and sidelocks, into the synagogue, ordering them to sing as they stamped on the holy Torah scrolls. Anyone who refused, or attempted to escape, was shot.

Chaim's father had managed to smuggle a consignment of

silver coins that he had hidden in the cellar some ten years earlier to an illicit local money changer. Both men knew he had
no option but to accept a fragment of their true value. He used
the proceeds to buy batches of food, which his wife prepared
for the extended family. They were at the dinner table when
Mordechai heard a noise in the yard; terrified, he realized the
SS had arrived.

Evictions were a grotesque spectacle. Though some feigned
indifference or even wept at the treatment of the Jews, many
former neighbours lined the streets to revel in the humiliation
they suffered. Jews were ordered to lock their properties, and to
place the keys into an envelope on which they had written their
old address, and their new one in the ghetto. These envelopes
were handed to corrupt gendarmerie; within twenty-four hours
most of the homes had been stripped bare.

Hershel Herskovic felt he and his family, which included his
grandparents, had been treated like animals. They had been
beaten like beasts of burden. He was scared to go out for a walk
in Munkacs, for fear of being cursed at, or casually assaulted by
German soldiers and their collaborators.

A pall of despondency hung over them all, though the boy
found comfort in the philosophy his father had shared in better
times. He was taught to believe that happiness should be independent of circumstance, because if you surrender to events you
will be perpetually sad.

Ironically, then, his father was notably and unusually quiet, as
if he was resigned to their fate. Hershel, remarkably, was more
resilient. Issues of life and death were huge themes for someone
of his age to appreciate, but he had a fatalistic approach to them.

On the first Sabbath in the Munkacs ghetto, Hungarian soldiers, stationed at each corner of the site, seized anyone who
emerged for prayers, and took them to destroy local synagogues.

Eichmann arrived towards the end of the month to monitor progress. His plan had been completed in only two days.

It involved allowing the *Judenrat*, Jewish councils consisting of former community leaders, to be nominally in charge of administration. The seven members of the Munkacs *Judenrat* lived with their families in a special quarter of the ghetto, but even their collaboration failed to save them; they were among the last to be transported to Auschwitz-Birkenau.

The wealthiest Jews were concentrated in the two brickyard ghettos, Sajovits to the south of Munkacs, and Kallus to the north. They were ordered to strip naked on arrival and subjected to invasive body searches, designed to discover hidden valuables. They were ritually abused and ruthlessly tortured. Only a few dozen Jews, war heroes from the First World War, were spared.

Moses Eldar's time at the front line, nearly thirty years previously, was not enough to save him from being whipped, kicked and punched as he was driven out of his home to cries of 'Heraus, schnell, verfluchte Juden!' ('Out, quick, damned Jews!'). His son Mordechai, given the responsibility of looking after his grandmother Miriam, shielded her from punishment.

The family had taken the precaution of sewing money and small pieces of jewellery into jacket linings and shoe inserts. Moses, who was all too aware of the fate awaiting them, reasoned that the money and jewels could be used to bribe their guards, a notion that ultimately failed to survive the chaos of the railway ramp at Auschwitz-Birkenau.

Initially herded into the courtyard of the school in Campulung La Tisa where Mordechai studied, the Eldars were taken to the ghetto in the city of Sighet. The ghetto was split into two sections, a neighbourhood of four streets in the centre of Sighet that housed 11,000 Jews, and a smaller slum, Ober Yarash, in which evictees lived in dark, dank alleyways.

This was where the Eldars, and around 3,000 other Jews, ended up. Conditions were appalling. There were no toilets, and they had been prevented from bringing their cooking pots. The local police commander, Colonel Sarvari, used fifty policemen, brought in from the neighbouring town of Miskolc, to rob their prisoners of anything of value.

Mordechai could not forget his father's distress when he was set upon by a group of Hungarian fascist youths in Sighet. They beat and kicked him before burning off his beard, a cherished symbol of his faith. To his persecutors, it was mindless blood sport; to the Eldars it was confirmation that their lives had been consumed by the forces of evil.

Yaakov Yosef Weiss missed his father terribly, even before the family was forced into the local ghetto, but his mother understood completely what had engulfed them. She was a Polish citizen and, in 1942, had narrowly escaped transportation to the camps. Police came one Saturday morning, barged into the house, and told the entire family they were to prepare to leave.

Mercifully, his mother, the intended target of the raid, was in Budapest, successfully seeking new papers. A friendly local businessman persuaded the authorities to allow the children to remain; though it was never confirmed, everyone in the area assumed he had paid a substantial bribe to save their lives.

This, inevitably, had a huge impact on their mother, who kept in touch with Polish contacts during weekly business trips to the Hungarian capital. Even when her husband had been alive she welcomed refugees from her homeland. Yaakov had memories of murmured conversations, without ever understanding their context.

When he became the man of the house, and had undergone the traditional rite of passage, his bar mitzvah, his mother calculated that he had the strength of character to come to terms with the truth. They were living on borrowed time and he could be trusted with her deepest secret.

'I have something to tell you,' she said quietly one evening, as she steered her son towards a kitchen chair. She revealed that a non-Jewish farmer, a business acquaintance, had offered to take in and hide the family, so they could avoid transportation. After agonized deliberation, she had refused.

Her tone was firm, her gaze unwavering. 'You are now old enough to be your own boss. If you want to go to the farm you go with my blessing. You have no need for justification in the eyes of God. Live your life as a Jew.'

Yaakov was in awe of his mother's strength, and the solace she gained from her faith. He realized she knew what was going to happen to them, and was engaged in the ultimate act of selfless-ness. He could not bear to part from her, or from his siblings. He would accept whatever fate God had in store for him.

The point of no return arrived after five weeks in the ghetto, on the morning of 23 May 1944, when the family were marched to the local train station. They were told they were being transferred to a labour camp, but they knew better.

THREE

Journeys to Hell

THE MOTHER OF AN EIGHTEEN-MONTH-OLD baby had no more milk to give. She was young, hungry and at her wits' end. Her child's piercing cries could not be avoided, since they were crushed, along with seventy other deportees, into a cattle car with a small rectangular grated window that looked out on to a slow-moving, rapidly shrinking world.

The baby was passed around carefully, but, in such claustrophobic, overheated circumstances, it could not be pacified. There was barely enough water to wet its lips and ward off dehydration. The Weiss family shared the mother's distress at her inability to breastfeed because they, too, had been on a starvation diet in the ghetto.

The entire carriage had been given five rounded loaves of bread to sustain them on their journey to Auschwitz-Birkenau, which took four tortuous days and four endless nights. Yaakov Yosef Weiss, who struggled, like everyone, to sleep, ate his small slice sparingly, one bite at a time.

His mother was only in her mid-thirties, but looked much older. Her face was pale and drawn. She had been worn down by deprivation and duty. Yet her spirit remained strong, and she radiated authority. Given the chance, when the train stopped at a signal approaching the Polish border, she obeyed her deepest instincts, to look after others before herself.

Manoeuvring herself to the grated window, she called out to an old woman walking beside the track. Yaakov's mother had hidden the last of her money from the scavengers. Now was the time to spend it. Waving several soiled notes out of the window, she begged for bread in a dialect Yaakov could not understand, but must have reflected her Polish roots.

So many opportunists literally took the money and ran in such circumstances. Yaakov's mother had no option but to trust the passer-by, so she tossed the notes out. The train remained stationary, the old woman returned, and squeezed pieces of dry, stale bread through the window. The deportees fell on it in their desperation; Yaakov was able only to secure a tiny sliver.

Another type of milk, that of human kindness, had long since run dry. The Hungarian gendarmerie seized one last chance to exploit the vulnerability of their victims when the train, which included twenty-four of Yaakov's school friends from Szilá-gysomlyó, arrived in Caseiu, a commune in Transylvania that acted as a handover point to German guards.

The gendarmes opened the wooden carriage door, trained their guns on the cowering, disorientated passengers, and demanded their valuables. Noticing an elderly woman's earrings, they ordered her to remove them. When she refused, they simply ripped them out of her earlobes. Indifferent to her screams, and those of her terrified companions, they prodded her stomach with bayonets before tearing her wedding ring off her finger.

Such barbarism reflected the dehumanization of the defence-less. It was repeated at other handover points, like Kosice, where trains from ghettos in Nyíregyháza and Munkacs paused for formalities to be completed by a new set of captors. Heirlooms and keepsakes were stolen in a savage manner; blood was often drawn.

The robbers in Kosice lied despicably. The deportees, desperate to discover their destination, begged the Hungarian guards for information. The thugs amused themselves with the casual invention that they were going to do agricultural work in a place called Hayaburyda.

Yaakov was proud of his mother's dignity, but saddened by the harshness of her life. She wore a widow's mask of resilience that was removed only on the train's arrival at Auschwitz. Her three daughters were sprawled around her in the carriage; as if understanding and accepting the inescapability of her fate, she decided to offer her son one last life lesson.

'Yankel,' she said quietly, moments before the deadly scrum of disembarkation. 'Remember the main thing in life is to keep the *mitzovs* [deeds that indicate empathy and kindness] and to keep *Yiddishkeit* [the Jewish way of life]. Just to learn the right way is nothing. You have to put it into practice.'

They were the last words she spoke to him. It was a Friday morning, and light rain was falling. Almost before they knew it, the carriage door was drawn open; fetid air escaped, to be replaced by an infernal din. Gruff voices screamed, 'Raus, raus, raus!' ('Out, out, out!') and the scramble began.

Those closest to the door were pulled out, or simply fell on to the ground. The dead had no dignity; their bodies represented a macabre assault course. Yaakov disembarked with his mother and sisters, but they were suddenly swept out of sight. He was pushed to the right side; they were swallowed up by the tide of humanity being funnelled towards the gas chambers.

There was no co-ordination, only panic and powerlessness. The screams of children, separated from their mothers, and of mothers, separated from their children, pierced the skull. Yaakov did not know it at the time, but he had been saved because he was unusually tall for his age, thirteen.

He simply followed orders, as part of the flotsam of an unfolding tragedy. It was not until much later that he realized his mother's exhausted appearance had sealed her fate. She would have been capable of work, but looked spent and weak. He mourned the loss of her mercy, and her guidance.

In that moment of separation, he felt the pangs of an orphan's loneliness. His mind was scrambled; bizarrely, he thought back to Zalman Leib, the ritual slaughterer who had rented his parents' former bedroom. Their last conversation had been snatched but seemed to have a strange significance.

It took place as they were being bundled out of the family house, after they scrambled to fill the single backpack they were permitted to take to the ghetto with them. Leib insisted to Yaakov that they would have to make a *bracha*, a blessing, for the purposes of sanctifying the name of God.

'Actually, Yankel,' he said, 'We should really say Hallel [a Jewish prayer for happy occasions].' The boy was nonplussed. 'Why? How is this occasion happy?' The answer filtered into his brain on the descent from the arrival ramp at Auschwitz-Birkenau: 'We are going to be murdered while glorifying God. That is a happy occasion.'

Yaakov had become inured to the scorn of those who could not, or would not, understand the depth of his religious belief. In the days and weeks to come, he dared to believe he had been spared because the Almighty had a task for him to fulfil. This acceptance, that his life was out of his control, would be a source of comfort.

At least those taken to their deaths from the Transylvanian train were saved from the horror endured by the first Hungarian

Jews to arrive at Auschwitz, nearly a month earlier, on 2 May. Of the 3,800 deportees from Topolya near Vojvodina, and the Kistarcsa camp on the outskirts of Budapest, only 486 men and 616 women were kept alive, as slave labourers.

The rest were directed towards the so-called Little White House, the former farmhouse more formally known as Bunker 2. There, it quickly became clear that Auschwitz-Birkenau was not ready to receive victims in such numbers. The gas chamber was too small to accommodate all the condemned in one go.

This meant that the SS guards divided them into two groups. The first were stripped and hustled into the chamber. The unfortunates in the second group had to wait their turn nearby, behind a makeshift fence or in the disrobing room. They could clearly hear the screams of those who preceded them.

Only one of the four crematoria was in working order, so the bodies piled high. This level of incompetence led to the replacement of the SS garrison commandant, Arthur Liebenhenschel, by Rudolf Höss. The Birkenau commandant, Friedrich Hartjenstein, was replaced by Josef Kramer, Höss's former assistant, who had been running the only Nazi concentration camp on French soil, Natzweiler-Struthof in the Vosges Mountains.

Kramer would go on to be known as the Beast of Belsen, where his cruelty was conspicuous. He was eventually detained by the British Army, convicted of war crimes involving the deaths of thousands of inmates, and hanged by British executioner Albert Pierrepoint in Hamelin prison in Germany.

The fate of the desperate mother with the screaming baby became a little clearer years later. It transpired the child was grabbed, on the ramp, by a Polish prisoner in a work detail clearing the trains. The mother screamed, fought to regain the baby, but was pushed away by the inmate. 'Idiot,' he spat, pushing her to the right-hand queue containing those deemed fit for work. 'Don't you want to live?'

No one knows what happened to the baby. Auschwitz legend suggests that the mother, whose name is not recorded, survived the war, remarried, and raised a new family in the United States. It may sound fanciful, but her ordeal, immediately after disembarkation, was by no means unique. This sobering testimony, by another unnamed woman, a Hungarian Jew, was recorded by the Auschwitz Museum:

When the freight car stopped, a Polish prisoner approached me and asked whether my children had a grandmother. I replied that my mother was here with me. Then the Pole suggested that it would be prudent for me to now hand them over to her. But my son began to cry and beg me not to leave him, so I left the freight car with the children.

On the way I explained to my daughter that when asked, she should say she was two. At the time I thought not even the Germans would separate a two-year-old child from her mother. Sobbing a little, my daughter said she was three and I should not tell her such things as it was wrong to lie.

This lasted some time until we stood before Doctor Mengele. I suddenly felt a sharp tug. It was that Pole, who now pulled me away from the children and pushed me into the group on the right, among people deemed healthy and fit for work. He wanted to help me. But what could be worse for a mother than being separated from her children?

Dugo Leitner would be confronted by such haunting realities soon enough, when he arrived at Auschwitz-Birkenau following a two-day journey from Nyíregyháza. The make-believe world in

which he resisted the restrictions of adolescence, let alone adulthood, was about to be atomized.

When he boarded the freight train, one Tuesday morning in
the fourth week of May, he chattered about how much he had
enjoyed the ghetto, because it meant he had no classes, and could
play, after a fashion, with thirty of his friends from school. Such
levity led to puzzled, disapproving looks, which soon turned into
undiluted anger.

'Can I have your tickets, please?' he announced to the one hundred or so souls squashed into a carriage with a single window,
laced with barbed wire, which carried the lingering smell of its
original occupants, sheep on the way to slaughter in Poland. The
smile on his face froze as his childish joke fell flat, and its audience threatened violence.

Several men glared at him, menacingly, and shaped as if to hit
him. Meir Leitner, his father, shouted above their heads: 'What
do you want from the kid? What does he know about where we're
headed?' Order of sorts was restored, but the incident further
darkened the mood, and invited despondency.

Dugo burrowed his way under his father's arm, and buried
his head in his armpit. His brother Shmuel did the same on the
opposite shoulder. The family huddled together for comfort.
Golda Leitner cradled her daughters, Rachel, Ethel and Esther,
while Nathan, Dugo's cousin, lay between his parents.

There was no air, no food, no hope. Golda chided herself for
believing a rumour they were to be taken east to work in the fields.
'Why run away?' she asked those who had suggested making a
break for it on the way to the station from the ghetto. 'At most, we
work, and the family stays together.'

She refused to fear the worst, even when the gendarmes told
her she would have no need of the packages she had prepared for
the journey. 'You have nothing to worry about. The packages will

be brought after you.' Just another egregious falsehood, with no consequences for the oppressors.

The following morning horse-drawn carriages took away the elderly and the sick. The deportees were then marched to Harangod, one of three previously deserted staging areas, by SS guards with dogs. They were under orders from Eichmann that, under no circumstances, were they to allow the train to be late. 'Komm schon, komm schon!' they cried ('Come on, come on!').

Meir and Golda Leitner were harried when they paused on passing their house, on a corner before the column took a ninety-degree turn. They looked vacantly at their former neighbours, who were lining the pavements, waiting to pounce on their misfortune once they were out of sight.

Dugo estimated their train had thirty freight cars – it probably had more. It waited for what seemed like an eternity outside the marshalling yard at Oświęcim/Auschwitz on Thursday afternoon. They were in a surreal traffic jam; the camp was in danger of being paralysed by the volume of new arrivals. The train was eventually split into two by a shunting team.

The carriages were rolled to the railway ramp at Birkenau, after being uncoupled from the locomotive, which stayed outside the barbed-wire fences. The external shunting team got off at the main gate, and were replaced by a group of inmates, who completed the task.

Once the bedlam of disembarkation receded, another prisoners' work detail descended on the carriages. They conducted what amounted to a spiritual fumigation, designed to erase all signs of human cargo. This involved wiping or scratching off the inscriptions, written en route by the doomed passengers. These featured names, dates, initials, final messages and brief biblical passages. As a last resort, they were covered by oil paint.

Death was everywhere. While the train carrying the Leitners

waited on the periphery of the camp, some passengers peered out through the grooves in the carriage wall. They glimpsed flames belching from the chimneys of two crematoria. The older passengers were confused; one wondered whether the laundry had caught fire.

Even someone as accustomed to war's destructive force as Meir Leitner had no concept of what was to befall his family. The speed of its destruction was mesmerizing, horrifying. It was torn apart within seconds of arrival on the ramp by guards who barked out orders in German and occasionally, because 300 ethnic Germans had been recruited for the garrison from Hungary, in Hungarian.

The guards barely went through the formality of asking basic questions about age or health, instead shoving the elderly, frail and visibly sick to one side with mothers and children. Seeing that scene unfold before them, and encouraged to look after themselves by inmates on the ramp, mothers started to discard their babies in a panic.

Dugo's aunt, who was aged around thirty but reasonably robust, handed her six-year-old son to Golda Leitner to look after. The aunt survived, but such an instinctive act of generosity sealed Golda's fate. She was bundled away, together with her three daughters and the boy, almost in the blink of an eye. There was no time to say farewell.

They would not be registered, and were almost certainly dead by the time Dugo, his brother and father had gone through the humiliating ritual of being taunted and beaten as they were stripped of everything apart from their shoes. Precautions to stop the spread of disease amounted to a brief, externally operated, shower, in which the water switched randomly from boiling to freezing.

Everything was done in a rush. Inmates, who could loosely be called barbers, had quotas to fulfil; they were watched by guards who counted new arrivals in ledgers. It was a brutal process, which removed all body hair, regardless of gender. Grotesquely, this was preserved in sacks and shipped to Germany. Meir Leitner was in agony because his stomach was carelessly slashed.

They then collected their striped prison clothing, which in Dugo's case consisted of one pair of short pants, one pair of three-quarter-length pants and a shirt with two buttons. By the time bureaucratic formalities had been completed, and their prisoner-number tattoo had been inscribed on their arm, they had not eaten for seventy-two hours.

Meir held his sons close, attempting to protect his self-respect despite the pain from the wound on his abdomen. He spoke gently, but firmly: 'Boys, dear ones, we must have come to Hell here. You must do everything to survive, to return home, to immigrate to the Land of Israel. Tell the whole world what the Nazis did to our people.'

It was almost as if he knew that he would have little more time with them.

Wolf Greenwald and his family were also on that train from Nyíregyháza. They had spent four weeks in a secondary ghetto in the area, set up for inhabitants of surrounding villages. Prevented from taking provisions from their homes, and given no time to hide heirlooms, they had little food and hardly any water.

The men slept outside in the ghetto, exposed to the elements. Around 500 women and children, including Wolf, irrespective of his relative maturity, were crammed into what was once a garage, but had apparently also been used before the war as a warehouse to store tobacco. Sanitary conditions were appalling.

Despite the efforts of volunteer Jewish doctors and nurses, in tending to another 11,000 detainees packed into 123 houses, a deadly epidemic of white-spot typhus began to spread. The authorities were indifferent to their plight, and studiously ignored warnings from the local *Judenrat*, the Jewish council.

Instead Pál Nyíregyházy, the desperately ambitious, rabidly antisemitic Mayor of Nyíregyháza, allowed *SS-Hauptsturmführer* Siegfried Seidl, police chief Zoltan Horváth, and an enforcement squad of nearly 100 Jewish collaborators to do their worst. A torture unit led by József Trencsényi extorted money and possessions and murdered several wealthy Jews, together with the leader of the local Orthodox community, while they awaited deportation.

Others committed suicide in the ghetto. Even those who were led to believe they were excluded from the deportations, such as Jews who converted out of the faith or married non-Jews, were deceived. A group of 160, sent to the extermination camp without knowledge of their destination, were betrayed two weeks after the transportation programme officially ended in the area on 6 June.

The Greenwald family had already travelled 40 kilometres from their home village. In an ordeal designed to complete the process of demoralization, they were marched another eight kilometres, through a square, where martial music played, and along barren countryside to the staging area.

Conditions in the cattle cars were uniformly grim. There was hardly anything to eat or drink, and little room to sit or squat. Those weakened by the deprivations of the ghetto had gaunt, featureless faces that seemed paralysed by their predicament. The first of them died as the train inched through the mountains, on a single-track line.

It stopped frequently at insignificant stations, and was regularly diverted into sidings to allow other official services to take precedence. This prolonged the suffering, so that by the time the train joined the queue outside the marshalling yard at Auschwitz, the journey had taken four times longer than normal.

The anarchic mess of disembarkation clouded Wolf's brain. He was vaguely aware of his father being shoved to the right, and of him saying, 'I will rest in peace wherever I am.' Wolf blindly obeyed the instruction to 'go with Mommy and look after the children'. Little did either of them know that was tantamount to a death sentence.

They were near the end of the line that shuffled towards Josef Mengele, who took it upon himself to direct human traffic with a studied arrogance. Wolf stumbled past him to the left, only to be stopped in his tracks by the shrill blast of a whistle. One of the doctor's SS assistants, most probably a medical functionary, singled him out and ordered him to retrace his steps.

It was only twenty or so metres, but it felt longer because of his vulnerability. Despite his terror, the boy summoned the courage to address the soldier in German: 'Willst du mich?' he asked ('Do you want me?'). The bitter response belied its generosity, because it saved his life. 'Komm da rüber, du verdammter Hund!' he was told ('Get over there, you damn dog!').

It was not the last time in Auschwitz-Birkenau that Wolf had cause to be thankful for his appearance. He was, inevitably, thin, but the SS man obviously noticed he had a sinewy strength, suited to hard labour. By the time he gathered his wits about him, and hastened to the end of the right-hand column, his mother and siblings had vanished.

In common with so many, he had no time to say goodbye to his mother. She had descended into a familiar fog of depression during the final hours of their journey. Her careworn look stayed with him. Wolf felt her pain, but he had not had enough life experience to fully comprehend the despair of a parent, unable to protect their offspring.

It was just after six o'clock when he managed to catch up with his father as they were funnelled into the shower area. Though he was grateful to see him, and their embrace was heartfelt, there was a fleeting reticence between them, almost as if they were embarrassed by the enormity of events.

At least the brutality of being shaved, and the curt conventions of the clothing procedures, stopped them from thinking too deeply about things. Since the needles with which they were tattooed were used continually, until they broke, they had also to worry about the threat of infection. It was all too common for painful sores to develop.

Father and son were soon separated, with Wolf joining other boys in the isolation barracks in Camp A. Anyone found to be ill, most usually with mumps or scarlet fever, was immediately sent to the gas chamber. Those given a clean bill of health made tentative attempts to learn about their new environment.

The novelty of discovering that the boys were drawn from the length and breadth of their country, notwithstanding a minority of refugees from Poland and Slovakia, soon wore off. Word spread by earlier arrivals in the camp ensured they quickly took note of the predatory nature of an equally reviled underclass.

Due to shortages of prison clothing, those assigned to Camp E, the Gypsy Camp, had to wear the civilian clothes in which they had arrived, or to take clothing collected from the dead. They particularly prized the shoes worn by new prisoners, and thought nothing of stealing from the unwise or the unwary.

A red X was painted on the back of their jackets, caps and hats. Each had to wear two strips of white canvas, sewn into the outer seam of the right leg of the trouser, and across the left breast of the shirt. The canvas featured three symbols: a triangle, letter and number.

The colour of the triangle conveyed a prisoner's category. Those worn by Roma and Sinti, defined as 'asocials' by the Nazis, were black. Prisoners in the Gypsy Camp had a Z before their registration number. This stemmed from the literal translation of gypsies in German, *Zigeuner*.

The Jews were the lowest social order. No one had a name any longer. The boys were denied the luxury of individuality, the comfort of their family, and the bond of a common culture. History and heritage meant nothing. There, in Hell, the flames would consume everything.

FOUR

The Valley of Tears

THE HORROR WAS VISCERAL, uniform and unrelenting. Stories of suffering merged and mutated. They emphasized the greatest truth, that the victims of a communal tragedy are individual and identifiable. Each boy had unrealized dreams, unspoken fears, a distinctive heritage. Death, like life, was personal.

Still, the deportation trains came. The first left Munkacs on 11 May. The last departed on 23 May. The ghetto was closed down on 26 May, when Auschwitz accepted its final consignment of misery from the town. Four days later, Munkacs was declared *Judenfrei*, clean of Jews.

Memories of savagery quickly faded in the minds of its perpetrators. After all, they reasoned, who would be left alive to condemn their cruelty? Who would remember that they whipped and cursed elderly Jews, with beards and sidelocks, into singing while they desecrated the sacred ground of the famous religious school established by Rabbi Shimon Shapira in Munkacs?

The desperate tears of old men, shed in shame and indignity, had evaporated in the wreckage. Boys like Hershel Herskovic, his younger brother Yisroel and cousin Chaim Schwimmer had become numbers on a ledger in Auschwitz-Birkenau. Functionaries like Laszlo Ferenczy, the senior gendarme officer who organized the deportation programme from Munkacs in minute detail, could congratulate themselves on a job well done.

His plan involved the evacuation of 3,000 people on each train. It was a marginal underestimate. Ferenczy warned the mayors of towns on the pre-planned route that they would be held responsible for keeping to the timetable. The nine transports from the brickworks in Munkacs carried a total of 28,587 Jews.

All had been stripped on arrival and beaten during a subsequent five-kilometre march to the loading area. In addition to ritual robbery, they were forced to burn prayer books and their four-cornered prayer shawls. The violence was so concerted that many of the vulnerable, and some of the most vociferous defenders of their faith, died.

Chaim Schwimmer had seen his father's will to live drain away. Prosperity was a fast-fading memory, but his father had used the remnants of his relative wealth to buy food for the less fortunate in the early days of captivity. Now, on the final leg of the train journey from Krakow to Auschwitz, he made peace with himself.

He struggled through prone passengers to the window, turned to Chaim and said: 'I need to daven [pray] one more time in my life. Understand this, my son.' With that he turned to the carriage wall, closed his eyes, and recited Mincha, the afternoon prayer service. It was the first time Chaim had seen his father cry. At that moment, the boy realized a torch was being passed down to him.

The four weeks in the ghetto had felt like four years. The first four minutes on the railway ramp at Auschwitz, when they were finally forced to disembark just after dawn the following morning, felt like four seconds. Almost before Chaim could blink in the unaccustomed glare of the morning sun, his parents vanished.

A man named Moshe Feldinger yelled repeatedly, 'Where are

we? Where are we?' One of the prisoners sorting through the belongings of the new arrivals, a Polish Jew from the Canada work detail, replied sourly, 'You are in the Valley of Tears.'

Chaim was in survival mode. His hunger overwhelmed his fatigue and confusion. Grief would descend on him later, like an assailant lunging from the shadows. His only instinct was to find food, and that involved taking a risk that, on many other days, with many other guards, would have resulted in a bullet in his brain.

Noticing how his fellow deportees had obeyed orders to throw their belongings on the boulder-strewn ground beside the track, he made his way to a neck-high pile of discarded coats and luggage. Surely, he told himself, someone would have taken the precaution of having a crust or a morsel of bread secreted somewhere close to hand.

He scrambled on to the pile, tore open a flimsy cardboard suitcase and found only clothing. It was the same with the next one, and the one after that. He was so engrossed in his task he failed to notice that a 30-metre gap had opened between him and the selection point.

Panic set in when he realized the danger he faced. Josef Mengele was staring at him in disbelief, which intensified as the boy sprinted past him and into the stragglers at the end of the line of the condemned, where he spotted his childhood Rabbi, Reb Avigdor, awaiting his fate.

The Rabbi wore glasses; Chaim had impertinently told others to remove theirs, since poor eyesight was an invariably fatal flaw in the eyes of those who dispensed life and death in the selections. Time stood still before Mengele's usual detachment dissolved. He screamed: 'Komm zurück, Junge, komm her!' ('Come back, boy, come here!'). Chaim saw two SS guards advancing towards him, and obeyed.

He was trembling as he looked up to the man who could wipe him out with a casual flick of a finger. 'Wie alt bist du, Junge?' ('How old are you, boy?'). Chaim was dry-mouthed and could only mumble inaudibly. Mengele, clearly irritated, repeated the question. 'Vierzehn,' advised one of the prisoners from the Canada work detail. 'Fourteen.'

Chaim babbled a statement of the obvious, which amounted to a plea for mercy: 'Ich habe Angst, Sir' ('I'm scared, sir'). The doctor looked at him intently. He would not waste too many more words on this wretch, but those three words gave the boy a future, of sorts. 'Komm da rüber!' ('Get over there!') he barked, gesturing to the right, and the ranks of the reprieved. This was no act of mercy; instead it was robotic, an illustration of the oppressor's need to be in control, as the final arbiter of life or death.

Even after he had stripped, showered, clothed and registered, Chaim struggled to come to terms with the abomination of his new surroundings. He knew he was lucky to be alive, but still could not process the monstrosity of the belching chimneys. He dared not analyse that sweet, cloying smell. Surely, he thought to himself, they are not burning people.

His answer came the following day, when he was moved to a new block. He came across a veteran inmate, a Jewish man who had managed to salvage his *kippa*, his skullcap. Chaim explained he did not know what had happened to his parents and was desperate to discover what had befallen them. It was a familiar question to the man, who was named Tzadik, which ironically means 'righteous one'.

He spoke slowly and sadly: 'See that fire? That's where your mother and father are. They're burning. God chose to punish the Polish people, who were not religious and did all sorts of bad things. But why did he do the same to the Hungarian people? You live the honest life. Why does He let them slaughter you? Why?'

The man trailed off and turned away. He knew there was no answer to his question.

Hershel Herskovic and his younger brother Yisroel were ahead of Chaim in the selection process. Normally, Hershel was the rash one; in this moment of truth, he was too bewildered to do anything that drew attention to himself. No one in his freight car, where more than eighty people were squeezed into a space once used for twenty soldiers, had heard the name Auschwitz before their arrival.

The family had debated volunteering to be on the first transport, reasoning they would have the choice of better accommodation at their destination, but were reluctant to travel on a Saturday. Other deportees were lulled into a false sense of security when the Germans planted handwritten notes on the train, purporting to come from former Jewish residents of Munkacs, who said they were satisfied with their lot in their new surroundings.

Gradually, however, almost through emotional osmosis, they all came to understand the nature of their journey. Hershel, like Chaim, noticed the impression of misery that settled on his father's face once the train entered German-occupied Polish territory. The realization that their initial optimism – that they were headed to Budapest, or the town of Hortobagy in central Hungary – had been dashed, was devastating.

Hershel, too, was parched and starving on arrival. He had a fleeting temptation to run, but his group of deportees had been herded on to rough, uneven ground. The stones were not especially large, but they were sharp. His father Abraham was transfixed by the chimneys. 'What is that big fire?' he repeatedly asked, to no one in particular. It was as if he could not compute the scale of an unfolding tragedy.

Abraham initially obeyed instructions to go to the right while his mother Devorah, his wife Chaya Soroh and the youngest seven of their eleven children were pushed left, towards the gas chambers. He tried to join them in an unwitting act of self-sacrifice, but was pushed back to the line of those spared to work.

The thread of life was gossamer thin. One of Hershel's uncles, initially reprieved, was ordered to join those casually condemned to death because an SS guard spotted an unsightly swelling on the back of his head. Such imperfection was fatal. Only one of Hershel's sisters, Yentl, was saved.

Years later Hershel would solemnly record the names and ages of his seven murdered siblings, as if paying homage at a memorial service:

Hentchl, a homemaker, was 13. Yankel, a marksman, was 11. Leah, our small babbeh, was 9. Shieh, who held himself like a general, was 7, and Moshe six and a half. Dovid was 4. Hudel was only six months old.

The Nazis deliberately set out to destroy family ties, having frayed them by constant harassment and persecution, and weakened them further by the privations of the ghettos and the ordeal of transportation. Separating siblings, and selecting mothers, in particular, for death, was an inhuman endgame.

Parents faced unimaginable choices and circumstances immediately after disembarkation. Those who were left clung together, while they could, but this was invariably impossible. Chaim lost track of his father, and did not know his fate, so he gravitated towards his cousin, who in turn sought out his brother.

Hershel and Yisroel were separated from their father and elder brother Berish after two days, when they were ordered to join a work detail, operating from the main camp. Before they were marched away by bayonet-wielding SS guards, their father pointed out his two youngest surviving sons. 'These are my children,' he exclaimed to the guards as he was hustled away. 'Haben Sie kein Angs,' he was told ('Have no fear').

Moses Eldar never really recovered from having his beard burned by those fascist youths. It broke him mentally, even if the physical scars slowly healed. He and his wife Tovah still had the strength to propel themselves out of the stifling cattle car when it arrived on the ramp in the late evening of Friday, 26 May 1944, but they disappeared, with their two youngest sons, almost immediately.

They had travelled for three days and nights, sustained only by dry bread. It was swelteringly hot during the day, and excruciatingly cold at night. The stench in the car was nauseating. 'We felt fear in our hearts,' recalled Mordechai, 'but no one could prophesy what was to happen.'

Mordechai, disorientated by the snarling dogs, club-wielding soldiers and mothers being coerced into abandoning their children by hovering inmates, never saw his parents and two young brothers again. For the last time at Auschwitz, he acted his age, fourteen and a half. Near hysterical with distress and bewilderment, he abandoned his grandmother and aunt and ran between the two lines of people, with different destinies, calling for his parents.

His cries fused with those of mothers screaming the names of their missing children, but were sufficiently shrill to gain a guard's attention. He pushed him, silently but contemptuously, towards the relatively able bodied. Mordechai felt no shame in continuing to screech. It was the only outlet for his pain.

He did not stop until, suddenly, he saw his surviving brother Yehuda walking along the fence in the opposite direction. He ran to him, oblivious to the blows he took on the back, shoulders and head from a stick wielded by a soldier who grabbed him, and fought to separate the boys.

Quickly realizing that the struggle was probably not worth the effort, and carried the danger of a loss of face, the soldier let Mordechai go with the warning: 'You will die tomorrow, not today.' The response – 'Yeah, with my brother' – was not terribly wise, but understandable. It was a flash of the type of defiance needed to survive.

The brothers registered what they thought was a smell of unplucked chickens burning. Smoke shrouded the sky. Mordechai whimpered breathlessly and intermittently. 'Does God know what they are doing to us?' he asked his brother. Learning from the excruciating blows taken by Yehuda across the back of his hand when he sought to help someone who had stumbled, he quickly retreated into himself.

The old lie, that the cattle car would take them from the ghetto to a camp to protect them from antisemites, had long since been exposed. This was a new reality; prison clothes that did not fit, and kapos, criminals from Ukraine, Russia and other Eastern European outposts, playing the sinister role of surrogate parents.

'The kapos spoke in a language we didn't understand and someone translated what was said to Hungarian. We were ordered to undress and get haircuts. They sprayed us with white powder and told us to shower quickly. They beat anyone who spoke with clubs and then ordered us to run towards the assembly area.'

It was approaching midnight. Mordechai hoped against hope that soon, in one of the forbidding lines of buildings in the camp, he would be reunited with his father. He thought of how Moses had talked constantly to God, and how he would lecture his children that, under no circumstances, should they desecrate the Sabbath. Now, it seemed, the Almighty had forgotten him in his time of need.

Mordechai had a vivid mental image of his father, and imagined the kindness and love in his voice, which he never quite managed to disguise in the name of discipline. His habit, of talking to his absent father in moments of stress or quiet contemplation, would stay with him for as long as he lived.

That was a reflection of the traditional status of a father in a Jewish family. He had the responsibility of teaching his son the scriptures, instructing him in a trade, finding him a wife, and teaching him how to swim. Some, to this day, take that final duty seriously. Most, though, regard it as a metaphor for seeking to secure their son's safe passage in the world.

Avigdor Neumann adored his father, Menachem. A stocky boy with a pleasant face and long, straight black hair, he was the fourth of seven children. One of them, a girl named Tziporah, died in infancy. Childhood photographs of him, dressed in a lace-collared frock coat and cradling a wooden hoop, were evidently deceptive.

By his own admission, Avigdor was a mischievous child. Things happened around him, and to him. Despite the temptations, his father preferred the carrot to the stick, and used to chide him gently: 'If you stand still for five minutes, I will pay you.' Despite the boy's sudden seriousness at the prospect of pocket money, both knew the chances of a payout were remote.

Menachem was, however, able to afford the finer things in life. As an extremely successful merchant of construction materials, he owned one of the biggest houses in the city of Velká Sevljuš, which was in Czechoslovakia until 1939, when it was annexed by Hungary and renamed Nagyszőlős. The local Jewish community, however, referred to it as Salaj.

A follower of the Satmar Hasidic sect, he relied on the self-restraint required by his faith to bring out the best in his free-spirited son. Avigdor would be woken at 5 a.m. and be taken, by candlelight, to pre-dawn prayers. He attended school from 8 a.m. to 2 p.m. and, after his mother Bella had given him lunch, returned to his studies until 7 p.m. Even then, if he had time after completing his homework, Avigdor would sit with his father, and learn rabbinical commentaries.

Menachem, a youthful-looking man, whose circular-framed glasses emphasized a long, open face, had passed on his finer features to his son. He was known for his generosity and even-handedness as a benefactor of several local charities, and distributed food to the needy from his kitchen.

The entire family was involved. Bella stood over a simmering pot of *cholent* on Friday afternoons, and the children handed out meals to anyone who walked up and along a large courtyard and knocked on their door. It was a measure of Menachem's insistence that anyone, however humble, deserved respect.

His social status had a spiritual significance, since he had the honour of hosting Rabbi Yo'el Teitelbaum, head of the Satmar dynasty, whenever he visited the area. Even a boy as strong willed and playful as Avigdor was awestruck by the holy man, who would test him on his religious knowledge.

Yo'el Teitelbaum would escape from the Bergen-Belsen concentration camp to Switzerland in August 1944. He was one of 1,600 Jews on thirty-five cattle wagons that formed the Kastner train, named after Rudolf Kastner, a Hungarian-Jewish lawyer who ransomed them with cash, gold and diamonds in a deal struck with Adolf Eichmann.

Rabbi Yo'el Teitelbaum spent two and a half years in Palestine before moving to the United States in 1947 in a sign of his virulent opposition to the creation of the State of Israel. He garnered a huge global following, as the Satmar sect's principal spiritual leader, until his death, aged ninety-two, in New York in August 1979.

Back in Salaj, the nature of a warm, inter-dependent community had changed dramatically at the outset of the Second World

War. Avigdor, who was eight years old at the time, saw Polish soldiers fleeing past their house, retreating towards the surrounding
countryside. His uncle, drafted into a labour battalion, was taken
prisoner by the Russians the following year.

Anti-Jewish propaganda, illustrated by vicious hook-nosed,
wild-eyed caricatures, filled the Hungarian newspapers in an
echo of the tactics used by the Nazis during their rise to power in
Germany. Local bullies, emboldened by regime change, abused
Avigdor in the streets and pulled at his sidelocks. When he was
eventually forced to wear a yellow star, he felt as if his life was not
his own.

There was an awful sense that something bad was about to
happen. It duly did so at 3 a.m. on the last night of Passover in
1944, when police and so-called loyal citizens demanded entry to
the Neumann family home. The family was forced to leave immediately, without possessions, and hustled to the ghetto.

The timing was not coincidental. It was designed to signal the
futility of faith.

Menachem was taken, along with other prominent citizens, to
a cellar in which they were tortured in order to reveal the loca-
tion of their personal assets, and the community's wealth. When
he was reunited with his family in the Great Synagogue, emaciated and without his beard, the final preparations for deportation
were underway.

Bella had been allowed to return home briefly, to retrieve provisions and a limited amount of clothing. Her husband, once
tall and proud, was now stooped, a shell of a man. Avigdor, only
twelve, had new responsibilities, the most important of which
was looking after the main basket of food his mother had prepared for the journey.

His sense of shame at dropping the basket in fright when he
saw Bella being beaten as they queued for the train between two

ranks of policemen stayed with him. He dared not retrace his steps to retrieve it; although his siblings carried some food, he blamed himself for the family's hunger during the seventy-two-hour journey to Auschwitz-Birkenau.

They had no water. Three tin buckets, which acted as toilets, were soon overflowing. The stench was overpowering, and the mood became irritable. Arguments broke out with increasing frequency and disturbing intensity. When the train stopped briefly at Kosice, Menachem broke his silence. 'This isn't good,' he said quietly. 'We're probably going to Poland.'

When Avigdor stepped out on to the railway ramp at Auschwitz-Birkenau, just before noon on 22 May 1944, his childhood ended. The scene was nothing like the one that camp commandant Rudolf Höss described with utter indifference, in the autobiography he was ordered to write between his war-crimes trial and his execution, at Auschwitz, on 16 April 1947:

> On the camp ramp, already waiting were SS guards and prisoners designated to collect and load on to lorries the luggage of the deportees. Once the freight car doors were opened, the Jews heard shouted-out orders to: get out, leave all luggage and bundles behind, immediately assemble on the ramp in [separate] columns for men and for women with children.
>
> At that stage the SS guards did not usually use force, so as not to cause panic among the newly arrived, which would complicate and prolong the selection procedure. Therefore they calmly explained that the deportees would first be taken to be bathed to prevent them from starting an epidemic in the camp, after which they would be put in a housing barracks before eventually being sent out to work.
>
> Asked by the deportees about when their belongings would be returned or when they would see their loved ones, the SS

guards replied 'soon', 'tomorrow' or 'on Sunday'. When the deportees asked the prisoners on the ramp, 'Poles' or 'Polish Jews', the answers were evasive, but mothers were advised to hand their infants over to grandmothers or other elder women.

That bland, cynical summary pointedly ignored the despair of separated families, and the violence enacted on those rash enough to break ranks. Menachem saw Bella struggle and ordered Avigdor to 'go and help your mother with the children'. He complied immediately, leaving his father and eldest brother with the rest of the men, waiting in lines of five on the far side of the track.

A veteran inmate, realizing the boy was physically able to work, shoved him back towards his father, who was doing his best to hide his own vulnerability. Avigdor tried to rejoin his mother, and as the pair struggled, the prisoner murmured in Yiddish: 'Listen, son. If I see you here again it will be the end of you.'

The disturbance caught the attention of Mengele, who stopped the boy when he reached the selection point. 'Wie alt bist du?' he asked ('How old are you?'). Avigdor lied without missing a beat: 'Fünfzehn' ('Fifteen'). The doctor replied: 'Was machst du?' ('What do you do?'). Again, the boy lied for his life: 'Ich bin Mechaniker' ('I'm a mechanic'). He had never used so much as a screwdriver.

Convinced, perhaps against his better judgement, Mengele waved him to the right with his customary insouciance. As he obeyed, Avigdor could not resist a glance at the pathetic retinue of women and children, holding hands as they walked across the tracks in the direction of the gas chamber. At that moment, to use his childish expression, he felt 'lower than a worm'.

He waited for hours, in a freezing bathhouse, before being given his flimsy prison uniform, which lacked underwear and socks. On his way to the barracks, he was approached by an inmate, holding a loaf of bread under his arm. Wordlessly, the prisoner handed it to the boy and hastened away.

It was a gesture so out of context with the setting that everyone paused in disbelief. Avigdor gave the loaf to his father, believing he would share the invaluable gift with him and his brother. Instead, in an act of profound generosity, Menachem gave equal portions to everyone in their detail.

Avigdor had never felt more proud of the man who had given him the ultimate example of humanity. It was bitterly cold that night. The boy sensed his father's discomfort on the wooden bunk and pressed his back against him to transmit his body heat. 'Now,' he thought to himself, 'I am a man.'

Yosef Zalman Kleinman was on the same train from Nagyszőllős, with his father Meir, mother Bryna, brother Solomon and sister Tuba. He had been born there, in January 1930, when it was part of Czechoslovakia. They were a religious family, who prayed twice daily in the synagogue.

His father did not speak Hungarian, so Yosef would read newspapers to him, outlining world and local events. The boy pasted reports into a scrapbook, which would later be burned at the request of his mother, because she believed the family would be punished by the Germans since it featured maps detailing battle fronts, and anticipated troop movements.

With the small family shop struggling, the boys did menial jobs to help make ends meet. Bryna made meals go a long way, and would send Yosef to check the ingredients were kosher. She kept scrawny chickens for the pot, and her speciality was Friday night's fish soup. Despite financial difficulties, the Kleinmans were a self-sufficient unit.

For them, the Holocaust began on 19 March 1944, when the community was preoccupied by a visit from a prominent Hasidic Rabbi, who came to offer seven blessings at the wedding of his niece, who had settled in Nagyszőllős after being orphaned in 1941, when her parents had been sent to the camps.

Yosef and his brother Solomon, who was eighteen months older, sneaked into the wedding banquet after initially being denied entry by the elders. They stood, pinned to the wall to the side of the long main table, where the Rabbi had pride of place. The celebratory air disappeared instantly when an aide whispered in his ear.

The Rabbi appeared momentarily confused, but quickly regained his composure and his customary authority. He pushed back his chair, stood up, and banged on the table, asking for silence. 'Gentlemen,' he said. 'We finish this feast right away. You should all scatter home.'

It soon became clear that Germany's invasion of Hungary would have devastating consequences. The war that Meir Kleinman had followed through his son's diligent distillation of events had arrived in their backyard. When, on the day after Passover, Meir was escorted back to the house by policemen who refused to allow him to worship at the synagogue, the die was cast.

The family went to a neighbour, a non-Jew, to listen to radio reports of regime change. It was then they heard of a general provision, ordering all Jews into ghettos. It was a week before the Kleinmans had to comply. Yosef acted on his own initiative, and immediately hid their silver candlesticks in a piece of cloth in the attic of another neighbour, where the head of the household had been taken as a slave labourer.

All around the city, families were being ambushed by memory. Some risked a final visit to ancestors, in graveyards dotted with ivy-strewn headstones. Others were in an agony of indecision; which heirlooms could they smuggle into the few belongings they would be permitted? What would they abandon for the vultures that would undoubtedly descend?

All three Kleinman children had been born in their house. Closing the front door for the final time was uniquely traumatic. Many tears had been shed before the residents of the street departed, en masse, for the ghetto, where they would live in basements, attics, and courtyards exposed to the elements.

On 18 May they were told they would be leaving for 'western Hungary' the following day. Bryna and several of her erstwhile neighbours made dough, and planned to bake bread in an oven owned by a sympathetic non-Jew. Each family took its turn; half an hour after Bryna had inserted her bread dough, the house was invaded by gendarmes.

'Ki a házból, menj ki!' they screamed ('Get out of the house, get out!'). Bryna scrambled to retrieve the half-baked bread. It crumbled quickly in the children's backpacks, which became uncomfortably hot on the march to the clearing station. As the column progressed along a tree-lined avenue, Yosef had what amounted to an out-of-body experience.

Something told him he needed to commit the scene to memory. He broke ranks, turned, and looked back at the tide of humanity lapping towards him. It was an eerily compelling sight, a tableau of loss and subjugation that he never forgot, even later amidst the horrors of Auschwitz-Birkenau.

The column marched in lines of five. It spanned the generations, from babes in arms to faltering grandparents, and even the occasional great-grandparent. Yosef began to notice people throwing money out of their pockets. Before long, the roads were littered with discarded packages.

No one imagined that around 80 per cent of them would be killed in the extermination camp that awaited them.

Yosef had never been on a train journey before. Instinctively curious, he counted the passengers in their freight carriage. Eighty-four Jews were at the mercy of fate. When the boy peered through a small window, and managed to read the station's name, Meir exclaimed, 'Oh, wow. We are going to Poland.'

Similar conversations were being had elsewhere on the train, but Meir seemed particularly surprised. He wore his prayer shawl, and became preoccupied with the rituals of religious devotion. He barely spoke again, until the doors opened at Auschwitz.

He did not drink on the journey, giving what little water there was available to his family, and so was weak and dehydrated. Yosef helped his father get down from the carriage, and left him leaning against it as he collected a prayer book he had spotted in a pile of discarded belongings.

A passage from Exodus entered his head: 'Honour your father and your mother, that you may long endure on the land that your God is assigning to you.' He dutifully collected raindrops from the carriage roof, wet his father's lips, and, placing an arm in the small of his back, helped him along the track.

By that time, Bryna and her twelve-year-old daughter Tuba had gone forever. His brother Solomon was several rows ahead of them in the men's queue. Before his youngest son had time to react, Meir was separated from Yosef, and sent to die. By the time they emerged, shivering, in their prison clothes, the brothers were alone in the world. Their family had fed the flames.

FIVE

The Art of Survival

DUGO LEITNER WAS KNEE-DEEP in human excrement. He could not have been happier, since, as one of twenty boys selected for the *Scheisskommando*, the sewage crew, he had the opportunity to prove he was fit for even the most revolting work. Compared to the dangers of enforced idleness, endured by the majority of the Hungarian boys, the risk of contracting dysentery was worth taking.

He spent each morning cleaning out the contents of the latrines, sweeping up faeces in buckets, which were taken away on carts to which the boys were harnessed. On one particular day, once they had deposited their evil-smelling cargo in ditches between Crematoria 4 and 5, they became aware of a terrible sense of responsibility.

Dugo saw several hundred people, waiting outside the gas chamber for space to die. It was awful, more gut-wrenching than anything he had been forced to wade through. He was pierced by their vacant stares. 'They know what's coming,' he thought. 'We know.' The emotional symmetry between them was unnerving, unforgettable.

The sewage crew's heads were bowed, as if they felt the weight of historical outrage on their necks. They lifted, suddenly, in response to their supervisor, a Czech Jewish inmate named

Silberman, who was known as the *Scheissmeister*. He owed his life to his quick-wittedness and awareness of what was expected of him, but he placed his moral principles to the fore.

He addressed the boys directly: 'Even in this Hell, where we are, we must not forget what we have learned. Here, too, we have to continue studying as much as we can. One day soon, there will be an end to this Hell. We don't know which of us will live, so we have to do good and get out of here as human beings.'

He urged them to sing, loudly and passionately. The response was remarkable. The boys' voices were powerful, dripping with emotion. Even the *Sonderkommando*, the prisoners who traded their humanity for temporary survival in the killing field, and were conditioned to daily acts of depravity, were deeply moved.

In emotional terms, it was a *mikveh*, a cleansing bath that also delivered spiritual purification. Dugo's boyish impulses were stripped away. He thought of song as an expression of belief, in the greatest moment of doubt. He loved singing, because it was an expression of who he was, and where he came from, but he had never loved singing more. He sang because he was Jewish.

The last vestiges of innocence had literally been knocked out of him. He had been sideswiped by a gypsy boy – 'a ten-year-old kid', according to the fourteen-year-old veteran, clearly affronted and radiating wounded pride – who hit him around the head and struggled to steal his shoes. Dugo shook him off, and proceeded to slash the soles so they were less likely to be envied. He made a silent promise he would never again be so vulnerable. In Auschwitz-Birkenau, he understood, the law of the jungle operated.

His father and brother had been taken from Camp D, the men's camp, to Buchenwald as slave labourers for the armaments industry. The pair had clashed constantly before their transportation, but Meir Leitner's first thought was to feed his older son, at his own expense. These were the contradictions of love and loss.

Dugo was plunged into a form of mourning. He had imaginary conversations with his father. 'Why do you deserve this suffering?' he asked him. 'You are such a righteous one. You were born in 1905, and were constantly conscripted. You were sent away from us to labour and fight in Ukraine. Why? Why you?'

In the real world, once Meir had been taken through the entrance gate to Buchenwald, under its mocking inscription 'Jedem das Seine' ('To each his own'), he was at the mercy of fate. Death rates in the camp were around 25 per cent; with cruel irony Meir died just before inmates were forced on a death march on 8 April 1945, three days before the Americans arrived. Dugo's brother Shmuel was gravely ill with typhus when he was liberated, but rallied and recovered.

Avigdor Neumann, who had also managed to inveigle himself into the *Scheisskommando*, was suffering similar grief. In mid-June, three weeks or so after he had moved into Camp D with his father and elder brother, their barracks was placed into lockdown. This so-called *Blocksperre* was ominous, since it signalled impending change on a large scale.

A new sub-camp, Kaufering, was being set up in Bavaria. Slave labour was required to create three massive underground bunkers for fighter-aircraft factories, which were vulnerable to Allied bombing on the surface. Menachem Neumann and his eldest son were in the wrong place at the wrong time.

They were sent to Warsaw, on to Dachau, and finally to Kaufering where the bunkers, up to 400 metres in length and five storeys in height, would be protected by a layer of gravel ten metres thick, and a concrete roof with a depth of three metres. The inmates had to build, and then partially bury, the huts in which they slept, on straw.

Their roofs, made of earth, were porous, and the floors were criss-crossed by rat runs. The work, which also involved the construction of railway embankments, was brutal; around half of the 30,000 slaves died from hunger, disease, exhaustion or summary execution. Avigdor's father and brother did not survive.

Avigdor was taken to be tattooed soon after they left Auschwitz. He no longer had a name; he was B 14665. He felt humiliated, as insignificant as a speck of dust.

Most of the Hungarian boys were quarantined for between six and eight weeks in an isolation barracks in Camp A, where they were examined daily by one of three doctors, Josef Mengele, Heinz Thilo and Berthold Epstein. Mengele needed no introduction; Thilo, an SS gynaecologist, was deeply unpleasant.

An enthusiastic participant in selections, he called the camp 'the arsehole of the world'. He was involved in the liquidation of the Theresienstadt family camp on 10–11 July 1944, when approximately 7,000 Jews were murdered in the gas chambers, and eventually committed suicide in prison while awaiting trial.

Epstein, by contrast, was liked and trusted by the boys, despite his enforced role as Mengele's assistant. Born into a Jewish family in Czechoslovakia, he escaped to Norway in 1940, where he became one of the few refugees accepted into the medical profession. He worked as a paediatrician until the German invasion in April 1942.

Arrested and deported on the cargo ship SS *Donau* in November 1942, he was put to work in Auschwitz, where his wife Ottillie and several other family members were murdered. Despite the efforts of Prince Carl of Sweden and Norway to have him released from service, he was kept in post until the Red Army liberated the camp, whereupon he treated survivors and joined the Czech Army Corps.

By early August, the majority of the boys were transferred to Camp E, the former gypsy camp, which was closest to the gas chambers. This was a matter of days after the previous occupants, around 4,200 Roma and Sinti men, women and children, were loaded on to trucks and sent to die. Typically, the boys learned of their forthcoming extermination through word of mouth. One of their own, Ze'ev Schick, kept records as part of a clerical job given to him by a kindly German communist prisoner named Max, who ran the clothing warehouse.

Conditions were forbidding. Heating, of sorts, was provided by two tin stoves, connected by a brick channel that ran across a damp mud floor. The blocks were poorly lit, and had little ventilation, so bad smells lingered. Roofs leaked. Two barrels, at the back door, acted as toilets. Insects proliferated, and lice were everywhere, leading to scabies.

Freshly shaven and bald – Dugo reckoned 'the SS made us ugly' – the boys, who were joined by gaunt, prematurely aged survivors of the liquidation of the Lodz ghetto in Poland, were in a kind of limbo. They were not forced to work, like adult men, but knew their chances of survival were likely to depend on their usefulness to their captors.

Rumours circulated incessantly. One suggested they were being kept alive for a possible prisoner exchange in a neutral country. Another hinted they were being saved for work in what was described as 'a builder's school'. Boys would seek the advice of veteran prisoners they came across. One *Sonderkommando* member, thought to be a Belgian Jew, predicted they were approaching 'the end of days'. He warned: 'If it continues like this there will be no Jews left in Europe.'

In such circumstances, Dugo and Avigdor's job with the *Scheisskommando* was envied, due to its grubby, but life-affirming, perks. It was, by common consent, one of the best jobs in the house, despite side effects that ranged from diarrhoea and vomiting to constipation. The boys even made childish jokes about it. A particularly thin stool in the latrines was referred to as *matzah*, the unleavened flatbread that was a staple feature of Jewish cuisine.

Their daily rations were meagre, consisting of 250 grams of two-day-old bread, a small piece of cheese or sausage, an approximation of tea in the morning and a litre of soup at noon. The boys would jostle for position, attempting to secure the thicker soup towards the bottom of the pot. The Kleinman brothers took turns licking out one another's bowls.

The *Scheisskommando* were expected to weed the area around the electrified fences, and maintain the lawns outside the administrative offices, but it was in the area around the kitchens that they derived the biggest benefits from being strapped to the garbage carts. They rummaged in the bins to find potato peelings and other small pieces of discarded food.

Yaakov Yosef Weiss, a later recruit to the group, was particularly ecstatic when he discovered two cabbage leaves. He sucked them intently, before sharing them with friends from his home town. Their unofficial self-help group was based on their faith. One had traded a piece of bread for a small prayer book found by the Canada Kommando, which sifted through discarded belongings. The boys recited passages from it to pass the time, and to replenish their belief.

They formed in groups of ten so they could pray in a *minyan*, a religious quorum. Such communal devotion, sometimes wordlessly observed as they stood together at morning roll call, added to the cohesion of a rapidly evolving community. Their unified approach was seen as a direct threat by the more nihilistic Nazis, who rejected all moral and religious principles.

Other supportive groups were formed, increasingly involving previously detached strangers. That realization, that no one would look out for them but themselves, tightened the bonds, and heightened the importance of behavioural norms. Gradually, a moral code, and a sense of brotherhood, began to emerge.

The boys from Lodz, survivors of 80,000 deportees from the city, taught their Hungarian counterparts how to work together to stay warm, either in the barracks at night, or especially in the frigid hours spent waiting for the formalities of morning registration to be completed in the *Appelplatz*, the roll-call square.

On the instruction to 'make a heater' they would gather in tight circles. Those on the outside circles would press inwards, transferring their body heat to those in the middle. After a while, and following another call to 'make a heater' from someone on the periphery of the group, the roles were reversed. Everyone benefited from such communal cohesion. It was a simple, selfless theory, tested in adversity.

Despite such thoughtful considerations, newcomers could not be shielded from the truth, however distressing. It was natural to hope, against hope, that a missing relative would be found, but there was also a moral imperative to explain the fate of those from whom they had been separated during selection.

The boys reasoned it was far better to have the flames and the man-made fog explained by someone who had recently gone through the pain of similar loss, than to hear the theatrical descriptions of veteran prisoners, of parents, brothers and sisters, leaving this earth as particles of ash.

Yosef Zalman Kleinman remembered standing by the fence, on his first day in the camp, and overhearing a veteran prisoner talking to two newcomers. 'Do you see where the chimneys are?' he pointed out. 'You see? It's not a factory. It's not a bakery. It's burning your families, your children.'

Yosef was shocked to the core by the lack of sensitivity and compassion. He thought to himself: 'How can he talk like that?' But within a matter of weeks he understood. He had heard many, many such conversations. They were part of an inmate's rite of passage.

Everyone recognized their own truth. When the extermination of those from the Lodz ghetto was at its height, Yosef noticed the smoke from the chimneys was especially white. Scientifically, this indicates a high moisture content in whatever is being burned, but he was convinced it was because the victims were on the edge of starvation.

Certain principles were, however, non-negotiable. Stealing from fellow prisoners was considered unthinkable, though pilfering from their captors was celebrated. There was an unspoken acknowledgement that, providing that it didn't endanger yourself, you had a duty to help your fellow man. Under no circumstances would informing on others, for personal gain, be tolerated.

The stronger characters, like Yaakov Yosef Weiss, who felt, with notable understatement, that 'it was all a bit of a mess', acted as enforcers against those who preyed on weaker boys. Food set the agenda. A boy's bread was his most treasured possession. Rations would be shared unhesitatingly on an equal basis, even if they came from an external source, like the sewage crew.

There was a hierarchy of betrayal involving so-called *Funktionshäftlinge*, prisoner functionaries recruited by the SS to maintain order and dispense discipline. The *Lagerälteste*, the camp elder, was at the head of what was literally a food chain. He controlled the *Blockälteste*, the block elders, who oversaw individual barracks. Kapos guarded the prisoners at work.

These functionaries were originally German and Austrian criminals, and as the camp expanded, political prisoners were given supervisory duties. Eventually other nationalities were employed; Ukrainian recruits were particularly feared, but some Jewish collaborators were equally vicious.

They controlled all aspects of the boys' daily lives, allocating work details and overseeing the distribution of rations. They had their secret schemes with corrupt guards and their personal favourites, but knew their welfare was linked to the satisfaction of their benefactors in the SS.

This led to violent extremes, designed to showcase their commitment to the job. One *Blockälteste*, a Polish Jew, became notorious for flogging boys for the slightest transgression. One boy, Meir Ackerman, could not sit down for two weeks after he was given twenty-five lashes. He eventually lost the sight in one eye due to regular beatings.

Yosef Zalman Kleinman's record of one such assault was documented for posterity by historian Esther Farbstein:

The German ordered the boy to bend over and started flogging him. There were a few of us boys around, curious like me, and we started counting the lashes. The boy didn't moan or cry. We were very surprised.

We counted twenty. We counted twenty-five. We counted thirty. Still the boy did not make a sound. It was astonishing. We had never seen anything like it. The boy's lack of response infuriated the flogger more and more, until after the fortieth lash he turned him over on the floor and continued flogging him on his face and legs.

The boy did not make a sound. Only after the fiftieth lash did the rubber hose stop twisting in the air. The flogger went out of the barrack and we helped the boy get up from the floor. It is hard for me to forget the red mark across his forehead. We asked him: 'What did you do? Why did he flog you?'

The boy replied: 'It was worth it. I brought my friends a few prayer books to pray with.' We helped him get up on his bunk, and some boys treated him to lessen his pain. No one was left unmoved by that scene.

The boys were occasionally subjected to a literal blood sport, being forced to hit one another until they were beyond the point of submission. It was degrading and dangerous, but justified in the eyes of their tormentors because it reinforced the balance of power within the block. The 'fights' proved the functionaries had the capacity to do what they wanted, regardless of the conventions of decency.

Mordechai Eldar, strong willed, shrewd and naturally observant, noticed another sinister element of exploitation in his barracks. It involved a Ukrainian kapo, who oversaw work details in the local lumber mill where he became infamous for insisting on silence while prisoners laboured. He would beat anyone he saw talking to a neighbour with a heavy stick.

At night, he returned to the barracks, where he took children into his bed. The boys were given preferential treatment, and additional rations, until they outlived their usefulness. Then they were quietly killed, to prevent their remaining as witnesses to the kapo's perversion.

It was all too easy to disappear in the camp. Even if absences were apparent, they were quickly forgotten. The scale of mass murder, the sheer numbers involved in the industrialization of death, was overwhelming. On 30 August, for instance, 874 prisoners in the *Sonderkommando* were employed, burning bodies in the crematoria. Another 400 or so were used to burn bodies in external pits. They worked around the clock.

Mordechai, however, was unwilling to forget, and he pledged never to forgive. Two of the boys, recycled so casually, obscenely and inhumanly by the kapo, came from his home town of Campulung La Tisa. One of them had shared a piece of his additional bread with him, before he was disposed of. He was consumed by rage, and guilt.

Everyone was being tested, regardless of their natural strengths.

Avigdor Neumann might have been respected for his resilience by his peers, but he could not hide from himself. He had no idea how he had not broken under the strain. He drew solace from the bedrock of his faith, but couldn't explain how he kept body and mind together under such duress.

Ultimately, he reasoned, the only way to survive was to submit yourself to the vagaries of fate. His life, or death, was preordained. His ordeal was inescapable, but manageable if only he could rationalize its brutality. That process, of course, was incredibly hard to bear. Like everyone, he flirted with surrender.

Food was an understandable, but tragically powerful preoccupation. One of the saddest sights the boys saw as they tentatively explored the camp was that of so-called *Muselmänner*, those in the later stages of what was, effectively, psychologically induced starvation. They had become conditioned to talking incessantly about food, and fantasizing about favourite meals until they were overwhelmed by their obsession.

Their plight would be summarized during the trial of Adolf Eichmann in Israel in 1961 by Dr Aahron Beilin, a Jewish doctor from Bialystok in Poland who was saved by his recruitment as a nurse in Auschwitz-Birkenau. He described the loss of control, created by a surge in the secretion of digestive acids that accompanied imaginary smells and tastes:

That was the first stage, and we knew that within a day or two the *Musselman* would enter the second stage. There was not such a rigorous division, but he would stop taking an interest in his surroundings, and would also cease reacting to orders. His motions would become very slow, his face frozen like a mask.

He would no longer have control over his bowels. He would relieve himself where he was. He was not even turning over when he lay down. He was a skeleton with bloated legs. Because they wanted to drag these people to roll call, they were placed forcibly next to the wall with their hands above their heads and their face to the wall. It was a skeleton with a grey face that would lean against the wall, swaying back and forth.

They would invariably be put out of their misery, though the chances of their deaths being recorded were remote. The Nazi bureaucracy was beginning to buckle under the strain. Documentation was incomplete, and numbers were hard to authenticate. It is thought around 232,000 children aged eighteen or under passed through Auschwitz-Birkenau. Of these 216,000 were Jews; the vast majority were aged fifteen or under.

The slave-labour force was thinning out, due to demands from sites deeper inside Germany. This opened the way for boys aged under fifteen to be sent on more localized work details, either within the Auschwitz complex, or in other external settings, such as the Brzeszcze coal mine, or the oil refinery at Trzebinia, a sub-camp established in early August 1944.

Prisoners, guarded by around sixty SS men, were put to work expanding the refinery. They dug ditches, laid foundations, installed a sewage system, and built railroad tracks. It was exhausting, unrelenting work, complicated by constant American bombing raids, which led to another demand, the creation of air-raid shelters.

With nearby industrial plants in Upper Silesia, mainly iron and steel mills and mines producing coal, lead and zinc, operating at capacity, other boys were allocated to agricultural or livestock farms, which offered opportunities for secretive scavenging of food, and other tradeable items.

The most prized jobs remained in the kitchen area, where Zalman Leib Meisels, son of a prominent religious figure known

as the Dayan of Vác, was assigned to ferrying food and messages. Yet, despite his security in the *Scheisskommando*, Dugo
Leitner had set his sights on what he regarded as the ultimate
life-insurance policy, a tattoo; many of the boys did not receive
one until later in their incarceration.

The nickname by which he was known referred to the sound
made by a cork as it is pulled from a bottle. It suited perfectly his
bubbly character, even if he blurred the boundaries between self-
assurance and foolishness. His first great confidence trick could
well have been his last.

Working on the logic that the tattoo would enable him to be
allocated external work, and be registered with the Red Cross, he
took to hanging around the camp's transport office with a couple
of like-minded boys. He seized what he thought was the main
chance by approaching a group of men at the office entrance.

'Who are you?' he asked them, disingenuously. 'We are from
Theresienstadt, and come for a number so we can go to work.'
He was directed inside, to a bored-looking clerk, who asked his
name. 'Rinbeck,' said the boy, off the top of his head. He invented
a birthdate and other minor details, and, to his delight, was tattooed on his left forearm with the number 14671.

His plan had what should have been a fatal flaw. It did not
account for a visit to the office from Josef Mengele, who saw
through the ruse almost immediately, and called in the guards.
Dugo was ordered to return to the chastened clerk, who blurred
and partially erased the tattoo.

The guards then beat Dugo, and his accomplices, savagely. He
knew how lucky he had been not to be hanged, and so soaked up
the punishment until he was allowed to stagger back to barracks.
His relatively carefree mornings, cleaning out the latrines, had
never seemed more alluring.

SIX

Sixty Years On

MORDECHAI ELDAR AND Moses Shalem slept beside one another as best as they could on overcrowded wooden bunks, sharing stories of loss and longing during slow, cold nights. Each felt alone in the world, a deep, dispiriting ache. They decided their best chance of staying alive was to confront death, in all its hideous forms.

Thrown together by fate, the strangers resolved to be the brothers the Nazis had killed, or had taken away from them. They would look out for each other, share food, and commit to a friendship like no other. They would volunteer for any job, no matter how menial or disturbing, because the alternative was oblivion.

Mordechai had grown seven centimetres in the previous year, but his mental state did not reflect his burgeoning physical maturity. It had taken him only three or four days, following the sudden and unresolved departure of his brother Yehuda, to realize he would not survive without him. He hid his insecurities well, but recognized, in Moses, someone who was even more street smart than he had forced himself to become.

Moses was older, taller, more reflective. When Mordechai talked about the temptations of suicide, he understood his despair, and admitted he had harboured similar thoughts, but argued that self-destruction would not bring Yehuda back. It would accomplish nothing. Whether he had been taken to the crematorium, or to another camp, it would fail to solve the riddle of his fate.

They would run to the wire together if they were overwhelmed by events, but they owed it to one another to eke out an existence, of sorts.

These were dangerous days, when quotas needed to be fulfilled. The boys were prohibited from taking refuge in their barracks during the day; hanging around the periphery of the camp was a perilous exercise, since anyone, regardless of age, health and sex, was considered fair game for the so-called death catchers if the numbers of victims didn't meet targets. It felt safer to have a routine to follow, a role to fulfil.

Collecting the dead from outside the barrack blocks each morning was the worst of tasks, but also one of the best, since a piece of bread, or a sliver of potato, would occasionally be found in the uniforms that hung limply from stiffened bodies. To win that job, Mordechai and Moses followed the advice of veteran inmates, and ingratiated themselves with the functionaries whenever possible.

They would load corpses on to a two-wheeled cart, one taking the victim's arms and the other his legs. Once they had been piled precariously high, the bodies would be taken to the main gate, where the boys would be given an empty cart to continue their collection. The bodies, meanwhile, were transferred to the crematoria or the burning pits.

The boys' old sensitivities had long since been abandoned. They were so accustomed to death, both sudden and prolonged, it had become part of their daily lives. Their empty bellies told them there was precious little food around. They saw the contorted bodies of those who had chosen suicide by throwing themselves at the electrified fences, most commonly in the evening.

They shut their emotions down, and took their time taking their load to the gate, pausing briefly to rifle through the pockets of the corpses. Occasionally, they removed a relatively clean shirt, which they wore themselves or saved for bartering sessions, which also involved stolen hats, shoes and shoelaces.

Mordechai and Moses lingered near the kitchens, trading for potato soup. They understood that such opportunism, or even a rash act of generosity, could be fatal. Everyone knew the story of the boy, a kitchen orderly, who had been hanged after being caught throwing a cabbage to a passing group of Soviet prisoners of war.

The risks were worthwhile, because of the subversive satisfaction of surreptitiously sharing a potato, bite by bite. Mordechai had found someone to watch over him. Moses had found an ally. And then, by chance one evening, Mordechai found his sisters, Ita and Sarah. He had something, someone, to cling to.

Several of the boys had similar good fortune, in finding siblings in the women's camp, Camp C, which adjoined their barracks in Camp A. These women were spared the gas chamber because of their apparent suitability for work. Some boys were reunited with their siblings when they called out their names, hoping they would register with the female inmates on the other side of the wire in the *Frauenlager*. Others caught a glimpse of them in the distance, and yelled to get their attention; the women did likewise.

The emotions these interactions unleashed were powerful and prolonged. Avigdor Neumann went to the fence to meet his eldest sister Sima Rachel on as many mornings as possible. He would wrap messages around a stone, and trust his aim was relatively accurate.

She survived the Holocaust but, as an old woman living in Israel, could still not recall one such conversation without enduring the deepest sadness. It came when Avigdor shouted to her: 'You know I am thirteen today. It is my bar mitzvah.' The realization that, instead of celebrating a cherished part of growing up, he was a vulnerable boy obliged to be old before his time, broke her heart.

His life had been splintered; it remained to be seen whether it would be cut short. The prospect was haunting. Sima Rachel knew that it would have been easier for him to succumb to humiliation and hunger, to lose the instinct to recoil and recover from the daily beatings. Yet something told Avigdor that salvation was possible. He was sustained by his parents' legacy, their faith.

Those principles created a formidable bond, regardless of gender. The boys' religious devotion might have been more vocal, but the girls, and the older women to whom they deferred, had religious discussions of greater subtlety, if no less intensity. There was an unspoken admission that it helped to retain their identity, as human beings.

Kindness, they discovered, was double-edged, benefiting both giver and receiver. The women made presents from salvaged pieces of wood or fabric, and shared favourite recipes from their childhoods. They created greetings cards from scraps of paper and, in some cases, even fashioned portraits of friends, or sketches of everyday life in the camps. These outlets for their creativity were another expression of individuality.

Though the sexes mingled in warehouses and administrative offices, they were generally strictly segregated. The only male prisoners allowed to enter the female camp were in construction gangs. This led to some women deliberately breaking bunks or damaging the structure of their barracks, so that workmen would eventually come to fix it.

As they did so, information about sons, fathers and husbands would be sought, and messages sent. Another ruse, clerks deliberately sending a parcel to the wrong area of the camp so it would have to be retrieved, was a similarly effective method of communication. There seemed little to lose. Jewish workers in SS offices were told by guards: 'You can know everything, since you will all die anyway.'

Mordechai would throw bread and other pilfered morsels to his sisters. They mourned their parents and their brothers, Shlomo and Avraham, but drew strength from their reunion. Another Shlomo, the abnormally tall elder brother of Yosef Zalman Kleinman, found himself in demand, because his height allowed him to hurl goods greater distances over the fence from a better angle.

The offerings were invaluable, since conditions in the *Frauenlager* were terrible. The women's clothing was invariably filthy, due to their having to sleep on the clay floor of the barracks. There was a perpetual shortage of bunks and a lack of running water. Work on a washroom started in 1944, but it was never finished.

Unlike the men, who tended to be quickly removed from Auschwitz-Birkenau if they were selected for external slave labouring, the women would often remain in the camp for many months, since the industrial demand for them was not as great. This relative lack of suitability for the heaviest work counted against them.

Mortality rates among the women were high, due to the brutality of the regime initially overseen by Franz Hössler and his deputy Adolf Taube, who were responsible for hundreds of deaths. Hössler was captured by the British and hanged on 13 December 1945, but Taube, who according to eyewitnesses summarily shot or kicked to death female prisoners who were late for their work details, managed to evade justice.

Two of the worst monsters were female. SS supervisor Maria

Mandl reported directly to commandant Rudolf Höss. Any inmate foolish enough to make eye contact with her, as she stood at the main gate into Auschwitz-Birkenau, would be hustled away, and never seen again.

She signed off the deaths of thousands of women and children on arrival, and subsequently staged a series of selections designed to weed out prisoners she deemed weak, exhausted, or ill-suited for work. She was executed for crimes against humanity in January 1948.

Mandl had promoted Irma Grese, a notorious sadist and sexual pervert who was alleged to have had an affair with Josef Mengele, to head up the Hungarian women's camp at Birkenau in May 1944. This elevation to *Oberaufseherin*, the second-highest rank an SS *Aufseherin* could attain, gave her unlimited power over more than 30,000 inmates.

Grese would slash inmates across their breasts with a cellophane whip, causing hideous infections, or beat them with a rubber truncheon, and frequently sent healthy prisoners to the gas chambers. She enslaved attractive young inmates, sexually abusing them before becoming bored, and despatching them to their deaths.

Her cruelty was multidimensional. She would cycle alongside work details, who faced marches of up to 16 kilometres to their assignments, unleashing her two Alsatian dogs on any stragglers. She killed with a silver pistol and by common consent was responsible for the deaths of thirty women a day on average.

A striking figure with natural blonde hair and blue eyes, she was convinced that her destiny, as an Aryan poster girl, lay as a film star, and employed her vanity as a weapon. She had a personal tailor to turn the best items of victims' discarded clothing into beautifully fitting uniforms, and wore expensive stolen perfume to taunt inmates who lived in squalor, and constant fear of their lives.

Grese had a haughty indifference to her fate; her last word to
Albert Pierrepoint, Britain's official hangman, on being executed
on the same morning as Hössler, was a curt '*schnell*'. Be quick. He
obliged, springing the trap at precisely 10.03 a.m. At twenty-two,
she was the youngest Nazi war criminal to be executed.

Her most enduring epitaph was written by Gisella Perl, an
inmate doctor at Auschwitz-Birkenau: 'She was one of the most
beautiful women I have ever seen. Her body was perfect in every
line, her face clear and angelic, and her blue eyes the gayest, the
most innocent eyes one can imagine. And yet Irma Grese was
the most depraved, cruel, imaginative pervert I ever came across.'

When Josef Mengele ordered Dr Perl to report every preg-
nant woman to him personally, she realized they were marked for
experimentation and death. The imperative of enabling them to
survive led to the inversion of her medical expertise, and her intrinsic belief in the miracle of life. She would perform secret abortions,
often exclaiming: 'A life for a life.' Her hope, unforgettably realized
after the war, in an incident recounted in her 1948 memoir, was
that the mother would go on to raise a family as a free woman.

The culture of deadly repression was self-perpetuating, since it
relied on the desperation of a substratum of so-called peer prisoners, primarily Jewish, Slovak and Polish collaborators. They
were as feared as the *Aufseherin*, the female SS guards, because
their violent interventions were calculated to ensure they retained
their privileges.

These functionaries inserted themselves into every facet of an
inmate's life. They triggered savage beatings after calling out the
most minor infractions during roll call, and accompanied those
inmates to the washrooms and toilets. They reduced rations,
taking at least a third of the bread allocated to prisoners, and left
the thicker, more nourishing soup at the bottom of the cauldrons
for their own consumption, or corrupt dealings.

Anyone rash enough to protest would be hit over the head with a ladle, denied food, and be marked for sustained revenge. Victims were denied access to washrooms, and suffered a range of petty punishments. In extreme cases, they were subjected to false accusations, and sent to their deaths.

The ability to apply power, ruthlessly and without recourse, attracted predators. Just as Mordechai Eldar had noted in the men's camp, there was an insidious culture of sexual exploitation in the women's camp, by both male and female functionaries. A hoarse-voiced kapo named Leo, who visibly enjoyed beating inmates with a sharp stick and would drag the weakest women out of the barracks with such violence they expired on the *Appelplatz*, was particularly feared.

No one had any conception of the future, beyond the survival of days that merged into one. It would have certainly been fanciful to the point of fantastical to suggest that such a future would be embodied by a defiant girl who ignored continual beatings for stealing, and sharing, fragments of bread.

Eva Birnbaum arrived at Auschwitz-Birkenau on the same transport, from Munkacs, as Chaim Schwimmer and Hershel Herskovic. It would be more than sixty years before she felt able to share details of her ordeal, survival and rehabilitation. True to her character, her motivation for doing so was to honour the memory of those she left behind. In her later years she would receive the MBE for her services to Holocaust Education.

At the age of ninety-six following her post-war marriage to Leopold Neumann, she lived in the Broughton Park area of Salford in Greater Manchester. She was widely known as Bobby, the anglicized version of Bubbe, Yiddish for Grandma. Dark haired with engaging grey-green eyes emphasized by neat rectangular glasses, she has an innate dignity and a tangible life force.

Her advocacy of the power of the family unit is understandable;

she raised five children and was the matriarch of an extended family of 100, including grandchildren and great-grandchildren. She was born on 8 March 1929 into an Orthodox Jewish family from Szolyva, a multinational town on the Hungarian-Czech border, set in the Carpathian Mountains.

The geopolitical complexities of the area were deep rooted and highly personalized. According to family legend, Eva's grandfather had left Poland in troubled times before the First World War on the advice of his Rabbi. 'What should I do?' he asked him. 'Fill up a wagon, get into it, and go straight away,' came the reply. 'Go as far as the horse will take you.'

He married at eighteen, built a house in what was originally a sparsely populated area, and had a large family. Eva, who as a child was known by the pet name Maidi, thought every Jew in the rapidly developing town of Szolyva was named Birnbaum 'because there were so many of us'.

Her father, like the fathers of Dugo Leitner, Mordechai Eldar and Hershel Herskovic, fought for the Hungarian Army in Italy during the First World War, but his hope that the medals he won for acts of heroism would save him from persecution was ultimately misplaced.

He had traditional conservative views, and prioritized his sons' education over that of his daughter. Nevertheless, thanks to a private teaching programme organized by her mother, an enlightened thinker who had been educated in Berlin, Eva emerged as an outstanding student.

It was an enviable area in which to grow up, with clean, cold air and mineral springs, which produced hot, pine-green water with renowned medicinal qualities. Tourists underpinned the wealth of the community, yet poverty was entrenched in the surrounding villages.

The Birnbaums welcomed the financially disadvantaged for

Friday-night dinners, together with locally stationed Jewish soldiers and transitory groups of Polish refugees. They took in the homeless, who helped with their household chores in return for shelter, and distributed meals across the town. It never occurred to Eva to refuse to help someone, if they asked.

Her father, though a caring man, chose not to believe eyewitness reports of mass killings from some of the refugees who sat around his table. He cited good relations with his non-Jewish neighbours, many of whom spoke Yiddish, but his uncharacteristic irritation, mirrored by that of his wife, hinted that all was not well.

The district's Jewish community was duly marched to Munkacs the day after the end of Passover in April 1944. Large groups of black-shirted youths roamed the streets, ransacking houses and robbing deportees. Eva, only fifteen, was forced to take off her most cherished jewellery, and hand it over to the braying thieves.

A synagogue acted as a holding camp before Eva, her parents and younger brothers, Shmuel and Yitzchak Isaac, were sent to a ghetto in the brick factory. Like many, she had never heard of Auschwitz, when, in a telling example of the micro-management of mass murder, they were loaded on to cattle cars in alphabetical order.

This meant most of the ninety or so deportees in their carriage were extended family; her eldest uncle was very frail and failed to survive the journey. His death was kept from the children, but Eva retained vivid memories of the mood of their passage. 'There was no sense of time,' she recalled, in an interview in 2019, 'just children's cries, silence, disbelief.'

Remarkably, their arrival was recorded in the so-called Auschwitz Album, the only surviving visual proof of Jews arriving at any death camp. Photography on the ramp was strictly forbidden, but these images were taken by one of two SS men, Ernst

Hofmann or Bernhard Walter, who had the responsibility of collecting ID photos and fingerprints from those deemed fit for work. The album contained eleven chapters, each detailing an element of the so-called special handling procedure.

On the day of her liberation, in the Mittelbau-Dora concentration camp in Germany, Lilly Jacob, a Hungarian Jew who was eighteen when her entire family was killed on arrival in Auschwitz-Birkenau, found the album in a deserted SS barracks. It became both a blessing, and a quiet curse.

Lilly used the money from selling glass-plate prints of the album to the Jewish Museum in Prague to fund her emigration to the United States, with husband Max Zelmanovic and their daughter Esther. The family flourished in Miami, where Lilly worked as a waitress, yet she was unable to escape her worst memories.

The album became a holy grail for a succession of Holocaust survivors, who travelled to Florida from around the world to seek her out in the hope the photographs would give them closure, in the form of an image of a long-lost relative. Lilly would weep with them when, almost inevitably, they were disappointed.

Only on rare occasions was identification possible; in such cases the relative was given the snapshot as a unique, almost sacred, memento. The album was donated to Yad Vashem, the globally renowned Holocaust Remembrance Centre in Jerusalem, in 1980, where it is held to this day. Lilly passed away on 17 December 1999, her legacy intact.

Those images, of harassed, head-scarved mothers and wide-eyed, unsuspecting children, speak to us from beyond the grave. They humanize the story that some still do not wish to be told, in an age of disinformation and denial. Typically, Eva Birnbaum's family was immediately destroyed on the ramp at Auschwitz. Her mother and brothers were sent to the gas chamber.

She was alone for the first time in her young life until she was

accidentally, briefly, reunited with her father after they had survived selection, and were showered and shaved. Each was in a
separate line, waiting to be tattooed, when Eva recognized him,
in a prison uniform that was far too short for him.

Oblivious to the danger, she rushed to him, across a dividing rope. 'Where is Mummy?' she asked. Her father grabbed her
by the shoulders, and brought his face down to hers. She never
forgot the compassion and urgency in his voice, which betrayed
his dread. 'Don't worry about Mummy,' he said, 'she will take care
of herself and you will see her soon.'

He barely had time to offer her a blessing before they were separated again. 'You must keep on going,' he told her. 'I want you to
be strong. Look after yourself and remember that you are a Jew.
Hashem [God] will help you.' His words would often come to
her, in her moments of greatest trial and tribulation, which came
soon enough, after she was sent to work in a warehouse, sifting
through victims' possessions.

The warehouse was known sardonically as 'Canada', because
it was a land of plenty. Eva was numbed by the new realities of
her life. She had quickly assimilated into the camp, picking up
tricks from veteran inmates like pinching her cheeks, to ensure
she looked healthy during morning roll call. 'Don't faint,' they
hissed. 'Don't move. Don't do anything.'

Her work detail operated with military discipline. She learned
to listen intently, and watch everything, but nothing could prepare her for the mortifying shock of finding one of her mother's
most treasured possessions, a vanity case containing Eva's childhood ribbons and thick, plaited hair. When that had been cut, it
was the first time she had seen her mother cry.

She could not bear to part with her mother's shawl, the last pres-
ent Eva had been given by her. She smuggled it into her barracks,
where 'the girls nearly killed me because they knew we could all

be shot for doing such a thing'. Eva knew she had no option but to oblige the others, and got rid of it as soon as possible.

'It was just a symbol of the past,' she recalled, her sadness echoing down the generations, nearly eighty years later. Much worse was to come.

Others envied her position, since, like the boys collecting corpses, the women occasionally found food in the pockets of coats or trousers. 'That meant we were lucky,' Eva recalled, 'but mentally we were unlucky, because we worked so close to the crematorium. It was our job to take the belongings of the people who went in. After three or four days I realized that our lives were not destined to be long. Anyone who worked in those places could not survive, because the Nazis did not want witnesses.'

She was wrong, since she worked in 'Canada' for nearly nine months, before the death march from Auschwitz-Birkenau in January 1945, but one day, to her horror, she spotted her maternal grandmother in a queue outside the gas chamber. Eva ran to the old lady, who asked plaintively, 'Where's your mummy, where's your mummy? I have not heard from her in days.'

The girl had reached a tipping point. She knew her grandmother's fate, but told her, 'Don't worry. You go in there and you will be together with Mummy.' Within a matter of minutes she heard the familiar screams, incantations of Shema Yisrael, a prayer said when death is near, and then silence.

In later years Eva would still be haunted by her actions. She became convinced that, at the time, she and her fellow inmates had been drugged to neutralize their feelings. 'That has bothered me for ages and ages,' she said:

None of us felt what we should have felt in those situations. We didn't cry. We weren't sad. The kapos told us what was going on. It was up to us whether we believed it.

That is when I became dehumanized. How can a human
being do that? To see it, be with it, and live with it. Who am I?
How can anyone do that? It is not normal for a human being
to watch that and not go mad. How can you live with hearing
mothers and children screaming Shema Yisrael when you put
your head on a pillow at night? It is terrible, beyond the comprehension of a child.

There was a familiar abandonment to fate in her acceptance
of jeopardy. Her approach to death mirrored that of Mordechai
Eldar: 'Risking your life wasn't frightening. To the contrary.
Every night we went to bed and made a plan to touch the wire.
That was the only way out. But, when it came to it, we always said,
"Tomorrow."'

Eva pushed boundaries still further by trading diamonds,
discreetly discovered while on duty in 'Canada', for such basic
essentials as salt and bread. This was done through a Jewish
inmate who came to collect clothing, which was purportedly destined for Nazi troops and domestic consumption. Once the SS
guards were distracted, he told her, 'Whatever you do, don't give
the valuables to the Germans.'

Eva and a friend did as he asked, hiding the diamonds in
the toilets, and burying them nearby so they were easily retriev-
able. The next phase of the plan involved transferring shoes to the
inmate; a cobbler in his barracks would then create hollowed-out
heels, into which jewellery and gemstones could be inserted.

The going rate for a diamond was three potatoes, and the girls
in 'Canada' hit paydirt on discovering a beautiful silver silk dress-
ing gown. Eva's companion noticed the buttons were not even; on
closer inspection they were a sequence of large diamonds, fruit-
lessly saved by the anonymous victim as insurance.

Such instincts were common, since Eva's father had shown

her where the family jewels were buried, in the cellar, just before their deportation. Money and material wealth meant nothing; she never had any intention of returning to her home town after the war.

The thick soup she bartered for in Auschwitz-Birkenau, and the bread she was able to share, were beyond price. Once, when her generosity was discovered, she was so badly beaten that the SS guard's stick broke across her back. She was unable to lie down on it for months.

Reassigned to the night shift, and given the job of disinfecting the best items of clothing before they were consigned to the German market, she often found herself dropping off to sleep. On one occasion, a one-eyed SS guard slapped her hard across the face, catching a finger in her eye.

She was in agony, but resigned to the consequences of brutality. She was amazed when the SS man returned a couple of days later, and gave her a bar of chocolate as a token of apology. Cynically, the girls around her interpreted it as a sign the war was coming to an end; a man who administered such punishment would need all the friends he could get.

Eva's drive to survive enabled her to endure the death march to Neustadt Glewe, a sub-camp of Ravensbrück in Germany, where, weakened by typhus, she lost consciousness and was carried on to a pile of corpses during its liberation by the Red Army in early May 1945. She would have died there, but for an involuntary movement that alerted a Russian army doctor, who found a weak pulse.

He was Jewish, and tended her daily in the camp hospital, where he put her on a diet of milk. One day, when they were alone, he whispered to her in Yiddish. 'They don't know I'm a Jew,' he said. 'Try to keep away from the Russians because they are not very kind.' Eva never knew his name, but his parting gift,

INNOCENCE LOST. *Clockwise from top left*, Eva 'Bobby' Neumann, middle, with her family; David 'Dugo' Leitner; Chaim Schwimmer; Yaakov Yosef Weiss.

LIFE INTERRUPTED. *Left*, Masaryk Street in Munkacs, 1930; *below*, the gate to Munkacs ghetto; *bottom*, Jewish families being deported to the Munkacs brickworks.

ARRIVAL. *Above and left*, Hungarian Jews arriving at Auschwitz-Birkenau in spring 1944; *below*, women and children deemed unfit for work being unknowingly led to the gas chambers.

WELCOME TO HELL. *Top*, Eva 'Bobby' Neumann, farthest right, on her way to the barracks after registration; *middle*, the interior of a barrack block, with wooden bunks lining the walls; *bottom*, a view across the camp, photographed in 1948. OPPOSITE PAGE: *top*, prisoners at forced labour build an extension to the camp; *middle*, women inmates sort through a pile of shoes from the transport of Hungarian Jews; *bottom left*, prisoners operate disinfection chambers to clean laundry and tackle rampant disease outbreaks; *bottom right*, the *Sonderkommando* burn bodies in open pits.

ARCHITECTS OF DEATH. *Right*, SS physician Josef Mengele (centre) with Richard Baer and Rudolf Höss, camp commandants, in 1944; *below left*, the construction of Crematoria 4 and 5; *below right*, piles of used Zyklon B gas canisters; *bottom*, the ovens at Crematorium 2.

DELIVERANCE. *Above*, piles of bowls litter the snow-covered ground in front of the main gate to Auschwitz-Birkenau, shortly after the camp was liberated on 27 January 1945; *below*, a view through the barbed-wire fence as the Canada barracks burns; *bottom*, the ruins of Crematorium 5, destroyed by retreating SS officers as they abandoned the camp.

THE BEST REVENGE. *Above left*, Mordechai Eldar; *above right*, Wolf Greenwald; *right*, David 'Dugo' Leitner showing a tattoo of his camp number; *below*, Hershel Herskovic being interviewed by authors Naftali Schiff and Michael Calvin; *bottom left*, Chaim Schwimmer; *bottom right*, Yaakov Yosef Weiss.

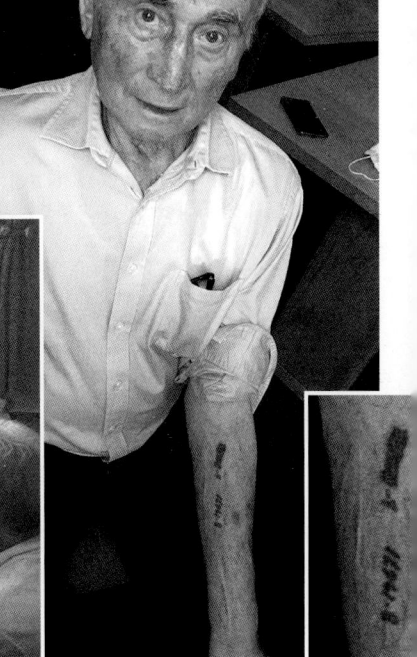

an armband that said simply 'Typhoid', ensured the troops kept her at arm's length.

Tall and skeletal, she weighed just 29 kilos, but was sustained by the doctor's human kindness. She followed his advice and hitchhiked to the main square in a nearby German town, where she convinced a bus driver she was a Czech refugee, and was taken to Prague. From there Eva travelled to Bratislava and on to Budapest where, after collapsing, she was found by chance by a cousin, looking for her sisters.

She stayed with her cousin for three years, sweeping floors and listlessly doing household chores while she struggled to come to terms with a radically changed world. 'I was nothing,' Eva recalled. 'I didn't belong. I didn't want to think. The path was always there, but I didn't see it for a long time. Looking back on it, I was probably depressed because I realized my parents were never coming back.'

She had little will to live, and ate the wrong things, so that she became grossly overweight. It was only when Eva reluctantly became a nursery teacher, and was pressured into membership of the Russian Communist Party, that she bought false papers and fled towards Vienna, with the ultimate aim of reaching Palestine.

She was apprehended near the Austrian border, and placed under house arrest because the local prison was full. She hatched an escape plan with a Jewish man, a ritual slaughterer of cattle and poultry; they slyly collected wine, whisky, schnapps and slivovitz from around the house, and distilled them into a bottle, which they gave to the main guard.

Bored and unmotivated, he duly drank himself into a stupor. 'We couldn't have woken him with a stone,' Eva said with girlish glee, many years later. She escaped through no man's land, a one-mile corridor between Austria and Hungary.

Her plan, to apply to emigrate to Palestine, changed in the

queue for permits, when she was warned of the probability that the British would instead send her to a detention camp in Cyprus. An aunt initiated contact with her sole surviving male cousin, Pinchas Tibor Rosenbaum, a leader of the Jewish community in Geneva.

Pinchas had saved the lives of hundreds of Jews during the war, masquerading as a German SS officer, or a high-ranking Hungarian gendarme. He changed the course of Eva's life by reintroducing her to her faith, and the values with which she had been brought up.

She was overwhelmed by emotion during a Friday-night dinner held by his in-laws, the Stern family. She had to excuse herself, weeping in the bathroom as Pinchas sang the Jewish hymns her father recited around the table. 'Reality came through,' she remembered. 'It was very painful, but it was what I was looking for.'

Eva married the following year, moved to England, and settled down to raise an expanding family. She told no one of her experiences, including her husband Leopold, for more than sixty years: 'I did not want my children to be brought up with some kind of guilt, or pity, and I didn't want to be pitied.'

Her life pivoted, once more, in 2006 when her grandson Daniel Goldberg asked her to return to Auschwitz, in a visit organized by Naftali Schiff and his charity, JRoots. She refused continually, but was eventually persuaded 'because he's such a wonderful kid. How could I refuse him? It's not possible.' Eva travelled on the understanding that if she found the experience too much, she would be driven straight back to the airport.

Ultimately, she found herself speaking to twenty-seven members of her family, in one of the barracks. She was unmoved by the surroundings, since they seemed superficial in comparison to her experiences, but the visit allowed her closure, since the crime the camp represents is too vast, too horrendous, for rational explanation.

She resolved to be a witness to her pain:

It seemed so natural being in that barracks, with everyone around me. Their faces dropped, because they had never heard me speak of such things, but I'm glad I did it. It reinforced my belief in life that if you do things for other people you are not busy with your sorrow, and you can forget yourself.

If other people rely on you, that takes away the pain. I remember one incident when we were on the death march. One lady – we called her the old lady although she was only forty or so – was leaning desperately on me. I thought 'I can't stop, because if I do I'll more or less kill her.'

That made me keep going, on and on. I've learned that looking after other people, sharing with them, is definitely a cure. Give your children love and support. Listen to them. Remember that to live is to give. Hate achieves nothing. Hate destroys you.

SEVEN

The First Cut

THE NIGHTS IN AUSCHWITZ-BIRKENAU were populated by ghosts, and illuminated by diabolic flame. Amidst the press of humanity, solitude was rare, invariably disturbed, but precious. Yaakov Yosef Weiss loved the release of darkness. It took him outside himself, and into the imperilled lives of strangers.

He tried to sing Jewish hymns on Friday nights, but could not do so with gusto, since his group of adherents were squeezed into the tightest of spaces on the cold stone floor of the barracks. Each boy laid claim to his own few inches, and stayed there for as long as possible, with his legs pressed against his chest.

If anyone needed to go outside, to empty himself in the barrels that acted as toilets, there was no room on his return. The best he could hope for was a space on a friend's lap, and the comfort of a rudimentary demonstration of the laws of physics, where heat flows to the colder source until there is thermal equilibrium. That's a win-win situation.

Yaakov did not mind being outside. He would squat against the side of the barracks, and occasionally sleep fitfully until first light. There was so much to process, in the daily struggle to survive, that he was lost in his thoughts.

The eerie echo of a train's whistle stimulated his imagination.

Another transport had arrived, but the Nazis didn't allow disembarkation in the darkness. Though escape was unrealistic, there were too many shadows, beckoning the panic-stricken and the desperate, for it to be worth their while.

Yaakov visualized the foul conditions the new arrivals would be enduring, the airlessness, hunger and paralysing fear they would be experiencing in their final hours in the cattle car. Many of those who would stumble out into the dawn would not live to see the sunset.

A descriptive Yiddish word of Slavic origin, *nebach*, came to mind. The dictionary definition refers to a 'weak, helpless or unfortunate person'. Used in Yaakov's position, it felt like a powerful expression of sympathy, a demonstration of affinity with the persecuted and the oppressed. He felt their plight in his bones.

He knew what to expect. Only a small portion of the day's arriving passengers – *chelek*, to use another Hebrew term – would survive selection. He would soon see them, ashen-faced, stumbling around the camp in a nightmare of bewilderment and uncertainty.

Sentimentality was dangerous, if it diluted the self-protective watchfulness he had developed in captivity, but Yaakov could not bring himself to overlook his internal thoughts and his most powerful emotions. Allied to the tenets of his faith, his feeling for his fellow man reassured him that he had yet to lose the essence of his humanity.

He was, however, more vulnerable than he cared to admit. The Hungarian boys were living on borrowed time. The first cut, on Rosh Hashanah, the Jewish New Year, was the deepest. It would gouge out the lives of around 1,200 of those who had arrived, from mid-May to early July.

Summoned for selection on Sunday 17 September, the start of Rosh Hashanah, the condemned were confined to the children's block until the Jewish New Year rituals were ending, on the following Tuesday, 19 September. Their murder was not the only crime against humanity committed that day, when the Russian advance resulted in several barbarous attempts by the Nazis to hide the extent of their guilt.

Only around 180 of the 3,000 Jewish slave labourers in the Klooga concentration camp in Estonia survived a slaughterous purge by the SS as the Red Army closed in. At the nearby camp in Lagedi, 426 Jews, mainly women and children, were murdered by their captors when liberation was only a matter of hours away.

In Auschwitz, the harbinger of death was a familiar figure. Josef Mengele oversaw the selection, in tandem with the malevolent physician, Heinz Thilo. Not for the first time, Dugo Leitner marvelled at how few guards Mengele had around him. It added to the monster's aura. It was as if he knew he was untouchable.

The boys were terrified, because they knew the subtext of being ordered to congregate for a headcount. Mengele was seeking to eliminate the sick, the skinny and the short. Mordechai Eldar was among those selected to die. He steeled himself for 'my final day', consoling himself that he would soon be reunited with his parents.

Yosef Zalman Kleinman, summoned from Block 35, and ordered to line up 'quick and tidy' by the guards, was always on the borderline in terms of height and weight. He pushed stones into his shoes to give him extra purchase and greater stature, standing for several hours without indicating the pain he was suffering in the soles of his feet.

It was to no avail, initially at least, since when he was ordered to strip to the waist he could not conceal the concave nature of his abdomen. Mengele dismissed him with the weak and physically wasted, but once Yosef was outside the barracks, he made a break for it, and reached the block in which his elder brother was safely positioned.

Yaakov Yosef Weiss knew the process; he had seen the weak
weeded out on a daily basis during their time in medical isolation,
following their arrival in the camp. He thought of the unfortunate souls, who obeyed commands to stick their tongues out as
the doctors looked for signs of scarlet fever. Even the merest hint
of infection led to those new arrivals being set aside.

An ambulance would come about an hour later; everyone
who watched the tragic tableau unfold knew its destination. Cremation awaited. The new arrivals would never be seen again. It
would be little different this time, Yaakov told himself. He would
learn later that 337 boys from his block had been earmarked for
the gas chamber.

Four of Dugo Leitner's classmates from Nyíregyháza were
also taken overnight, to the holding pen for the doomed. Chaim
Schwimmer saw two acquaintances, a boy named Famele and his
cousin, effectively die for their faith. They had become painfully
thin through refusing to eat non-kosher food in their first couple
of months in captivity. They even declined rice, because it had
not been cooked under the supervision of a Rabbi.

Chaim's attempts to persuade them to eat were hampered, since
he spoke only Hungarian and the two boys used Yiddish, the
language largely spoken by Ashkenazi Jews. He was profoundly
affected, because though the two boys were tall, he understood
their fate was sealed. 'Can you imagine making such a sacrifice?'
he asked. 'You have to be an angel to do that.'

Like Yosef Zalman Kleinman, Chaim had hurriedly added a
bed of stones to his shoes, to give him greater physical authority. He tried to read Mengele's body language. The arrogance
was overwhelming, but he noticed the economy of movement.
The doctor tended to settle on a potential victim's face and torso
before making his decision. He rarely studied their feet.

Overall, around 1,200 boys were held in Blocks 11 and 13. They were given double rations, a risibly transparent attempt to lull them into a false sense of security. Those who passed selection returned to their barracks and were afraid to venture out, in case they came across kapos and other functionaries following orders to fulfil quotas.

That was necessary since some, like Mordechai Eldar and Yisroel Taub, Hershel Herskovic's younger brother, escaped from the holding pens the night before Rosh Hashanah. Mordechai and Moses Shalem, his inseparable companion, volunteered to be the first to try.

Their plan was to squeeze through a small window, on to the roof, and drop down into the compound, where they would head for the latrines. Mordechai did so successfully, calculating he would need to leap three metres or so into a shadowy corner close to the fence, away from the road, and the guard.

He ran a short distance to the toilets, but Moses had to make alternative arrangements because of the commotion caused by another boy, who hurt his ankle on landing and was unable to walk. His cries alerted the guards, who rounded up the rest of the would-be runaways.

Desperate times called for desperate measures. Mordechai, following an example he had heard was set by fugitive Russian prisoners of war, hid himself by folding his body into the hole in which the boys did their business. Reckoning he would not be disturbed during hours of darkness, he picked a pit with hardly any faeces in it, and didn't mind getting his feet wet.

He waited until morning roll call, edging along a wall before joining the boys from whom he had been separated a couple of hours earlier. Their poker faces hid their surprise and delight. They were, after all, in this together. Moses never revealed how he had evaded capture, but he, too, was there to be registered.

Yaakov led unsuccessful attempts to win a reprieve for a friend.

He never forgave the boy, a kitchen hand, who refused to supply a piece of bread, so that it could be used as part of a package to bribe the *Blockälteste*, the block elder, who had overall responsibility for the 337 victims under his control.

The identity of those 337 boys didn't unduly concern the block elder, or the *Lagerschreiber*, the camp clerk. They merely needed to fulfil their individual quota. Wolf Greenwald knew all too well that if they, or their allies in the SS, made a covert profit, so much the better.

After the selection, Wolf was seen speaking to the block elder's assistant. He was approached by a boy named Lieby Kaufman, who asked him, under his breath, to go outside with him. When he did so, he was met by a veteran inmate, a Slovak, who wanted to know who to bribe to spare the lives of his nephew and cousin.

When Wolf suggested the clerk was most pliable, the Slovak produced an envelope stolen from the administrative offices. It contained two twenty-dollar bills that he had hidden for nearly two years. Kaufman took the risk of acting as go-between, slyly handed it to the clerk, and the deal was done. Two other lives would be cut short.

Meanwhile the prevailing climate of amorality created a moral dilemma for Yaakov. He realized that, by saving Boy A, he would be condemning Boy B, an innocent bystander taken in his place to ensure the numbers added up. This, he reasoned, was probably against halachic law.

This fell under the jurisdiction of Rabbi Tzvi Hirsch Meisels, a judge in a religious court known as the Dayan of Vác, a thousand-year-old city on the eastern bank of the Danube, just north of Budapest. He was aged forty-two and had no official position in the camp, to which he was sent on 10 July in one of the last transports from Hungary.

His wife Henna and six of his eleven children were murdered

on arrival. A seventh had died after his conscription into a Hungarian slave-labour battalion. Rabbi Meisels eventually fulfilled his vow to survive, to bear witness, after a death march to Braunschweig, and on to Bergen-Belsen. He wore prison clothing in Auschwitz, and had surrendered his beard and sidelocks, but was revered as a spiritual leader.

In many ways, Meisels was in an impossible position. He was approached by the father of one of the condemned boys and asked to rule on the legality, in religious terms, of paying a ransom to secure his only son's release. He was prepared to give everything of value that he had managed to hide, since he had also heard that some guards, block elders and kapos were accepting bribes to spare certain boys.

The father cut an agonized figure, because, like Yaakov, he also appreciated that, according to the tenets of his faith, he could be guilty of murdering the boy who would take his son's place. 'Please give me a ruling in accordance with the Torah,' he asked the Rabbi. 'I will do whatever you say.'

Rabbi Meisels was conflicted. Such life-and-death decisions are onerous at the best of times but here, without the support of his peers, and halachic books to consult, he felt unable to give the man guidance. He told him: 'I do not have the peace of mind required to render judgement, due to the great hardships and troubles that plague us.'

The father broke down in tears, and pleaded repeatedly to be given some direction. The Rabbi wept with him. He insisted he would not prohibit him from saving his son, and left the decision to his supplicant's conscience. He stressed: 'Do as you wish, as if you hadn't asked me.'

The father's despair was unimaginable, but he accepted the situation 'with love and joy' because 'if it were permissible beyond doubt you would surely tell me. My only son will be burned in accordance with the Torah.' He compared his plight to that of Abraham, who was ordered by God to sacrifice his son Isaac on the mountain top in chapter 22 of the Book of Genesis in the Hebrew Bible.

Another moral dilemma with which the Rabbi was confronted concerned a fifteen-year-old boy named Akiva Mann, who wanted to save a school friend, an accomplished religious scholar, Moshe Rosenberg. Like the desperate father, he sought authorization to pay a ransom. When Meisels refused this, Mann determined to offer himself up, as sacrifice.

He pleaded: 'Moshe is a true Torah scholar; the entire world will benefit from him while I am only a worthless ignoramus. If I merit the privilege of performing the exalted act of giving up my life, which is not worth a penny, why shouldn't I gladly do such a thing?'

The Rabbi remained unmoved, reinforcing his ruling that, under halachic law, Akiva's life took precedence over that of his friend. If Akiva defied him, and followed through with his plan, he would be flirting with the sin of suicide. Never before had the Rabbi's position felt so painful, so profound.

His devotion to religious purity did not, however, dilute his spirit of defiance. On hearing that the consignment of the first batch of 1,200 Hungarian boys to the gas chamber had maliciously been scheduled for Rosh Hashanah, he defied religious law by risking his life in insisting on conducting one of the holiest rituals of the Jewish New Year.

He would sound the shofar, a ram's horn that produced a plaintive range of sounds, dependent on the alignment of the player's lips and facial muscles, so the condemned boys would be given spiritual sustenance in their hour of need. This was a hugely significant but uniquely subversive act, since it was a direct and unprecedented challenge to the Nazis' contempt for their victims' culture.

The shofar had been smuggled to Rabbi Meisels, after being found in belongings in the 'Canada' warehouse. His tearful fourteen-year-old son Zalman Leib Meisels begged him not to use it: 'Please father, you are all I have. This will turn me into an orphan. Ribbono shel Olam [God as the creator and master of the Universe] doesn't ask this of you.'

Zalman had been given a job in the kitchens by veteran inmates as a gesture of respect, which saved his life when he was caught by a Polish kapo after sharing a stolen piece of bread. The kapo, knowing this represented a hanging offence, gave him twenty-five lashes instead of handing him over to the SS. He first advised the boy not to scream; Zalman bit down on his lips so determinedly that blood gushed from his mouth.

'A miracle!' the kapo exclaimed. 'I hit him on the back and he bleeds from the front.' Seemingly delighted by his poor joke, and aware that he had saved face in the eyes of his superiors, he walked away after inflicting three or four more blows. Honour, of sorts, had been restored.

Rabbi Meisels told his son that in a place like Auschwitz 'my life will probably soon come to an end anyway', and ordered him to act as a lookout as he entered the holding pen. It was twilight, the most perilous time of day. He moved among the boys, administering blessings, offering encouragement and citing verses from the Psalms before, in adherence to tradition, he sounded the shofar one hundred times.

The boys were at fever pitch. 'Hear, O Israel,' they proclaimed in unison. 'The Lord is our God. The Lord is one.' The Rabbi, profoundly moved, spoke powerfully and emotionally. 'Boys,' he said, 'even when a sword is hanging over us, we do not stop praying to God for salvation.' Those words were to prove prophetic.

There was precious little time to react to the impact he had made, or the mortifying sight of a friend, Rabbi Yehoshua

Fleischman from Debrecen, among those condemned. Those stationed outside, including Meisel's son and Yaakov Yosef Weiss, quickly realized the threat the Rabbi was under when the Germans overcame their initial confusion and hustled him away. Yaakov had tried to listen to the speech, but couldn't take it in, because his brain was overloaded.

Rabbi Meisels also survived the war and helped displaced persons in Bergen-Belsen before becoming the Rabbi of the British sector. He moved to Chicago in 1947, married, and had nine more children. He poured out long-suppressed emotions when he recalled the shofar incident in his autobiography:

> Where is the pen, and where is the writer who could possibly put down on paper my inner feelings when I entered the block? It is a miracle that my heart was not splintered into pieces when I saw the dozens of youthful eyes and heard their terrible sobbing.
>
> With burning tears and voices beseeching the heavens, they pushed to kiss my hand, to touch my clothes, all the time bewailing 'Rebbe, Rebbe, Have Mercy, Have Mercy' and similar pleas that one cannot suffer to hear. They would not even let me continue the prayer before the blowing of the shofar. Although this put my life in danger, this revived the spirits of the shattered camp inmates and gave them some peace of mind.

He blew the shofar again when darkness had fallen, positioning himself close to the wire while the boys were being loaded into lorries. The sight of them being herded to their deaths stayed with him until his own death, in January 1974: 'They were brimming with joy and begged me to blow the one-hundred sounds quickly before the gate opened and they would be on their way to who knows where. I can still hear reverberating in my ears the sobs that burst forth.'

Understandably, given his earlier escape, Yosef Zalman Kleinman also could not erase the scene from his memory:

> The SS began loading them into trucks, and their screams were terrible: 'Hear, O Israel . . . Mother . . . Father.' This took several hours. I had never heard anything like it. In Auschwitz usually, during summer, the people were taken to the gas chambers by the hundreds of thousands. Those people did not know where they were being led. But we, who had already become veterans of the camp, we knew . . .

Wolf Greenwald was another prisoner who tried, and failed, to blot out the soundtrack to an unfolding tragedy. He thought back to the previous evening, when he had said his farewells. He made the pretence of optimism, telling friends that he had heard they were being sent to learn a trade, but was given short shrift. One told him, sadly, and simply: 'We are not babies.'

The camp buzzed with rumours that Mengele had been called directly by Heinrich Himmler, the principal architect of the Holocaust, to accelerate death rates. Yosef Herczl, who escaped from Block 11 the previous night and would be one of only two boys to survive from his transport from Hungary, was among inmates rounded up for a surprise selection that afternoon.

The Nazis were supposedly seeking 300 volunteers for an external work detail. Yosef sought advice from Rabbi Meisels, who suggested that any chance to leave Auschwitz was worth taking, but it inadvertently put Yosef in harm's way, because he was suffering from eczema.

Obeying orders to strip to the waist, Yosef was singled out by Mengele, who screamed, 'Du kratzige Hund!' ('You diseased dog!') and sent him to the infirmary. This usually amounted to a death sentence, but it effectively saved his life. He recovered quickly. The malnourished inmates in that selection were sent to the gas chambers, and those chosen for the work detail were never seen again.

In other times and places, the boys would have had the luxury of guilelessness. They would have had the freedom to come to terms with the conflicting emotions and experiences of adolescence. They would have had teenage infatuations, formative triumphs, trials and tribulations. They would have had the privilege of making mistakes without deadly consequences.

They had never felt more alone. They had been wrenched from the families that had guided them, and the communities that had shaped them. They could not indulge the whims of childhood, even though some tried to create rudimentary games with block mates to lessen the weight on themselves. Ironically, those who toiled on work details at least had something to occupy them.

Collective depression set in, as their options became limited. There was no opportunity to mourn friends, no way to process the monstrosities they endured. They became preoccupied with the likelihood and timing of their own deaths. Nightmares were intense, terrifying. Conditions in the blocks were so cramped that everyone was sucked into a cycle of psychological torment.

The ten days following Rosh Hashanah are called the Days of Awe. Everything pointed to the next date that Nazi propagandists would have circled on what the inmates referred to, fearfully, as the Goebbels calendar. Yom Kippur, the Day of Atonement, is the holiest day of the year in Judaism. It is a time for sombre reflection.

According to some religious scholars, it is also the day on which only the virtuous die.

EIGHT

The Football-Pitch Selection

EVERYTHING WAS DEBASED in Auschwitz-Birkenau. Traditional symbols of normality and universal sources of enjoyment were corrupted beyond recognition. Even a football pitch, the setting for the game that captivates the world, was contaminated, since it was located next to the crematoria.

Ron Jones was permitted to play there on Sundays, representing Wales in a surreal league that also included teams from England, Scotland and Ireland. He saw what he called 'walking skeletons' digging ditches. He watched thousands queuing to die behind an adjoining fence. In the summer the smell of seared flesh was overpowering.

He had been captured fighting in the Middle East in 1943, and was incarcerated in Italy for nine months before being transferred to forced-labour camp E715 in Monowitz, the largest of Auschwitz's sub-camps. As an Allied prisoner of war, he lived alongside Polish resistance fighters, political dissidents, homosexuals and captured Soviet troops.

Most were assigned to work with hazardous chemicals in the nearby IG Farben plant, doing twelve-hour shifts six days a week. The owners considered 'our new friendship with the SS' as being 'very fruitful', and pressed them to enforce higher production levels of rubber and liquid fuels.

This inevitably involved violence; workers were beaten regularly by criminal elements, brought into the factory as kapos. The management's ambivalence was summed up by Maximilian Faust, the chief engineer, who reported to company headquarters that although he opposed 'flogging and mistreating prisoners to death', he understood that 'achieving the appropriate productivity is out of the question without the stick'.

The Nazis installed a football pitch to give a favourable impression to the Red Cross on their only inspection of the camp. Their cynicism was deeply rooted and deadly; when the Red Cross reneged on a promise to return in six months, to check on humanitarian progress, the Germans carried out plans to exterminate 21,000 gypsies.

The most visible influence of the Red Cross, in addition to food parcels for prisoners of war, were the kits they supplied for the four teams in the Home Nations League. Football was another perk for favoured workers, who were allowed to wear watches, given tokens to spend in the canteen, and even given free access to the camp's brothel.

Ron Jones was aged ninety-four, living in Newport as the last surviving member of the Wales team, when in January 2012 he finally told the story that had nagged at him for years, 'before it is too late'. It had given him nightmares because the game's basic pleasures, in his case, as a goalkeeper, making important saves, felt so wildly inappropriate.

'I think the Germans thought that letting us play football was a quick and easy way of keeping us quiet,' he recalled, in an interview with the BBC. 'It kept us sane. It was a bit of normality, but it sounds wrong somehow to say I've got fond memories of playing football, considering what was going on just over the fence.'

Ron believed he owed his survival of a seventeen-week death march, through Poland, Czechoslovakia, Germany and Austria, to the latent fitness he had as a player, and the camaraderie of the teammates he walked alongside. They kept one another going, when it seemed easier to succumb. By the time he was liberated by the Americans in April 1945 he had lost half his pre-war body weight.

The SS would occasionally play matches in Auschwitz-Birkenau against prisoner functionaries. Legend had it that one Polish kapo, a particularly agile goalkeeper, was warned he risked a transfer to the gas chamber if he continued to defy the German forwards. In the words of the Austrian player Igor Fischer: 'The opponent out on the pitch was a very special one. They could also kill you. Not on the pitch, but later on.'

In today's world, football is a vehicle for wealth, social accept-ance, national and cultural celebration. In 1944 it was insufficient to protect even the most ardent patriot, who played for Germany after winning the Iron Cross, second class, while serving in the trenches in the First World War.

Julius Hirsch, born in 1892 in the town of Achern in south-west Germany, was the first Jewish player to represent the national team. A powerful left-footed forward, he made his international debut aged eighteen, and competed in the 1912 Olympics in Stock-holm, where Germany were beaten 5–1 by Austria in the first round, but thrashed Russia 16–0 in the Consolation Tournament.

Hirsch won the German championship with Greuther Fürth in Bavaria and retired from professional football in 1925, but his mental health suffered during the rise of the Nazis. He attempted suicide when he was fired from a subsequent job for being a Jew, and was assigned as a slave labourer at the outbreak of the Second World War.

He was safe from deportation because he had married Ella, a German Protestant, but waived his rights by divorcing her, so that she and their two children would be spared persecution. He felt his military record and sporting status would protect him. Sent to Auschwitz in March 1943, it is thought that Hirsch died there, unregistered. A German court ruled in 1950 that he had died on 8 May 1945. The current German Football Federation has named an inclusion award in his honour.

Another Jewish football pioneer, the celebrated coach Arpad Weisz, was also killed there. A noted tactical innovator, who had played for Hungary before retiring with a serious injury, he discovered Giuseppe Meazza, one of Italy's greatest strikers ever. Weisz led Inter Milan to the Italian championship, and won two more titles with Bologna.

He was one of the first tracksuit managers, taking part in training sessions instead of standing in a suit as a detached figure of authority on the touchlines, as was the fashion at the time. He oversaw players' diets, insisted on grass pitches being cut to a precise length, and was known as 'Il Mago', the Wizard.

He changed his name to Veisz in response to a changing political climate, but was forced to flee from Italy to France, and on to Holland, when Mussolini's Fascist regime took power. It proved a brief respite; he and his family were arrested by the Gestapo in August 1942 and, after three months in a labour camp in Westerbork, were deported to Auschwitz.

His wife Elena and two children, Roberto and Clara, were murdered in Birkenau on arrival. Worn down by the persistent brutalities of slave labour, Veisz (Weisz) died there in January 1944. Together with Ron Jones and Julius Hirsch, his life was celebrated in 2020 in a mural at Stamford Bridge, commissioned by Roman Abramovich, Chelsea's then-owner.

It took a familiar mixture of Mengele's cynicism, anger and

ego for the football pitch to be weaponized against the boys. The
selection was preceded by an announcement that they would
each be given a third of a loaf, and some cheese the following
day, to ensure they would not be unduly hungry during the Yom
Kippur fast.

The ploy was exposed soon after 3 p.m., when the 2,600 remaining boys were ordered to assemble. They were confronted by an
ominous collection of block elders, clerks of varying authority,
and SS guards who organized them into groups of one hundred.

The reason became clear when Mengele appeared on his
bicycle, which an aide leaned against a barrack wall as he walked
in measured strides towards the football pitch, which had been
turned into an impromptu parade ground. Yosef Zalman Kleinman, transfixed, recorded the scene for posterity:

> All of a sudden a tremble passed through the parade ground
> like an electric current. The Angel of Death appeared. He put
> his arms behind his back, his lips as usual were tightly closed.
> He lifted his head so that he could survey the whole scene and
> then his eyes landed on a little boy about fifteen years old, per-
> haps fourteen.
>
>   He was not far from me in the front row. He was a boy from
> the Lodz ghetto. I remember his face very well. He was blond,
> very thin and very sunburnt. His face had freckles. Mengele
> approached him and asked him 'How old are you?' The boy
> shook and said 'I am eighteen years old.'

Mengele erupted. 'I'll show you,' he shouted, ordering Berthold
Epstein, the conscripted Jewish doctor who acted as his assistant,
to fetch a hammer, some nails, and a plank of wood. A deathly
silence descended. When Epstein returned from his errand,

Mengele picked out a tall, good-looking Slovak boy, seized him by the shoulders, and led him to one of the two goalposts.

Yaakov Yosef Weiss feared that Mengele was about to hit the boy with the hammer in a demonstration of his untrammelled power. He could hardly bear to look as the doctor ordered that the plank of wood be placed on top of the boy's head, and hammered into one of the uprights. The unwitting accomplice was, by common consent, around 1.65 metres in height. He would survive; those boys unable to reach the plank, as they lined up in single file, were doomed.

No explanation was necessary. The boys stirred, stretching so that they reached their full height. 'Everyone wanted to get another half inch, another centimetre,' Yosef Zalman Kleinman observed. 'I also stretched as much as I could but I despaired. I saw that even taller boys than myself did not attain the necessary height. Their heads did not touch the plank.'

It was his brother Solomon's sixteenth birthday. He would reach the bar with little problem, but realized Yosef's plight. Solomon whispered to him: 'You want to live. Do something.' His brother surreptitiously undid the laces on his shoes. Since they were already too big for him, he could fill them with stones with relative ease.

Yosef's problem was his subsequent inability to stand to attention. Solomon noticed his discomfort, ripped his hat into pieces, and handed them to him, as a form of protective cover for the stones. Yosef made himself around an inch taller but his brother, who consulted with a nearby friend in the third row, admitted 'it's not enough'.

All around them people were making life-and-death decisions. Yaakov, as alert as ever, spotted these were complicated by a fundamental change in the selection process; those boys destined to die were sent to the left, instead of to the right, as usual. This could have been subterfuge, but it may well have been heart-less practicality, since the condemned were herded closer to the blocks set aside for them.

Minds were racing into strange areas. Hershel Herskovic was under the impression that older boys, of around sixteen and seventeen, were being singled out. He wondered whether this was part of a Nazi masterplan to ensure that the more mature boys would not survive, and be capable of producing future families.

He and his cousin, Chaim Schwimmer, intended to follow a well-worn principle, which they had applied from their early days in Auschwitz-Birkenau. Never stand too close to the front in a roll call, nor be in the first wave of any selection. Far better to seek cover in the herd, and wait until nearer the end of selection, when boredom might have set in.

The pair were consumed by a quiet terror. Chaim, in particular, knew he had little chance of passing selection. They hung back without attracting attention, and waited until around 5 p.m., two hours into the ordeal, before their nerve failed and they resolved to flee.

A passing group of Russian prisoners, blackened and dirty from their work detail, provided the cover they needed. Gambling that the SS guards would be distracted by the sheer number of boys that needed to be processed, they stole into the Russian line, which closed protectively around them as they headed to the shower block.

'We managed to smuggle our way into the bathroom,' Chaim later said, as if unable to comprehend their good fortune. 'We went deep among the dirty shit there, and stayed for about two hours. We had to come out because we knew that, if someone was missing in evening *appel* [roll call] they could beat you to death. Thankfully, the Germans who made that day's selection were not around anymore. We could get back to our people.'

Yosef Zalman Kleinman also placed his faith in the chaos

theory of survival. He waited until the guards were preoccupied, then dashed into the group of tall boys who had already passed selection. The plan might have worked, but for Mengele spotting another smaller boy, who had the same idea.

'What are you doing?' he yelled at the SS guards and the kapos. 'This is sabotage.' He ordered that the entire group be retested. Nimble and quick-witted, Yosef Zalman negotiated a narrow passageway, and returned to his former group of friends, who had yet to undergo the selection procedure. He stayed with them for around fifteen minutes before once more joining the taller boys, who were to live to see another day.

Logically, Yosef Herczl should have been in his final hours. He was small for his age, but as he awaited his fate in a crowd of similarly despairing boys, he was approached by an SS officer, who pulled him away. He had heard Yosef's perfect German and needed an interpreter. Just as on Rosh Hashanah, when he escaped from a holding pen, Yosef had cheated death.

The tide of humanity ebbed and flowed around the football pitch, where confusion reigned. Herding cats would have been simpler than corralling hysterically fearful children. In addition to the would-be escapees, brothers who had been separated from their siblings struggled to remain with them, regardless of the fatal consequences. Then, amidst the hubbub, Yaakov Yosef Weiss bore witness to the day's definitive act of desperation. He recalled:

I was tall enough to reach the plank, but a boy two or three places behind me in the line, Toivie Gruen, stretched his neck out and could not hit it. Mengele sent him to the left with a smile and a flick of a finger and watched in amusement as Toivie tried again. He tried a little jump, of no use. The third time he leaped up and headed the top half of the piece of wood.

Toivie found the strength to address Mengele directly in

German. 'Ich möchte arbeiten und ich möchte leben' ('I want to work, and I want to live'). Mengele abused him, and again sent him to the left. Toivie then started shouting: 'Ich kann arbeiten und ich möchte leben' ('I can work and I want to live').

Everyone wondered how someone could have such courage. It would have been nothing for Mengele to take out his gun and shoot him. No one would have stopped him, and it would not have been the first time he had done such a thing. To him, killing a Jew was less bother than killing a fly. We were nothing to him. But God wanted Toivie to live. Mengele looked hard at him and said: 'Gehen Sie live' ('Go live').

It was an astonishing reprieve on what was a day of death. Elsewhere on the camp, as on every Saturday and each Jewish holiday, the infirmary was being emptied of those deemed too sick to be of use. The so-called *Muselmänner*, in the latter stages of starvation, were taken to the gas chambers with them as night fell.

Similar scenes were being enacted across the network of death camps. Leon Szalet, a German Jewish prisoner in Sachsenhausen, offered an unforgettable insight into the suffering in his post-war memoir, *Experiment E*:

The moon shone through the window. Its light was dazzling that night and gave the pale, wasted faces of the prisoners a ghostly appearance. It was as if all the life had ebbed out of them. I shuddered with dread, for it suddenly occurred to me that I was the only living man among corpses.

History takes time to offer validation. It would be sixteen years before the world would recoil from one unremarked example of cruelty, enacted in Auschwitz-Birkenau that night. The victim was Nachum Hoch, the Transylvanian boy who used the global platform of the trial of Adolf Eichmann in Israel to reflect on his punishment for attempting to find food to ease his Yom Kippur fast:

> The upper part of my body was put in an oven, the type they had there in Auschwitz, and I was beaten on the lower part of my body with a stick which was very thick. It was one they used to carry the lunch pails. At first they gave me ten strokes. I fainted. Water was poured on me, and then the second group of ten blows was delivered.
>
> I fainted again. Again they poured water on me, until I received twenty-five blows. I could not move any more. They left me there, and to this day I can only sit on the left side. I cannot sit on the right side because of those blows. The bones were not broken, but I still have a piece of flesh completely mutilated, a red wound.

Wolf Greenwald had risked his life on several occasions during a terrible Day of Atonement. Like Toivie Gruen, he failed selection repeatedly but was recklessly defiant. Mengele's patience, however, was exhausted. He warned him: 'Wenn du noch einmal vor mich trittst, erschieße ich dich auf der Stelle' ('If you come before me once more I will shoot you on the spot').

Wolf did not doubt him, but refused to give up hope. He calculated his final chance would come in the maelstrom of bodies being harried on the way to the holding pens. So many boys stumbled blindly forward; he kept his eyes on the periphery of the group. Once he saw daylight, he threw his shoulders back and bolted.

A kapo managed to grab him by the jacket, which Wolf left behind as he used the last of his strength to wrestle free. He then ran helter-skelter down the walkways before he reached Block 17, where an altogether more kindly German block leader effectively, and inexplicably, saved his life.

'Junge, komm her!' ('Young one, come here!') he barked, holding open the barracks door, which immediately slammed shut behind the panic-stricken boy. His unexpected saviour calmed him down, stashed him in a bunk, and waited until his pursuers called off the chase. Wolf returned to his surviving friends under cover of darkness.

Max Steinmetz described the scene in his barracks that night: 'We sat on the bunks, broken hearted and shattered, and recalled prayers and supplications. Where could one focus on these prayers and requests, recited with devotion, more than in the place and the situation that we found ourselves in at that moment? This is the plain truth.'

Yaakov Yosef Weiss remained spiritually aware, despite the trauma of the day. To him theological tracts were not arcane examples of religious principle, but living, breathing elements of everyday reality. Prayer and belief were the foundation stones of his existence, and his determination to survive.

He had been taught that man had two choices: to climb the stairs, or to fall down the drain. It was easy to be impure, to succumb to evil inclinations; the door would open, and one would fall into the depths. It was harder to do good, to retain a basic belief in humankind; the stairs were steep but manageable.

The main purpose in life, he philosophized, is to keep climbing, whatever the setbacks. You will fall and rise again, fall once more and still find the strength to resume the climb. God will help you. The important thing is to never give up.

His thoughts were echoed by Hershel Herskovic: 'Never give up whatever the circumstances. Do your best to prevail. Doing something positive, or thinking positively, creates an environment of hope and expectation. If you give up, you are easily lost.'

Even someone with such a positive personality as Dugo Leitner was unusually quiet as he struggled to come to terms with the day. He had seen twenty-five of his classmates fail selection. His cousin Samuel Leitner was also sent to the gas chamber. Mengele had played God to devastating effect. Everything had happened so quickly.

Yet, throughout his alarms and adventures, Dugo had never felt afraid. It was as if he found comfort as he stared into the abyss. He searched for perspective in his faith, and the rituals of happier times. Not a naturally deep thinker, he found himself dwelling on the profound, almost unfathomable, meaning of Unetaneh Tokef, a haunting, evocative prayer that reflects on mortality, and is recited on High Holy Days.

It reads:

On Rosh Hashanah their decree is inscribed, and on Yom Kippur it is sealed, how many will pass away and how many will be created, who will live and who will die; who will come to his timely end, and who to an untimely end; who will perish by fire and who by water; who by the sword and who by beast; who by hunger and who by thirst; who by earthquake and who by the plague; who by strangling and who by stoning; who will be at rest and who will wander about; who will have serenity and who will be confused; who will be tranquil and who will be tormented; who will become poor and who will become wealthy; who will be brought to a low state and who will be uplifted.

Those questions were still to be answered. As Dugo thought to himself 'We do not die . . . yet.' He had seen around 2,400 of the Hungarian boys had been taken away to die on two horrifying Holy Days. A storm had broken, but there was a powerful sense that another one, of equal, if not greater, violence was just beyond the horizon.

NINE

Revolt

'Everything burns here. When will we be ashes?
How much longer will I be on this earth?'

AVIGDOR NEUMANN DID NOT know at the time that he was scheduled to be in the second batch of boys to be exterminated on Simchat Torah, the next Holy Day, but he refused to shy away from existential questions. He had convinced himself, if no one else, that he was unafraid of death. He insisted it intrigued him, rather than intimidated him.

He wanted to live, but was content to surrender to fate, and his faith in a higher power. He refused to despair. At around 1 p.m. on Saturday, 7 October 1944, three days before he was due to be taken to the gas chamber, he discovered others were not so sanguine. They were prepared to fight to the death for the right to live.

Avigdor heard the muffled thud of an explosion, followed by gunfire and the scream of motorcycle engines. A new plume of smoke was visible from the area housing Crematorium 4. The SS guardhouse close to the main gate at Auschwitz-Birkenau erupted. The roll call they had organized to select 100 *Sonderkommando* members for 'transportation' had obviously gone horribly wrong.

Dugo Leitner and the rest of the sewage squad, unwashed and foul-smelling, were hustled back to barracks. Mordechai Eldar's grim ritual of corpse collection was cut short as lockdown was ruthlessly imposed. The definitive revolt in the camp's bloody history, by the slave labourers that the Nazis ordered to do their dirtiest work, was underway. It would not end well.

Otto Moll, the SS section leader who oversaw the gas chambers and crematoria, had given murderous vent to his suspicions about the intent of the *Sonderkommando* the previous evening. Known as 'Cyclops' because of his glass eye, he was responsible for numerous atrocities, and killed hundreds in cold blood.

Erratic in nature, and lethally spontaneous, he prided himself on being a marksman. To prove the point, he became notorious for jamming a lit cigarette into the mouth of a prisoner, pulled from the line in roll call, and attempting to extinguish the cigarette by shooting it.

Miklós Nyiszli, a Hungarian doctor forced to perform autopsies on fellow inmates killed during human experimentation by Josef Mengele, described Moll as 'the most insane murderer of the World War'. He was sadistic, cruel, and fully deserving of his fate, the hangman's noose after a war-crimes trial in Dachau.

He had an animal cunning and sensed, correctly, that the *Sonderkommando* knew they faced liquidation, because fewer transports were arriving and the Allied advance was accelerating. Enraged, he dragged Yaacov Kamiński, whom he suspected of being a leader of the resistance movement, out of his barracks. When Kamiński refused to buckle under interrogation, Moll shot him.

The expendability of the so-called special squad in Auschwitz-Birkenau had been established from the outset, in the summer of 1942. A group of some 200 Slovak Jews were ordered into a nearby birch wood to exhume corpses from a burial pit, before dragging them to newly modified crematoria. Refusal to follow orders was instantly fatal.

As the extermination programme intensified during the autumn of 1944, a further 200 Jews were recruited to clear another deep pit, behind the original farmhouses at Birkenau. These bodies were dug up, placed on petrol-infused wooden pyres, and incinerated. By December, around 100,000 corpses had been disposed of.

Realizing their usefulness was at an end, the *Sonderkommando* members hatched an escape plan. When this was discovered all 400 were gassed in the chamber in the main camp. Their bodies were collected by a new set of 300 *Sonderkommando*, and thrown into new pits, where the fires were never allowed to be extinguished.

Five of the newcomers managed to break out, but were hunted down. Their bodies were put on display around the camp as a warning to others. Another escape attempt, by hundreds of Hungarian Jews in a preceding train to the one that brought Mordechai Eldar to Auschwitz-Birkenau on 26 May, was equally disastrous. The SS tracked down the men, women and children, and killed them without mercy.

By this time, the Hungarian Jewish establishment could not claim ignorance for their failure to protect their community. Two escapees from Auschwitz-Birkenau, Rudolf Vrba and Alfréd Wetzler, had provided a forty-page document outlining the atrocities. Vrba, whose real name was Walter Rosenberg, lived in Great Britain and Canada after the war, and he went to his grave in 2006 believing his report about systematic extermination had been deliberately suppressed in Hungary.

Whereas the pair had been meticulous in planning their bid for freedom – it took two years and included such ruses as hiding for three days immediately after their escape in piles of petrol-soaked wood to put the SS guard dogs off their scent – the *Sonderkommando* rebellion was fractured and ill-conceived.

Explosives had been successfully smuggled out of the nearby Union armaments factory in the false bottom of a food tray, but the external Polish resistance communicated secretly that they wanted to delay the revolt for as long as possible to give the Red Army time to arrive. The *Sonderkommando* disagreed and, once they refused to participate in the roll call at Crematorium 4, events spiralled out of control.

When an SS staff sergeant reached for his gun, Chaim Neuhof, a Polish Jew who had survived in the *Sonderkommando* for the previous two years, hit him over the head with a hammer, screaming the code word 'Hurrah'. Zalmen Lewental's unique eyewitness report, written in a small notebook and buried close to Crematorium 3 in a jar that was not discovered until October 1962, detailed the subsequent chaos:

> They showed immense courage, refusing to budge. They set up a loud shout, hurled themselves upon the guards with hammers and axes, wounded some of them. The rest they beat with what they could get at. They pelted them with stones without further ado. It is easy to imagine what the upshot of this was.

The *Sonderkommando*, who also wielded iron bars and long-handled ceremonial knives, smuggled out of the 'Canada' warehouse and turned into bayonets, were confronted by SS motorcycle units, who mowed them down with machine-gun fire. Some managed to flee to their barracks, where they set light to straw mattresses.

This fed a fire that spread across the wooden roofs to Crematorium 4, where the grenades, cannibalized square metal cans filled with gunpowder, fuses and shrapnel, and dynamite, stored for the insurrection, exploded. The crematorium burned to the ground. Seeing the flames, *Sonderkommando* members in Crematorium 2 steeled themselves for action, only to be compromised by fate.

A group of Russian prisoners, seeing the SS advancing towards the building, seized a German kapo and threw him, alive, into the ovens. Realizing retreat was no longer an option, the *Sonderkommando* killed three SS corporals, cut the wire, and ran off into the surrounding countryside under heavy fire from the watchtowers.

Some took refuge in a granary, close to a sub-camp in the village of Rajsko, about five kilometres away. The SS surrounded it and, not wishing to risk further casualties on their side, set it alight, gunning down those who did not burn alive, as they stumbled out, through the flames. Another group of *Sonderkommando*, caught in a local forest, were also wiped out.

In all, around 250 prisoners were killed, including the remaining leaders of the resistance. Another 200 or so were forced to lie, face down, on the ground in the crematoria compound, and shot in the back of the head. Four women, Regina Safirsztajn, Estera Wajcblum, Ala Gertner and Róża Robota, who stole explosive material from the armaments factory, were later hanged publicly in the women's camp after refusing to confess under torture.

Sonderkommando in Crematorium 3, alerted by the sirens and the sound of gunfire, saved themselves by pouring their hidden explosives down the latrines. They were locked in a room while the SS searched their barracks to no avail. On their release they were ordered to participate in the most gruesome of clean-up operations.

Their first task was to burn 600 corpses that remained on the floor of the gas chamber in Crematorium 2 from that morning's scheduled killings. By late afternoon they were required to strip the bodies of their friends and colleagues, *Sonderkommando* massacred in the revolt, and burn them.

Among those spared was Dario Gabbai. He was born in

Thessaloniki in 1922 to a Greek mother and Italian father, who were murdered, alongside a younger brother, on arrival at Auschwitz-Birkenau in mid-April 1944. Together with his elder brother Yaakov and two cousins, Dario was among thirty-five Greek Jews selected for the *Sonderkommando*; the SS preferred to use them, rather than Eastern Europeans, since there was less chance of them witnessing, and potentially obstructing, the murders of friends or family members.

This was far from foolproof. On one occasion Gabbai, prisoner 182568, recognized two friends from his home city in Greece entering the gas chamber. Acutely aware that escape was impossible, he decided the kindest thing he could do was direct them to a spot that would ensure they would be close to where the Zyklon B pellets landed, and die quickly.

Following the evacuation of Auschwitz on 18 January 1945, Gabbai endured a death march in temperatures of -23°C (-9°F). He fantasized about the hot summers he had experienced in Greece, and had the physical reserves to cope with the subsequent ordeal of excavating tunnels for the SS in Austria.

Enslaved in two of the worst concentration camps, Mauthausen and Melk, he was liberated from Ebensee concentration camp by the American 80th Infantry Division on 6 May. He had never mentioned his status as a *Sonderkommando* member since, with the Nazis actively seeking to erase all evidence of their crimes, it would have meant certain death. Prisoners like him were regarded as *Geheimnisträger*, bearers of secrets, and had their identification documents kept by the Gestapo.

After a brief spell working for the United Nations, Gabbai returned to Greece, where he was reunited with his brother and sister-in-law. He emigrated to the United States in 1951. He settled initially in Cleveland, at the invitation of the local Jewish community, but quickly moved to California.

He was thought to be the last surviving *Sonderkommando* member when he passed away, aged ninety-seven, in Los Angeles in March 2020. He had devoted his life to humanizing the men who did the most dehumanizing of jobs, and to paying respects to the victims he had little option but to process.

An outwardly debonair figure, who acted in several films, Gabbai took pride in his personal fitness and drove a blue Mustang. However, he could not conceal his guilt and vulnerability. 'How can I have peace of mind?' he asked. 'I saw people who had just been alive, the mothers with the kids in their arms, some black and blue from the gas and still standing up, dead.'

Gabbai likened his experiences in the crematoria to a virus that lay dormant within him, until he was ambushed by memory. He admitted that there were times when death seemed a better option, but never shied away from the details of his heinous tasks, since he had promised himself, in his darkest moments, that he would shed light on the barbarism of the Holocaust.

Still haunted by the sound of mothers and their children crying and scratching the walls of the gas chamber as they died, he was helped to do so by Rabbi Shaul Rosenblatt, a noted UK-based educator and charity director, and by filmmaker Sheldon Lazarus.

He challenged his own conscience by describing the deceit required to convince victims to undress, and by outlining the mechanics of murder. His role involved moving bodies out of the gas chamber with a hooked cane and into an electric lift, which took them to the ground floor, where they would be loaded into the ovens by so-called stokers, who oversaw a cremation process that took between fifteen and twenty minutes.

Others had extracted teeth from the corpses; Gabbai had already cut off the hair of female victims in the chamber. As he did so on one occasion, a sound of escaping gas emerged from a dead woman's lips when he placed his feet on her belly as he sought purchase. 'Where is God?' he exclaimed, a question that was increasingly preoccupying some of the boys.

Conditioned to opportunism, they took care to establish good relations with *Sonderkommando* members since they were invariably willing to share with the boys some of their additional rations, which included tinned food scavenged from discarded clothing in the disrobing rooms of the killing zone.

In extremis, as with the case of Max Steinmetz, whom they hid during the selection of 9 October, the *Sonderkommando* were also ready to accept the risk of providing refuge. History may view them as indistinct, wraith-like figures, consumed by the terrible nature of their tasks, but on closer analysis they demonstrated compassion and an understated, but no less human, spirit of resistance.

Their image as automata, and even collaborators, is deceptive. They were husbands, fathers, sons. They had seen their families exterminated. They could not dwell on their grief or desire for vengeance, but they felt it deeply. The only way for them to function was to shut down their emotions, but to dismiss them as merely robotic is to deny them their humanity, which is precisely what the Nazis intended.

Only four of the countless photographs taken in the camps portray members of the *Sonderkommando*. Taken clandestinely, quickly, and in circumstances of the greatest danger, one shows a group of naked women running, apparently towards the gas chamber. The other photographs, framed at a distance, show corpses being burned in a fenced-off birch grove close to Crematorium 5.

The photos were smuggled out of Auschwitz-Birkenau in a tube of toothpaste to the Polish resistance in Krakow, who passed the film through the underground network for development in Britain. An accompanying note, dated 4 September 1944, was

signed 'Stakło', an alias for the camp's resistance leader, Stanisław
Kłodziński.

The urge to bear witness to the world led to prisoners burying
hundreds of notes in cans and bottles around the camp, docu-
menting the fate of their families, transportation details, death
rates, sketches and their own last testaments. The cans and bottles also included ashes, and were discovered after liberation by
the Red Army and the Auschwitz-Birkenau State Museum.

The existential angst of Dario Gabbai's brother Yaakov, who
died in 1994 aged eighty-two, is striking. He told historian
Gideon Greif: 'Every one of us had cremated a few of our relatives and acquaintances separately. We gathered up the ashes of
each person separately and buried it in cans. We recorded the
name of the victim, his date of birth, and the date of his murder.
We buried the cans and we even said Kaddish [a Jewish prayer for
the dead] over them. Now, who'll say Kaddish for us?'

Only 105 *Sonderkommando* members remained alive after the
revolt and the subsequent investigation, during which at least a
dozen members of the resistance died under torture. Thirty-five
of these were moved to work in Crematorium 5, the boys' destination. The other seventy were ordered to cover up the magnitude
of the crimes committed in Auschwitz-Birkenau by destroying
the other crematoria.

The camp was in turmoil. The prisoners might have been conditioned to death and destruction on a barely imaginable scale,
but the futile heroism of the murdered *Sonderkommando* had a
huge effect. Though the SS ruthlessly suppressed the revolt, its
audacity heightened the sense that the tide of the war had turned
irrevocably, and was lapping at their feet.

The time capsule of Zalman Lewental's secret writings records
the fate of the boys on arrival in Crematorium 5 on 10 October,
and the casual brutality to which they were subjected. Describing

events from the moment they were ordered to undress, he captures their horror, their panic and their sheer powerlessness:

> The boys noticed the smoke belching from the chimney and at once guessed that they were being led to death. They began running hither and thither in the square in wild terror, tearing their hair, not knowing how to save themselves. Many burst into horrible tears, dreadful lamentation.
>
> The *Kommandoführer* and his helper beat the defenceless boys horribly to make them undress. His club broke, even, owing to that beating. So he brought another and continued the beating over the heads until violence became victorious. The boys undressed, instinctively afraid of death. Naked and barefooted, they herded together to avoid the blows.
>
> Many boys, in a wild hurry, ran towards those Jews from the *Sonderkommando*, and threw their arms around their necks, begging for help. Others scurried naked all over the big square in order to escape death. The *Kommandoführer* called the Sergeant with a rubber truncheon to his assistance.
>
> The young, clear boyish voices resounded louder and louder with every minute, when at last they passed into bitter sobbing. This dreadful lamentation was heard from very far. We stood completely aghast and as if paralysed by this mournful weeping. With a smile of satisfaction, without a trace of compassion, looking like proud victors, the SS men stood and, dealing terrible blows, drove them into the bunker.
>
> The sergeant stood on the steps, and should anyone run too slowly to meet death he would deal a murderous blow with the rubber truncheon. Some boys, in spite of everything, still continued to scurry confusedly, seeking salvation. The SS men followed them, beat and belaboured them, until they had mastered the situation. Their joy was indescribable.

Chaim Schwimmer estimated that the ordeal, from being beaten while getting undressed to being herded into the gas chamber, covered nearly four hours. Sensing, in the delay, that something was amiss, a boy asked the small Jewish *Sonderkommando* member what was going on. 'I've been told to wait,' he said. The process eventually resumed, and it would not be until the front doors of the chamber were about to close that fate intervened.

Meanwhile, Avigdor Neumann, in the second batch of the condemned, waited to learn his fate. He didn't have a simple explanation for the intensity of his faith, but he believed like he had never believed before. His trust in divine intervention was resolute, and his prayers were heartfelt:

Master of the World, you are also a father, and a father slaps a child sometimes, but why so?

I have to get up every morning to hunger, to beatings, to cold, to heat, to humiliation. At any minute I am waiting for someone to beat me up, or shoot me. If you're sick, you shut up, because if you get taken to the clinic you don't come back. You can touch that electrical wire and solve that problem. You would burn in a second.

So why fight for life? The belief that God will, in a blink of an eye, get us out of here.

TEN

Miracle

YAAKOV YOSEF WEISS HAD submitted himself to a higher power. He was praying intently when he heard a shout, sensed a sudden shiver of movement, and saw a sliver of light expand until it flooded the floor of the gas chamber. There was still no thought of salvation, only an immediate suspicion that a new form of torture had been prepared by the boys' persecutors.

Unlike those whose desperation led them impulsively to surge towards fresh air and the front door, he held himself back as the guards created a chaotic corridor, pushing the boys towards one wall. The older occupants of the chamber were herded the other way. According to Hershel Herskovic they included a group of newly arrived Greek Jews who had believed the lie that they were going to have a cleansing shower.

Yaakov's brain was suddenly racing. He needed time to think, to work through the possibilities. 'It looked like they were about to start a new selection,' he recalled, a lifetime later:

I did the exact opposite to what you might expect. Instead of pushing myself forward, with the rest, I manoeuvred myself to be as far back as possible. Why? Because I wanted to know what was going on.

Nobody in his wildest dreams believed that we were going to be taken out from there. I saw the doctor [Heinz Thilo, one of the three Germans who ordered the postponement of the extermination process] and had so many questions to answer. Are they simply looking to see whether we are healthy enough or strong enough to be gassed?

Or don't they have enough gas for us? Do they want to use dogs on us instead? Do they want to use bullets? Are they taking us out to shoot us? Whatever. It's only a matter of how they want to dispose of us. We never contemplated for a single second that they were going to let us live. The Germans wanted to hide that there was such a thing as a gas chamber.

Dugo Leitner had similar thoughts. He envisaged the nearby forest of birch trees, where bodies were being burned in pits, and feared they would suffer a similar fate. He was still so convinced he was about to die that he followed his murdered mother's advice, that he should ask the Almighty for help whenever he was in peril. 'Messiah!' he exclaimed. 'Come save me. They are going to murder me.'

Despite the confusion, and a frantic sense of curiosity, Yaakov was sufficiently self-controlled to continue to hang back and assess the situation. A line, of sorts, had been formed, and was being roughly funnelled out of the chamber towards the senior SS officer, Johann Schwarzhuber, who oversaw the gassing programme. It was clear that some sort of procedure was underway.

Wolf Greenwald sensed the bewilderment of the guards as he watched Schwarzhuber take control. 'Once they were closing the doors, we knew they only opened them to take dead people out,' he remembered. 'The men were saying, "What is this?" but he gave orders for the youngsters to step out.'

Nachum Hoch was third in line. He had been so cold on

entering the chamber, and so scared of the seemingly inevitable agony which awaited him, that 'I could not speak a single syllable.' He recognized the SS man at the head of the line as the one who had separated him from his father when they arrived at the camp.

Schwarzhuber grabbed the first boy in the line by the shoulders, felt his biceps and ordered him to do ten knee-bends before sprinting to a nearby wall and back. Seemingly satisfied with this rudimentary illustration of his fitness, he turned him around, and pushed him away, to form a new line, on the right.

Sruli Salmanovitch, the Transylvanian boy who had volunteered to lead the largely unsuccessful escape attempt the previous evening, was next to be inspected. He was relatively small in stature, so Schwarzhuber asked him his age. 'Nearly one hundred,' he answered. He was to pay for his defiance with his life.

The SS officer was outraged at the boy's surliness and lack of respect. He shoved him to the left, and pointed back, towards the gas chamber. 'Du Schwein!' he screamed ('You pig!'). 'Sprichst du so mit mir? Du wirst sofort wieder da reingeschickt' ('Is that the way to speak to me? You will be sent right back in there').

Hoch was frigid with fright. He could barely bring himself to make eye contact with Schwarzhuber, who impatiently instructed him to do the set of exercises that would decide whether or not he had a future. He did enough to convince the SS officer of his usefulness, and stumbled towards the first boy to be saved, on the right-hand side.

Meanwhile in the scrum of humanity, Yaakov watched intently. He could almost count the droplets of rain on the Germans' uniforms. He was puzzled by the selection process because he could detect no obvious pattern in those who were given an apparent reprieve, and those unfortunates who were bullied towards the line of newly condemned boys.

'Only a small number of people were being selected,' he recalled:

> There was no indication whatsoever that he was picking a certain group, based on their height, their health or their muscles. One was a big, tall fellow, the next very small. You couldn't tell what the Germans were aiming at.
>
> We were all Adam HaRishon people [a reference in Hebrew to the concept of Adam, being the first man, who is the essence of subsequent humanity] but there were differences to previous selections, where if someone wanted to join his brother, cousin or friend in going to their death they were allowed to do so.
>
> Here, no one was allowed to move around after being chosen. If they tried, they were hit with great force by the soldiers who guarded the lines with their bayonets. I couldn't see where all this was going to lead.

At that pivotal moment, Yaakov trusted in the latent power of his faith, by having a direct conversation with God for the first time since he had been transported to Auschwitz-Birkenau. This was not a normal prayer, spoken or even sung; it had the feel of a conversation between parent and child:

> I said to Rebono Shel Olam [a Hebrew term for Master of the Universe], 'I don't know what to say. I don't know how to answer their questions. I don't know what they will ask of me. Please help me. Please put the right words in my mouth. I will do whatever you tell me.'

With that, he began to push to the front. The boys who passed selection were being lined up in rows of five. Hershel Herskovic was in the third row, as the fourteenth boy selected. 'I had hope in spite of everything,' he explained, some eighty years later. 'I somehow felt assured we would survive. I told myself, "He will send an Angel to save us."'

His cousin Chaim Schwimmer was next up for selection. A much smaller boy than Hershel, he felt he had nothing to lose from a direct plea to his captors. 'Ich möchte arbeiten' ('I want to work'), he announced, drawing attention to an artless attempt to show off his muscles. Despite the tart response from a guard – 'Das sagen Sie alle' ('You all say that') – his gesture softened the mood, and he was spared.

Dugo Leitner continued to churn inside, despite his selection. 'I knew it was the end of us,' he explained. 'Who could believe we were being saved? I thought they were going to make soap from us. We were dying for the sanctification of the Lord, but suddenly, we are outside. My brain could not take it in.'

He remembered Psalm 74, which he had recited while in the gas chamber. The relevance of verses 12 and 13 seemed inescapable: 'But God is my King from long ago; he brings salvation on the earth.' Divine providence seemed the only explanation for what was happening, all around him.

The scene was apocalyptic. The boys on either side of the divide were naked, hunched. They had long since been stripped of their dignity. Those who had been rejected were starting to understand the probability of their fate; they whimpered, and began to wail, until they were beaten into relative silence. Some trembled with fear, others shivered through cold; it was impossible to tell the difference.

Even the *Sonderkommando*, who had seen things a man should never see, looked at them piteously. These were children, herded together like cattle chosen for slaughter. This process was no act of mercy, though it seemed apparent that some of them might survive. Offering false hope to the majority added to the cruelty of the ordeal.

Yaakov's gamble, in holding himself back, left him in peril. A flurry, involving a sudden concentration on counting those boys on the right-hand side, suggested a quota of some form was close to being fulfilled. He did not know it at the time, but he was approaching the point of no return; unless he was selected in the final six he was doomed.

When Yaakov presented himself to him, Schwarzhuber was evidently concerned by a graze on his knee. The SS officer's lips were pursed, indicating he was unconvinced by the boy's plea that it was 'nothing'. Yaakov's life was in the balance; their subsequent exchange remained implanted in his memory, down the years:

'Kannst du laufen?' ('Can you run?'). 'Kannst du marschieren?' ('Can you march?').

'Ja.'

'Dann lauf' ('Run, then').

Yaakov sprinted to the wall, returned, and then obeyed an order to lie down beside the boy who had preceded him. Still unsure of what was happening, he quickly got up, without being instructed to do so. Schwarzhuber pushed him distractedly into what was to be the last row of the lucky ones. Once another couple of boys had joined him, the Nazi officer turned to the guards.

'Es ist fertig,' he told them ('It's finished').

Gesturing towards the fifty boys on the right, he said: 'Diese. Lass sie sich anziehen' ('These. Let them get dressed').

His tone darkened instantly. He motioned contemptuously in the direction of the newly condemned on the left-hand side and laced his words with menace: 'Werfen Sie sin den Ofen' ('Throw them into the oven').

Yaakov realized he was safe. Overwhelming relief mingled

with disbelief, and a sense of guilt. Out of the corner of his eye he noticed the boy with whom he had a sour exchange, prompted by his profession of hope, when they first entered the gas chamber. He was being herded back to where they had come from.

The instantaneous outcry provided the cover for a relatively small youth, whom Dugo Leitner recognized as a fellow member of the *Scheisskommando*, the sewage squad, to dart towards the ranks of the reprieved, and hide himself in a pile of discarded clothing, from which he emerged when guards were distracted. Fifty-one would live to see another day.

Such was the commotion, his ruse was not spotted. Yet another boy had provided a macabre diversion by breaking free and throwing himself on to the electric fence. His emaciated, naked body convulsed briefly, and was left to hang there. Suicide was so commonplace it was treated as an inconvenience rather than a symbolic reaffirmation of an individual's control over his destiny.

Yaakov tried, and failed, to block out the despair of the doomed. 'Their screams reached the heavens,' he recalled. 'They knew this was it. They were screaming all sorts of things, but I cannot remember what. When there is a multitude of people screaming you can't distinguish what they are saying. I just concentrated on getting dressed quickly. I didn't know what to take, so I just grabbed at anything within reach.'

He picked up a pair of trousers, and found a piece of bread in a pocket. It was only later that he wondered about what befell the boy who had saved the scrap of sustenance. It was the remnants of a meal he would never finish, an illustration of a life he would, in all probability, never live. Fate had rarely seemed so bleak.

Even the SS guards seemed thrown off balance by events. Wolf Greenwald had a surreal, unusually sympathetic, conversation with one, who told him to help himself to clothing. 'He stood there until everyone had what they needed. I picked up three or

four pairs of underwear, two suits, a winter coat, shoes and stock-
ings. When I'd finished he asked: "Jugend. Bist du zufrieden?"
("Young fellow. Are you satisfied?"). I thanked him and he politely
wished me good night.'

The rain had stopped, and the sky was clearing. Hershel Herskovic remains convinced he saw a rainbow over the camp.
Mordechai Eldar, who, like Hershel, was one of the first to pass
selection, has a rather more sobering memory of the moment.

He wasted no time in collecting some clothing, and waited
outside the chamber for further orders. He was far enough back
from the building to spot a soldier with a mask, carrying cans of
gas pellets on to the roof. The cries of those trapped inside would
soon diminish and disappear. Death was about to reclaim its
dominion.

The fifty-one would not know why they had been spared, and
what they were needed for, until they returned to barracks. Their
only clue was provided by a member of the *Sonderkommando*, as
they were being lined up to march. 'Children,' he murmured, unwilling to draw attention to himself following the carnage of the revolt
two days earlier, 'you are saved because Dr Mengele needs you to
work.' A second *Sonderkommando* member was incredulous: 'No
one has left here alive. You are the first. This has never happened.'

They were about to set off on their return journey from Crematorium 5 when they came face to face with another set of boys,
who were scheduled to be executed after them. Yaakov Yosef
Weiss captured the confusion: 'They shook their heads at us and
we shook our heads at them as if to say, "What are you doing
here?" No one knew what was going on. Were they now in a
queue for selection?'

This group contained Avigdor Neumann, who was shocked to
the core, since he recognized the familiar faces of Hershel Herskovic and Dugo Leitner: 'We had just got to the crematorium

doors and I saw the guys walking towards us. I thought, "How could this be?"'

He instinctively feared the worst, and remembered stories of victims being thrown, still alive, in the open pits because the chamber and crematorium were overloaded. Yet his group, too, was turned around, and ordered back to barracks in the old gypsy quarters. Generations later, Avigdor's relief is reflected in the ease of his laughter:

I always say the Grim Reaper doesn't love me. It's a deep feeling. Someone upstairs decided I would come back from the crematorium that day. You may be hungry, you may have lice, you may be sick, you may be suffering, but you must believe. Things are not necessarily written by you.

I am alive in my faith. I sucked it from my mother's milk. As I grew up, I didn't understand otherwise. I am human, with human faults, but I have my faith, my values. I didn't study psychology, but I firmly believe my faith gave me the will, and the confidence, to survive.

Facing death is such a strange experience. It is not quite as simple as you knowing what's going to happen and not believing it. You might convince yourself that maybe, maybe, it's not true, and it won't happen, but on the other hand you put up with it. You know, 'that's it'.

The fifty-one had a ghostly presence. Anyone seeing them assumed that they had been marched to their deaths a matter of hours earlier. Just as the *Sonderkommando* members had recoiled in surprise at what they regarded as an unprecedented turn of events, the guard at the main gate seemed somehow softened by the struggle to believe the evidence of his own eyes.

'There's always a guard standing there, when you come back

into camp,' Yaakov reflected. 'I can't forgive him that he smiled at us, but we could really see that, in some way, he appreciated that we had returned. For a goy [a non-Jew] and a sadist like that to have a bit of feeling was interesting to me.'

Hershel did not have time to feel anything on his return to the land of the living, but his numbness was replaced by euphoria when he was greeted in the barracks by his younger brother Yisroel Taub, who had been hidden overnight. He never forgot the warmth of their embrace.

The brothers would be separated again, as displaced persons in the turmoil of post-war Europe following their liberation, but for that night, at least, as they held one another desperately, kissing and crying, they convinced themselves they would never allow themselves to be parted.

'Our joy was great, but to tell the truth we were shocked,' recalled Dugo Leitner. He was engulfed by the gratitude of the inmate who managed the barracks, because Dugo had engineered a bribe that spared his two sons. The functionary pushed a piece of bread into his mouth, and promised he would do anything to help him: 'You see, there is a God. You were saved. My two children were saved too.'

The reality of their situation was reinforced a little later, when Josef Mengele entered the block. The temperature seemed to plummet, and the hum of excitement was silenced instantly. As the doctor used a stove in the centre of the room as a platform, Hershel sensed his agitation and confusion. It was the first time that the fault lines in his facade of authority had become apparent.

There was a bitter edge to Mengele's voice as he addressed the boys who stood before him. He told them that a train, fully loaded with potatoes, had arrived at the railway sidings from Greece. They would form a *Kartoffel Kommando*. Some of the potatoes would be consigned to German troops, and sent to the front. The rest would be either ferried to the kitchen, or planted around the perimeter of the camp.

The doctor seemed almost affronted by the boys' survival: 'Sie müssen sich keine Sorgen um das Krematorium machen' ('You don't have to worry about the crematorium'), he said, before warning them, 'Wenn ihr nicht arbeitet, mach ich euch alle aus' ('If you don't work, I'll kill you all').

The work detail would not begin until the following morning, which gave conspiracy theories time to ferment. Yosef Zalman Kleinman had an element of protection, since he was among sixty inmates assigned to work in the kitchen, a central thoroughfare from which rumours often spread.

Kleinman overheard one of the guards talking about a power struggle between Schwarzhuber and Mengele; the former was making a point by sparing the boys. In the eyes of Wolf Greenwald, this theory gained credence early the following month. Schwarzhuber was reassigned to Dachau, where he took charge of several of the eleven sub-camps in the Kaufering complex.

He was then transferred to the Ravensbrück women's camp in January 1945. Thousands were killed in a provisional gas chamber towards the end of the war; Schwarzhuber took personal command of the extermination programme when several underlings refused to oversee it. He was found guilty of war crimes by a British military tribunal and, following an unsuccessful petition for a pardon, was hanged on 3 May 1947.

Another theory, that Heinz Thilo's deeply cynical survival strategy, of attempting to distance himself from the murderous excesses of Mengele as the war had clearly been lost, also had its advocates. Thilo was seen having a prolonged angry exchange with Mengele at the crematorium, and some suggested he had used his medical seniority to sanction the release of the fifty-one. The theory about a power struggle gained traction when Thilo was transferred within days to the Gross-Rosen concentration camp in Germany; he fled just before its liberation, was captured, and committed suicide while in prison.

Mordechai Eldar, who refused to read anything divine into his reprieve because he had abandoned his faith, was typically acerbic. He had lost his belief in the more noble aspects of human nature, and was prepared to accept that the Germans were in the process of trying to save their own skins. The fifty-one were merely an insurance policy.

The hard-headed boy was an equally resolute old man when he considered the situation in an interview in 2023:

Well, I would like to know what happened, even today, but I never made enquiries. My own view is that, because the war was nearing its end, the Germans realized they would have to answer for the gassing programme.

Some of the participants in that programme continued to say they had to carry out Himmler's commands, but others wanted to stop. They probably made a compromise, so we were taken out of the chamber. That's my explanation, at least. Was it like that? Who knows? Nothing like that had happened before.

We also have to take into account the fact they were running out of people to work. Many of those who remained in Birkenau were half dead. The soldiers at the front were waiting for food, and because we were young and relatively strong we were sent to unload the potatoes.

Chaim Schwimmer hid himself the following day, because he feared he would be too weak to endure the ordeal of carrying heavy two-handled wooden boxes, overladen with potatoes, up the hill from the train to a central distribution centre. 'I didn't think I would survive another day of that sort of work,' he explained.

Mordechai Eldar was made of stronger stuff. Once the potatoes were assigned for transportation to the front, sorted into sacks and loaded on to a convoy of trucks, he began to dig longitudinal trenches in driving rain. These were lined with straw before being filled with the remaining potatoes.

'It was very hard work, especially for young men in our physical condition,' he remembered. 'The SS soldiers guarded us and forbade us to eat the potatoes. Whoever did so and was caught was severely beaten. Nevertheless, most of us luckily managed to eat potatoes without getting caught.'

He reasoned that the planting process was designed to produce a new crop before the Russians arrived, but calculated, correctly, that it was futile. The camp was starting to be wound down; one crematorium remained active for a month or so, to deal mainly with those who had died in the infirmary, but the gas chamber was used relatively sparingly, to process those who were sick.

'We sighed with relief,' Hershel admitted. 'We worked for a week or two, but Mengele was clearly downcast. The atmosphere was better. Life seemed somehow less brutal.' A process of hardening had been completed; Yosef Zalman Kleinman realized he no longer noticed the flames from the chimneys, nor the smell from the ovens.

Yaakov Yosef Weiss was acutely, spiritually, aware: 'There's no survivor who didn't experience absolute miracles,' he reasoned. 'They experienced wondrous things through divine providence. He (God) was there in Auschwitz the whole time. He was there to save them.'

Mordechai took stock of how he had changed: 'I suppose I was a naturally tough kid, and the camp intensified whatever I was born with, but something about survival comes from your soul. To be honest, I don't know what it is. We talk about ambition and drive but I can't describe it.'

He had the confidence to indulge his curiosity by regularly walking past the remains of Crematorium 4, damaged by the *Sonderkommando* mutiny. It was dismantled by the end of 1944; plans were laid in the preceding six weeks to blow up three other crematoria. Technical equipment from the gas chambers and the furnaces were shipped back to Germany, together with valuables collected in the 'Canada' warehouse.

The SS began the process of covering their tracks by destroying prisoner records, burning all ledgers containing arrival details. Pits containing human ashes were bulldozed. Crematorium 5 remained in working order until mid-January, and the majority of *Sonderkommando* members were systematically killed.

Going into December 1944 most of the remaining 200 or so Hungarian boys were moved from Auschwitz-Birkenau to the official labour camp. Those without tattoos, due to the haphazard nature of the process, were duly branded. These included Wolf Greenwald, who became B14639.

A new, terrible, ordeal awaited them.

ELEVEN

March or Die

WOLF GREENWALD HAD HEARD the distant thunder of Russian artillery fire for several days, and seen poorly disguised dread in the eyes of the SS guards and their commanding officers in Auschwitz. The Red Army's Vistula-Oder offensive, launched on 12 January 1945, had reached Krakow, and was advancing towards the industrial areas of Upper Silesia, with the ultimate aim of establishing a bridgehead for an attack on Berlin.

The Nazis were unaware that the Russians' combat communications suggested the liberation of the concentration camp was not a priority. They merely mentioned the village of Birkenau, and referred vaguely to the camp as 'barracks'. Nevertheless, the decision to evacuate it was taken on 17 January.

It was snowing heavily early the following morning, a Thursday. Temperatures were around -20°C (-4°F), but felt colder due to the windchill factor. Greenwald and the surviving Hungarian boys were among 56,000 prisoners forced on to the road, to march, or die.

They had no food or water. The SS shot anyone who stumbled, hesitated or dared to break ranks. Precise figures are difficult to quantify, but it is thought around 9,000 perished. To this day, villages on the routes of the two main death marches feature memorials to those exhausted souls who succumbed, or were murdered in cold blood.

The grave sites – in Brzeszcze, Miedźna, Ćwiklice, Pszczyna, Brzeźce, Studzionka, Bzie Zameckie, Jastrzębie Zdrój, Mszana, Wilchwy, Wodzisław Śląski, Bieruń Stary, Mikołów, Mokre, Borowa Wieś and Gliwice – constitute a literal road map of misery.

Around 20,000 Auschwitz evacuees, including the final 100 *Sonderkommando* members, made their way south-west on foot to Wodzisław Śląski, where the majority were put on trains that took them to concentration camps within the Third Reich, including Gross-Rosen, Buchenwald, Bergen-Belsen, Mauthausen, Ravensbrück and Sachsenhausen.

Most of the boys were in the larger column that marched a similar distance, 65 kilometres, north-west to Gliwice, another rail hub. Greenwald was frozen to the marrow, 'but every time you felt like giving up, you would see the SS shoot a few people who were lagging behind, so you kept going'.

He was tempted to take advantage of a brief respite in one of the Auschwitz sub-camps, Blechhammer, in the early afternoon on Friday, 19 January, but was persuaded not to do so by a Polish prisoner, with whom he had struck up a relationship of sorts, as they trudged, heads bowed, through the wind and snow. The youth was twenty-three, seven years older than him, and Wolf was convinced by his fears that anyone who stopped there would be executed.

Hershel Herskovic had every reason to take the risk, even though, as the site of two strategically important synthetic oil-producing plants, Blechhammer was targeted in Allied bombing raids. He had been virtually dragging his cousin forward, step by step, by placing his hands around his waist and in his jacket pocket, for nearly twenty-four hours. Chaim Schwimmer was on the verge of collapse; Hershel, too, was terribly ill. He had breathing difficulties, felt weak, and suffered from diarrhoea.

Chaim admitted that 'I couldn't walk by myself. I was exhausted and only kept going, up and down those hills, because I was helped by the others.' Unlike Hershel, he regretted ever leaving Auschwitz: 'We were stupid because the SS were scared for their lives. They knew the Russians were coming and left maybe two or three men behind, to look after the whole camp. We should have done what the smart ones did, and hidden ourselves. They stayed alive, because there was no one to bother them.'

In Blechhammer he formed a self-help group with Hershel and Yisroel Taub: 'They had quilts there, and it was warm as there was coal,' Chaim remembered. 'We went to bed and in the morning there were no guards, the watchtowers were empty. The camp was in the middle of the town and we went searching for food. The locals must have contacted the SS and a group arrived and shortly after they carried us away. But for a couple of days we had some rest from the marches.'

Hershel recalled with a wry smile, 'We weren't sure the SS had any ammunition, anyway.' Perhaps that explained why he felt safer there than in Auschwitz, where 'there was so much confusion and uncertainty among the Germans' in the final hours that 'it was difficult to see who was in control'.

Wolf Greenwald spent Friday night in a barracks in Gliwice, before being marched to the other side of the town, where they were held in another of the four Auschwitz sub-camps in the area. The war came to them with terrifying speed; though the main target of a raid by British and American aircraft was railway infrastructure, one bomb exploded in the centre of their temporary quarters.

The Red Army would occupy Gliwice on 24 January, and wreak terrible vengeance against the most vulnerable. More than 1,000 inhabitants, mainly women, children and the elderly, were murdered. Men of working age were deported to Soviet mines, as slave labourers. The atrocities were a reminder, if any were needed, that war's inhumanity enveloped both sides of the conflict.

Greenwald was among the Auschwitz evacuees to leave four days before the town fell to the Russians. He estimated that several thousand – no one knew precise figures, since the panic was palpable and the Germans no longer kept records – were crammed into sixty open-air wagons, with the intention of reaching Mauthausen concentration camp in northern Austria.

The slow journey south was brutal. Exposed to the elements, prisoners were soaked by an icy rain, and huddled together to minimize the effect of the wind. Some, frozen and hungry, gave up the struggle and died. The toll mounted for nearly a week, but arrival in Mauthausen, west of Linz, offered no relief.

The Germans, alarmed by an outbreak of typhus, refused to allow the evacuees to disembark, and re-routed the train north, past Prague and through Germany in the direction of Sachsenhausen concentration camp, north of Berlin. Wolf remembers Czech peasants throwing food down from bridges, but for many it was too little, too late.

Despite the temptation, he did not join those from his section who jumped off the train and into deep snow. They bet their lives on it being easier to escape, since the local populace seemed supportive, and there were no SS men around. The transport was being guarded by veteran members of the Wehrmacht, who lacked the vigour and rigour of their more feared compatriots.

The dead were unceremoniously unloaded in a forest close to the camp, the first of its type to be commissioned when Heinrich Himmler became chief of the German police in July 1936. The living were given shelter, of sorts, in hangars close to the Heinkel aircraft works, since the main camp was full to bursting point.

The cycle of fear and retribution intensified over the fortnight or so that Wolf was there. In early February a special SS unit, headed by Otto Moll, one of the monsters of Auschwitz, obeyed a centrally issued order to liquidate around 3,000 supposedly 'dangerous' internees, who had either undergone military training, or were classified as 'unfit for marching'.

On 13 February, Wolf was part of the human cargo taken directly west to Bergen-Belsen, a four-hour rail journey that was, given previous circumstances, relatively tolerable. The conditions he found on arrival were, however, horrendous. Belsen was in the grip of a typhus outbreak so virulent the SS chose to guard the camp perimeter without entering it.

The system was inevitably open to corruption. Registration of new arrivals was conducted by inmates; in some cases, in return for previous favours, prisoners were listed as having died during the transport, and assumed the identities of those who had actually died in the camp, of disease or starvation. Other inmates were murdered for their Red Cross food parcels, with impunity.

Wolf could not fail to be struck by the air of apathy, anarchy and aimlessness: 'They gave us some food every day, but we did not work. We spent most of our time standing around in very bad weather for five or six hours while they counted us. People just dropped where they stood.'

While Greenwald waited for the Allies to arrive (they would do so on 15 April), Hershel Herskovic, his brother Yisroel Taub and Chaim Schwimmer were among 20,000 inmates existing in flimsy tents at Mauthausen, the so-called camp of no return. Their journey there, in the same open-topped wagons that transported earlier groups, was perilous and protracted.

Alerted by cannon fire, which signalled the imminence of a final Russian assault on Blechhammer, the few remaining SS men had evacuated the camp on Sunday 21 January. The Auschwitz evacuees were given nothing to eat or drink, and were harried on an eight-kilometre walk to a railhead.

By coincidence, the boys met up there with Dugo Leitner, who had been marching for three days. 'I was walking with my eyes closed,' he recalled:

I couldn't open them properly because of the strong winds, and the heavy snow. I went without food. Most of the captives around me were Russians, Poles, Ukrainians. There were not many Jews. It was impossible not to fall asleep, standing up.

I found myself crying because of a dream. In it my mother leads me to a room which is full of so much good stuff. She tells me we will soon go to Israel, where *bilkelach* [mini challah rolls, a domestic speciality] grow on trees. I'm hungry so I beg her for one. She tells me she can only do that when we are together in Jerusalem.

I nag her, but she still says no. That's why, when I wake up, I am crying. I never lost faith that I had to survive. I had to get through the camps to come home and tell the whole world what the hawks did to the people of Israel.

He sustained himself by conjuring up the complementary memory of his father, who advised him to recite Psalm 20 in his moments of greatest peril: 'The Lord will answer you in the day of trouble; He will uphold you, O God of Jacob. He will send you help from the sanctuary, and from Zion he will feed you.'

The new threat came from the air. As the train headed south, on another excruciatingly sluggish five-day journey, it was strafed by Allied aircraft, whose attention had been drawn by a convoy a little further down the line, ferrying weapons to the front. Dugo, sitting in an open wagon, close to the cart carrying coal, was in the direct line of fire, and remarkably lucky to survive an incident which, it is believed, cost the lives of seven of the fifty-one reprieved Hungarian boys.

Dugo could not put names to the young faces he still remembered in his dotage, but his memories felt authentic: 'Imagine. I'm sitting there, in the trailer, when the plane plunges at us. All of a sudden it fires: "drrrr . . . drrr . . . drrr." Seven of my friends, sitting the width of the trailer across from me, were all killed. I was carried to another carriage, where there was not enough room, but I had been spared.'

Hershel Herskovic was another who had a fortunate escape, in the same attack. An evacuee in the closest wagon to his was hit and died. The boys had been reduced to eating snow, or sucking ice hacked from the side of the carriages, but were rescued in a rare show of pity by Czech officials, who gave permission for coffee to be distributed during a brief halt. It was weak, but wonderfully warm.

On arrival in Mauthausen, at the start of February, Hershel quickly realized that it was 'a terrible place, much worse than Birkenau'. Originally designated for those officially described as 'incorrigible political enemies of the Third Reich', it was the Nazis' only Category III camp. Category III incarcerated prisoners whom the SS considered to be 'severely incriminated', especially previously convicted criminals and asocials.

Around half of its 200,000 prisoners, held between August 1938 and the camp's liberation on 5 May 1945, died there. Among them were Polish prisoners who had worked in Crematorium 1 in Auschwitz-Birkenau; they were executed two weeks before the camp was freed.

Hershel's first impressions remain vivid: 'We had to walk from the train up the mountain to the camp. It seemed to touch heaven, and it was heavily fortified. There were thick stone walls, electric fences and watchtowers. It looked like it had been there since the world had been created.'

Dugo remembered 'stunning views but ominous cold'. He recalled how the boys were assailed by local residents with pitch-forks as they ascended to the camp:

> Imagine. The Germans told the local municipality that we were criminals, coming to their town. Dozens of them were pushing and prodding at us.
>
> 'Who are you?' they asked us.
>
> 'We came from Auschwitz-Birkenau.'
>
> 'What is Auschwitz? What is Birkenau? Where are your parents?'
>
> 'They were murdered in Birkenau.'
>
> 'What? You guys are drunk! You guys are crazy. You escaped from an asylum in Budapest.'
>
> While this was going on, people were slipping on the mountain path, breaking arms and legs. Blessed be the Lord God who kept me; I got a few jabs with the pitchforks, but I did not fall. Two lines of SS men were waiting for us when we reached the upper camp. Whoever entered was beaten up. It felt as if we were being led to our deaths.

They were taken to the bathhouse where, to their relief, the showers released intermittent spurts of cold water. This was not to last much longer; within a month or so there were no washing facilities in the camp. Disease was rampant, and inmates were infested with lice.

Though there was no new change of clothing, they were at least able to rinse the filthy rags in which they had arrived. Dugo even managed to swill out his ill-smelling shoes, into which he had defecated. 'Imagine the aromas,' he recalled, with a trademark smile.

Mauthausen's ethos was 'annihilation through labour'. Chosen because of plentiful quantities of granite, which was used in civic construction projects, its quarry was a death trap. Inmates worked from sunrise to sunset to extract heavy stones, which they carried up the so-called Stairs of Death consisting of 186 uneven rocks, stacked up to half a metre high.

Thousands died there, either from exhaustion or excessive force by SS guards who positioned themselves with whips on the way up. Some were pushed to their deaths off the cliff at the top of the climb. Other detainees were sent to sub-camps servicing the armaments or aircraft industries. Still more were used as slave labour by local companies, who paid the authorities for the privilege.

The boys were not assigned to the heaviest work, but were still driven out of their tents for endless roll calls, which began soon after dawn. They repeated the human-heater system they had used in Auschwitz, crowding together in groups of ten or twelve, and rotating their bodies so that each of them had time warming up in the middle.

'It was very cold and windy, but that rota kept us as warm as possible,' Hershel recalled. 'I didn't think about tomorrow. Only getting through that day, doing everything to keep going, mattered.' Occasional opportunities to help unload bread, which involved opportunist pilfering, were literal life-savers.

The boys' final ordeal began at the start of April, when they were sent from their tent city in Mauthausen on a death march of more than 60 kilometres to Gunskirchen, a newly opened sub-camp for 17,000 Hungarian Jews consisting of little else but primitive barracks, strewn with bodies denied the dignity of burial.

For the first time, Hershel sensed the shame of those local residents who came across them by the roadside. They didn't want to look at the pathetic stream of emaciated prisoners. Bystanders seemed to flinch, shrink into themselves, and melt away into the shadows.

The rain was unrelenting, piercing Dugo's thin shirt. The temptations were insidious. They rested, after a fashion, in fields overnight, but anyone who broke ranks, to try to dig up freshly planted potatoes, was shot. Dugo sustained himself by eating slugs: 'How we chewed those big, bubbly ones.'

He felt humiliated because his trousers were in the process of falling to pieces. One leg reached his knees, the other, in tatters, reached his shin. It was on that route, cold, ill-nourished and showing the first signs of typhus, that he reached crisis point. 'I just sat down and didn't want to walk anymore,' he remembered.

'I knew it was the end because I didn't have the strength to continue. Then I saw someone approaching me with a gun. All of a sudden I had a surge of energy and ran back to my companions. For some reason they didn't shoot me. How come death didn't want me? I told him, "I'm not on your list. Send me back."'

Taken out of context, that dismissal of death may seem impossibly jaunty, but Dugo's attitude, originally shaped by his survival of the Holocaust, was nuanced by his post-war military service. He emigrated to Israel in 1949 and was immediately drafted into the IDF, where he saw action in several conflicts.

'I'm not afraid of death, I'm apathetic,' he admitted, while seeing out his days in the settlement of Nir Galim, which he helped found with other survivors, near Ashdod in Israel's southern coastal plain. 'I'll give you an example. You can't say you're not afraid in war, and I've been in two total wars. When you're shot at, you're scared. You don't mess with it. But you can't panic. You must watch out for yourself, and not be indifferent to the dangers, but you cannot be ruled by fear.'

Anarchy, though, is inherently unpredictable. It strips away any sense of certainty. Gunskirchen was deadly because it was completely disorganized and impossibly overcrowded. Dysentery and typhus devastated starving, skeletal inmates; Hershel remembers 'there were bodies, strewn everywhere'.

Chaim Schwimmer described 'hooligans, running around

everywhere' in the forest where they were abandoned. They lived in roofless huts, and slept among frozen corpses. Even someone with Dugo's drive to survive seemed to be diminished:

> I'm already in a stupor. The typhus is eating me. The lice have already eaten me. It's a terrible place.
>
> I'm so sick I no longer feel alive. I feel like I am living my final moments. But then an SS man decides to try to save his own skin by handing out food from the Red Cross. We are starving, dying of hunger. We start pounding on the doors of the food warehouse, and the SS start up with machine guns. I don't know how many were killed, but I managed to escape.

That night, Dugo returned to relative safety and wept, because 'I was so discouraged by my life.' In the darkness, he conducted an angry, imaginary conversation with his father:

> 'Daddy, When I was in Birkenau you asked me to stay alive, to survive and go home. Look how I am sitting here with no food and no clothes on. How are you guarding me?'
>
> My dad says, 'David. Calm down. Get something to wear.'

The following morning, he returned to the scene of the previous day's carnage, removed the trousers from a corpse, and put them on. He wrestled the coat from another body. Understandably, desperation had overwhelmed normal conventions of decency; he would, at least, be warmer.

Following warnings that a repeat of the previous day's unrest would lead to more reprisals, Dugo was one of the first inmates to get hold of a Red Cross package, which contained two packets of biscuits, two boxes of sardines, two packets of marmalade and a carton of milk. He guarded the package with his life.

As for Hershel, he thought of fleeing into the forest, but doubted he would survive since he was on the edge of exhaustion. Yet he retained his natural resourcefulness. He spotted a break in the fence surrounding the warehouse, and helped himself to food, which he stashed inside his clothing and carried back to the camp.

Hershel was in the process of sharing it with his cousin Chaim and Yisroel Taub when he was ambushed by fellow inmates:

People were so hungry, and I had little energy to resist. They robbed me and ran away when a German guard noticed I was being attacked. I was on the floor, and he took out his gun and shaped to shoot me.

I will never know why he didn't. He probably didn't have any bullets left. I couldn't run so he just hit me hard on the head with his gun. It knocked me out for a little while, and when I got up I was dizzy. At least we were able to divide the food I had left. Without that we would probably have died of starvation.

Chaim, who was suffering badly from typhus, and Yisroel, who was terribly weakened by diarrhoea, looked after Hershel for forty-eight hours until, on the afternoon of Friday, 4 May, word spread that the Americans had taken the surrounding town; they were free to do as they wished.

By the time the liberators arrived, at ten the next morning, the SS had fled, after a haphazard attempt to force inmates to bury some of the dead. The eyewitness account of Captain J. D. Pletcher, of the 71st Infantry Division, stands the test of time as an insight into the depravity of the situation:

Driving up to the camp in our jeep, we first knew we were approaching the camp by the hundreds of starving, half crazed inmates lining the roads, begging for food and cigarettes.

Many of them had been able to get only a few hundred yards from the gate before they keeled over and died. As weak as they were, the chance to be free, the opportunity to escape was so great they couldn't resist, though it meant staggering only a few yards before death came.

Of all the horrors of the place, the smell, perhaps, was the most startling of all. It was a smell made up of all kinds of odors – human excreta, foul bodily odors, smoldering trash fires, German tobacco – which is a stink in itself – all mixed together in a heavy dank atmosphere, in thick, muddy woods, where little breeze could go.

The ground was pulpy throughout the camp, churned to a consistency of warm putty by the milling of thousands of feet, mud mixed with faeces and urine. The smell of Gunskirchen nauseated many of the Americans who went there. It was a smell I'll never forget, completely different from anything I've ever encountered. It could almost be seen and hung over the camp like a fog of death.

As we entered the camp, the living skeletons still able to walk crowded around us and, though we wanted to drive farther into the place, the milling, pressing crowd wouldn't let us. It is not an exaggeration to say that almost every inmate was insane with hunger. Just the sight of an American brought cheers, groans and shrieks. People crowded around to touch an American, to touch the jeep, to kiss our arms – perhaps just to make sure that it was true.

The people who couldn't walk crawled out toward our jeep. Those who couldn't even crawl propped themselves up on an elbow, and somehow, through all their pain and suffering, revealed through their eyes the gratitude, the joy they felt at the arrival of Americans.

***

Dugo's first thought was to head for the kitchens, but others got there before him. They made the fatal mistake of gorging themselves. Some were unaware of the risks, but Hershel came across a doomed boy who told him: 'I don't mind dying so long as I have enough food.'

Hershel was 'only bones' but he had the presence of mind not to eat the rich, fatty food given out by the liberators, who lacked foresight of what it would do to ravenous inmates. He refused meat, restricting himself to potatoes, bread and dry biscuits before he managed to get Chaim and Yisroel, who were by now very ill, into a military hospital.

Hershel was also admitted, and initially felt a little better, but declined sharply as typhoid took hold. He did not eat or drink for five days. It was then, as he woke from a deep sleep, that he realized 'the light had disappeared from my right eye'. He closed both of them, held his hands in front of his face, and opened them again. His field of vision was shrinking with frightening speed.

Within ten minutes, he could see nothing. He had gone blind, through a combination of disease and the brutality of the SS soldier who had then vanished into the night. His last conscious image is of frozen corpses, littering the landscape.

TWELVE

Free

SLEEP WAS ELUSIVE AS HERSHEL Herskovic began to come to terms with the loss of his sight. He used the dawn chorus of birdsong as a reference point, and though he sensed the presence of his brother Yisroel at his bedside, he could not be sure until he heard his voice.

He was hungry, not having eaten for several days, and fighting an overwhelming feeling of helplessness which challenged the instincts that had enabled him to survive the war. New realities were onerous; when he asked Yisroel to take him out of the hospital, so he could beg in the street, he found he lacked the strength to move freely.

The sensations and restrictions of blindness did not affect him psychologically while he was still physically depleted, but as he got better, and more attuned to the rhythms of a new form of daily life, they affected him a great deal. He was conflicted; he didn't know where to go or what to do.

Hope that his blindness would be temporary proved understandable but pernicious. He was taken to an Austrian eye specialist, who administered intravitreal injections, which delivered medication directly into his eyeballs. The disappointment when the injections proved unsuccessful was crushing.

He returned to Hungary in early August after a spell at a rehabilitation centre. Clinging to the hope he could still be treated, he stopped off in Bratislava for further examinations in the Jewish hospital there. Once again, the specialist concluded that his blindness would be permanent.

While this futile search for encouragement had been going on, his father Abraham had been staging a daily vigil at the main station in Budapest, hoping to see his sons among passengers disembarking from trains from Germany or Austria. By chance, while questioning passengers, he mentioned his sons' names to a Romanian boy, who had accompanied Hershel and Yisroel when they left the military hospital.

Informed that they were seeking treatment in the Slovak capital, their father immediately travelled there. Hershel knew he had arrived before Yisroel, because he heard his voice, asking nurses for news of them. The boys were overjoyed but frail. Yisroel, in particular, was ailing; he had water in his lungs and was soon sent to recuperate in the clean, fresh air of the Tatra Mountains, on the border between Poland and present-day Slovakia.

Each of these unlikely reunions, being enacted across the continent by the dispossessed, were, in their own way, testament to the failure of the Nazis' murderous creed. Yet the tectonic plates of an imperfect, uncertain world were still shifting. Following more unsuccessful tests in hospital in Budapest, where Hershel was reunited with his elder brother Berish, who had survived Buchenwald with their father, he made his way to a home town he barely recognized.

Only two Jewish families from Munkacs, those of a teacher, Eliyah Rubin, an Auschwitz survivor, and the Ungars, the town's watchmakers, were intact. The rest had been destroyed or decimated; more than 85 per cent of the pre-war Jewish population had been wiped out.

Jewish property had been stolen, the Hebrew Gymnasium, a key educational establishment, had closed, and synagogues were being used as warehouses. The town was visibly under Commun-ist influence, having officially become part of the Soviet Union in June 1945. Public prayer services required a licence and the building housing a newly improvised synagogue was confiscated by the authorities.

Hershel recognized the perils of a new tyranny, and heard ominous echoes of old prejudices: 'As soon as I arrived I had the impression I didn't want to stay there. It felt like a ghost town. The way the Russian soldiers spoke and behaved convinced me that I had to get out. My father didn't feel so strongly, maybe because he was older, but I kept pushing him. We still celebrated the Jewish holidays there, but it felt provisional.'

The Iron Curtain was descending. A time limit, for restricted emigration to Czechoslovakia, had expired, and his father was stopped at the border when he sought to take Hershel to Prague for further tests. The guard originally refused them permission to leave, but relented when told of the medical emergency.

Leaving Hershel in hospital in the Czech capital, his father returned to Munkacs with the intention of bringing Berish back with him. He had missed his opportunity. When he retraced his steps back to the border with his eldest son it had been sealed. The pair were Soviet subjects, prisoners of history. Once again, the family had been splintered.

While in Prague, Hershel met representatives of London's Jewish community, whose refugee committee had been given permission by the British government to resettle 300 Jewish boys in England. The only proviso presented an obvious problem: to be permitted to travel, they had to be fully fit. Hershel did not meet the criteria.

Undaunted, he employed the cunning of a camp veteran, by

successfully persuading a Czech doctor to go against his considered medical opinion, and write a letter suggesting the boy had a chance to regain his sight, given further injections, and the expertise within the British medical system. This was enough to ensure Hershel's ticket to a new life.

He would be accompanied by his cousin Chaim Schwimmer, whom he had effectively saved, in the pivotal days after liberation, by pressurizing the American troops to take him to hospital. Typhus had depleted Chaim's body, and also drained his spirit. He felt so demoralized he had neither the energy nor the inclination to join the joyful throngs that welcomed the Americans. Later in life he would reflect:

> Imagine that. We had been waiting and praying to see the Americans, but when they arrived I didn't even go down to see them. There were thousands dying all around me. I was very sick, but I knew it would be stupid to eat the truckloads of canned food they brought with them.
>
> So many people, who had been eating next to nothing, died. Their stomachs could not cope. Instead the three of us – Hershel, Yisroel and me – went into the fields on the Saturday afternoon to pick potatoes. They were not rotten, so we cooked and ate them, hoping they would give us strength.

They were eventually given a lift into the town of Gunskirchen on the back of a truck containing a group of black GIs, who were so struck by their desperate appearance they defied orders not to do so. Still in their ragged striped uniforms, they wandered aimlessly before returning to the camp. They were so conditioned to the disciplines of incarceration that, quite illogically, they were fearful of being punished for missing an inspection.

Chaim, in particular, had taken too much out of himself. He

lay down on the floor, went into a coma, and lost the next five days of his life:

My cousin first thought I was dead. When he realized I was unconscious he started begging them to take me to hospital. They finally took us there on the back of a tow truck.

The hospital was operated by nuns. I was so full of lice, from top to bottom, you could barely see an inch of my skin. They brushed them off with steel brushes, put me in water, and washed me. I was so tired. They put me to bed, and I slept for maybe a day and a half, two days. When I woke up I was a new person.

Out of immediate danger, he was taken to an upstairs ward, where new worries emerged. His blood pressure was perilously low, and his veins were so damaged that nurses had severe difficulties taking blood samples. Chaim was also mentally confused, being convinced he should be celebrating Shavuot, the two-day Jewish holiday that marks the Torah being given to Moses on Mount Sinai. That had taken place nearly a week earlier, when he was in a coma.

He was under intensive observation for a week before a decision was taken to transfer him to a convalescent home in the mountains, 'a beautiful, beautiful place' where Chaim stayed for almost a month. He ate well, despite some concerns that, unlike the fresh vegetables he eagerly consumed, the meat was not kosher.

He gained weight steadily, and began to plan for his immediate future, which, it turned out, would be interlinked with that of his cousin. Chaim, too, found a place on the scheme taking Jewish youths to England. He was reunited with Hershel during a three-week recuperative stay in Taverny, in the north-western suburbs of Paris.

They had to wait for space to be found on cross-Channel ships, on which returning troops understandably took priority. Eventually, they sailed from northern France to the port of Dover with the speech of a Rabbi ringing in their ears: 'The world discovered socialism and communism, but we know how it ended, with barbarism. Have the courage to carry on the old traditions.'

Chaim had recovered his old poise and strength of will; he pushed back against an original plan to send them to adoptive families in Buckingham and Birmingham, preferring to stay in a more religious environment in London. That also suited Hershel, but his pressing priority was to survive seasickness. He vomited continually until he set foot on unfamiliar, but mercifully dry, land.

The legacy of Gunskirchen was universally brutal. Dugo Leitner's most vivid memory of the immediate aftermath of liberation was waking up to find American soldiers and doctors standing around his bed. 'What's your name?' they asked. 'How did you get here?' His mind had been scoured; he could not answer them.

'I couldn't remember a thing,' he admitted. It took a couple of days for his memory to return. The catalysts, ironically, were the Auschwitz tattoos on the inside of his left arm; one had been crudely erased, the second, below his elbow, branded him as B14571. That brought everything back.

The images were haunting, a tableau of loss and grief. His stolen childhood, his mother Golda's cooking and kindness. The last Passover meal with his family before they were driven into a ghetto, the agony of deportation in a crowded cattle car. Most horrifyingly, the murder of his mother and two sisters on arrival in the camp.

Dugo had a primeval urge to fill in the gaps. Once released from hospital, he made his way to Vienna, and on to Budapest, travelling precariously on the roofs of a succession of trains. He continued to live on his wits, begging lifts as he completed the final 280-kilometre journey to his home town of Nyíregyháza by road.

Little more than 300 members of the Orthodox community would return. Dugo's family home had been destroyed by a direct hit from a bomb. 'There was a big hole in the house, like the hole in my heart,' he recalled. 'The walls were bare and dry. Not a bed or a table. Not a closet or a shoebox full of family photographs.'

His senses were assaulted by what had been, and what the town had become. The spectacular synagogue, in which he had prayed, was a bombsite. It had been blown up by the Nazis in October 1944. All that remained was a human reckoning. He needed to know what had happened to his father Meir, and his brother Shmuel.

On the way to the former family home, Dugo came across a prominent local Jewish administrator, Eliezer Blue, who once worked for the Foreign Ministry. Blue had become accustomed to the tormented questions of distressed refugees, so he seized the initiative by telling Dugo 'your brother is at home'.

He didn't answer the inevitable follow-up: 'And where is my father?' The silence was oppressive but instructive. The sadness in Dugo's voice testifies to the enduring nature of his loss: 'I realized, at that moment, that my father, like my mother, did not survive.' He was by nature an inveterate optimist, but the darkest of clouds descended.

It would be a while before he discovered the details of Meir Leitner's death, a couple of weeks before Buchenwald was liberated by the American Third Army on 11 April. The knowledge that his father was so close to sharing the freedom enjoyed by 21,000 surviving inmates that afternoon was like a knife, twisting in Dugo's guts.

Like his brother Shmuel, he could see no future remaining in Hungary. Though, superficially at least, his old neighbours were welcoming, their self-protection during the fascist purge of the Jewish population led to a feeling they could not be totally trusted. Too much had changed for their presence to be comfortable.

Meir Leitner's belief in the principle of the state of Israel was amplified by the younger members of the post-Holocaust generation. Though Dugo, like the majority of those from an Orthodox tradition, was initially resistant to a Zionist philosophy, their activists' promotion of eventual resettlement in what was then Palestine, under a British mandate, gradually began to make sense.

Bnei Akiva is now the largest religious Zionist youth movement in the world, with over 125,000 members in forty-two countries. Established in 1936, it was on a smaller scale immediately after the war, operating locally, yet playing a pivotal, proactive role in preparing Holocaust survivors to make *aliyah*. Literally translated from Hebrew, that means 'ascent', 'rise' or 'going up'; it has become universal shorthand for emigrating to Israel.

'The young guardians, and nation builders, wanted to take me there, but at first I didn't like the idea,' Dugo admitted. 'Gradually I turned around.' He moved into the Hungarian countryside, where Bnei Akiva operated farms, which trained survivors in the skills they would need in the mother country.

Over eighteen months or so, Dugo formed and fostered an ambition to establish a kibbutz, the utopian communities traditionally based on agriculture. He was not afraid of hard work, and was taken by the purity of the notion, rather than its ideological associations with socialism and Zionism.

Israel's Declaration of Independence, on 14 May 1948, together with the authoritarian undercurrents of Eastern Europe, convinced him to take practical steps to emigrate. This was a perilous, covert process; Hungary had closed its borders, which were easier to penetrate in the north, into Slovakia.

Once in Bratislava, would-be immigrants were taken on a

relatively short journey through eastern Austria to Vienna. They then travelled south-west into Italy and on to Bari, the port city on the Adriatic from which Dugo boarded a ship bound for Israel. By the time he disembarked, on 21 March 1949, he had already been recruited as a gunner in the Israel Defence Forces (IDF). He was prepared to fight for the right to live as he pleased.

So, too, was Mordechai Eldar. He had endured a tortuous route to Gunskirchen that forced him to confront the greatest of taboos, the eating of human flesh. Transported from Auschwitz-Birkenau in mid-December 1944, at the height of winter, many of those with him, in open-topped carriages destined for Sachsenhausen, died of cold and starvation:

> What helped us a bit was the canvas that was left on the floor which we used to cover us. We undressed the dead and took their clothes, wore them and lay on the bodies because the floor was frozen. After some weeks in Sachsenhausen we were taken to Mauthausen.
>
> One day a plane bombed the camp and there were many injured and dead. Parts of bodies were strewn on the ground. We suffered terrible starvation and ate them. You have to be in a certain situation to understand it. I also ate worms, snails, potato peels and things thrown in the trash.

It took trademark courage to confirm the consequences of desperation. Mordechai had rarely spoken publicly of such behaviour until, in February 2016, he travelled to Detmold in Germany to give evidence in the trial of Reinhold Hanning, who had volunteered for the Waffen SS at the age of eighteen, and was a notoriously cruel guard in Auschwitz. He was duly found guilty of mass murder, but died at the age of ninety-five, in January 2017, before he could serve a prison sentence.

Even though Mordechai had, by that time, become a hugely
respected commentator on the Holocaust experience, the trial
proved cathartic because it enabled him to address, fearlessly and
concisely, the worst of his memories. He spoke of public executions, accompanied by the camp orchestra, with the victims 'hung
head downwards'.

He referred to Josef Mengele as 'a disgrace on the world' for his
'satanic acts' and described how a friend, a twin, had been experi-
mented upon. When they met years later, in Israel, his friend
could not bring himself to speak of the horrors he experienced.
Instead, overwhelmed, he 'cried bitter tears'.

Mordechai's summary of the inhumanity of his captors proved
deeply affecting:

Our lives were managed by the block alteste, the kapo, their
assistants and of course the SS command. They didn't allow us
even a moment of quiet. The kapo was cruel and his authority
was limitless.

He was permitted to beat us, to starve us, to kill, to prevent
sleep or to call us to roll call in the middle of the night. The
kapo also invented special acts of cruelty such as extracting
gold teeth brutally without any consideration of pain. His aide
turned the soup pot over, and we all got down on our knees to
lick the food from the ground, like dogs.

He would set up fights between two prisoners that he chose,
and if they didn't fight with gusto he would beat them harshly.
The height of such cruelty, as I remember, was a fight between
two brothers, apparently twins. They were both beaten with
such barbarity by the kapo that they died two days later.

He would throw bread or a potato at the electric fence and
stalked whoever tried to get a bit of food. Whoever dared to
advance toward the fence risked death by electrocution or a

bullet from the guards' outpost. Many chose this. And whoever survived was treated by the kapo to a beating. Once I was the victim of such a beating.

His resilience enabled him to survive the death march from Mauthausen to Gunskirchen, but Mordechai was barely alive on the day of his liberation when an American soldier found him lying in a ditch close to the main gate. Like so many of the fifty-one boys, he was coaxed back to health in a military hospital until, with grim determination, he set off for his home town of Campulung La Tisa, 'to see who had survived and who had been murdered'.

Some members of his extended family were dead, but he found his sisters, Ita and Sarah, and an aunt. His elder brother Yehuda, who had been sent from Auschwitz as a slave labourer, found Mordechai in January 1946, in Bavaria, to which he had moved with a group of childhood friends from Budapest.

The four siblings resolved to emigrate to Palestine, illegally if necessary, and were among 4,500 Holocaust survivors on the renamed *Exodus 1947*, an old coastal steamer that became a global symbol of struggle after it had embarked on a symbolically provocative voyage from the French port of Sète. On 18 July 1947, while the boat was anchored 20 nautical miles from the Palestinian coast, off the port of Haifa, it was intercepted, rammed by a British destroyer, HMS *Childers*, and stormed by British troops.

The Eldar family were then placed on one of three navy transport ships. The French authorities refused to forcibly remove the refugees on arrival at Port-de-Bouc in the south of France and, following a twenty-four-day hunger strike, during which passengers refused to disembark, they sailed for Hamburg.

Billeted in a Displaced Persons camp in the British zone, Mordechai and his siblings were determined not to be deterred. In

June 1948 they travelled from Germany to Marseilles, from where they sailed to Tel Aviv on the SS *Kedmah*, widely thought to be the first ship to fly the Zionist flag. After a spell in a resettlement camp in Hadera, Mordechai began what was to be a thirty-year career in the Israeli Army.

Avigdor Neumann, another survivor who would eventually be recognized as a hero of several wars, also endured the death march to Gunskirchen. He was relatively fit, compared to some of the fifty-one, but consumed by a strange unease, since freedom forced him to confront daunting realities:

I'm a fourteen-year-old boy, alone in the world. What am I going to do? I knew I had no parents, no family. I didn't believe my sister was alive. Depression began to take hold. Yes, I was free from the Germans, but this sadness, this helplessness, settled in. I asked myself, 'Where am I going, and what for?'

He, too, heeded his homing instincts and returned to Nagyszőlős, which had been renamed Vynohradiv when it was subsumed into Ukraine. In what he described as a scene of 'great joy', Avigdor found his sister, Sima Rachel. From that moment on 'she meant everything to me, father and mother'. Being four years older, she had a greater sense of the dangers of the time. They were no longer safe in what they had once called home.

They spent time in Belgium before arriving in Israel on the *Theodore Herzl* in April 1947. A home-made banner hung over the side of the ship: 'The Germans destroyed our families. Please don't destroy our hope.' The plea to the administrators' conscience fell on deaf ears.

The boat was intercepted by the British and the pair were interned in a detention camp in Cyprus. Refusing to be discouraged, they returned to Israel in December of that year, where

Avigdor resumed his studies in Bnei Brak, just east of Tel Aviv, before being drafted into the military in November 1948.

He married Rivka in 1953 and had two children. By 2025, his family had expanded to include seven grandchildren, forty-three great-grandchildren and one great-great-grandchild. He felt he had been spared for 'a sacred mission' to pass on life lessons to a new generation.

'I left Auschwitz, but Auschwitz has not left me,' he reflects. He has a long-term heart condition, which involved the insertion of three stents, and means 'that every morning I give thanks when I wake up'. At ninety-four he is a ceaseless, selfless, ambassador for his cause, lecturing to youth groups, schools and military units.

Like Dugo Leitner, who visited Auschwitz thirty-eight times to provide his perspective during study visits, Avigdor returns regularly to the camp to share his experiences. He refuses all offers of payment for his time, 'because that would damage the sanctity of the act'. In 2019, aged eighty-eight, he even belatedly celebrated his bar mitzvah there. Typically, the day after Naftali interviewed him in 2024, he intended to travel to Poland, despite a badly swollen leg:

> We have a duty to share our truth. The people who listen to me were born into a reality they take for granted. There's a state, an army. Jewish soldiers, Jewish police. I played a part in building my country. I played my part in founding it, defending it, fortifying it. How did I feel, wearing the uniform of my nation? It's indescribable.
>
> When I speak to Germans I tell them that this is our revenge on Hitler. He wanted me not to be. He wanted none of us to be remembered. Yet we are still here. We have offspring. God willing, more and more of us will be born. For years I did not

speak. I did not tell. But once I stopped being introspective, I knew what I had to do.

I am filled with pride for what I was privileged to do. Despite everything I built a wonderful family. From nothing, I found the will to rise up. I tell people to learn from me. Do not let yourself be overcome by sadness. There is no room for despair. It is possible to rise from the ashes. We are an eternal people and nothing can defeat us.

THIRTEEN

Second Chances

COMPELLINGLY POIGNANT contradictions lace Hershel Herskovic's second life. He laughs with his eyes, although they are invariably closed. He admits to being an emotional character but protects himself by being clinically analytical about aspects of his past. He has never been conscious of shedding tears; when he cries, his cheeks remain dry.

'I don't know whether that's because I am blind,' he concedes, though many sightless individuals weep normally. 'I have no idea.' He responds powerfully to such usual stimuli as joy, pride, anger or distress; the signs, perhaps a catch in the throat, a change in the tone of his voice, or a slight shortness of breath, differ subtly.

Releasing tension in that manner is a natural form of compensation, like his heightened ability to sense body language, movement, noise and other alterations in the surrounding environment. He provides passionate, expressive proof of the misconception that the blind are somehow emotionally restricted.

'To me, it is natural that I cannot see. I don't miss anything, because I have become used to it. You know, I've not seen anything for seventy years, actually, to be exact, eighty years. What would happen if I'd be able to see tomorrow? Probably I wouldn't be able to orientate myself for a few days, but you don't miss what you don't know.'

He has a high, largely unblemished forehead, but age has left its mark. The lines under his eyes resemble an arid riverbed of profound experiences. Yet, at the same time, there is a softness to his face, which is full of life. The inner youth is allowed out to play by laughter, which tends to be loud and unabashed.

Anyone who spends time with him, and who has awareness of the challenges he has overcome, would recognize this description of him, by Naftali, my collaborator on this book: 'He is thoroughly authentic, to a fault, one of the most self-assured, mentally confident and strong-willed people I have ever met.'

Coming from someone who has stared into the souls of hundreds of Holocaust survivors, in gathering a unique range of testimonies, that is some recommendation. Each survivor has a tangible life force, but Hershel's spirit is notably undimmed, unquenchable.

His son David, a lawyer, describes him as being 'extremely strong willed, with an acute sense of justice. He's never liked joining the herd and he taught us to think for ourselves. He went through so much, but survived with his smile and his songs.'

Those traits became quickly apparent on his arrival in England, once the glorious luxuries of fresh bedding, warm clothing and plentiful food, in his reception camp in Dover, had enabled the overwhelming exhaustion that had consumed him in the first year after liberation to ebb away.

He spent some time in a shelter in the East End of London before being separated due to his condition, once it had been confirmed as permanent. He was sent to Henshaws, a prominent school for the blind in Manchester, by the Jewish Blind Society, whose imposition of authority quickly started to chafe.

Hershel did not want to go, because he felt it would compromise his faith. He was the school's only Jewish pupil, and it lacked kosher facilities, but he was helped enormously by the generosity of a local Jewish family. To the envy of his fellow pupils, who missed home comforts, they took him out of the boarding school every Friday so he could enjoy the traditional observances of the Sabbath.

He returned for the start of the academic week with a range of suitable sandwiches, prepared by the lady of the house for daily consumption, since he could not, would not, eat school food. This arrangement lasted for six months, but it was inexorably undermined by his unease at a wider form of social exclusion.

'I must say that, although I was looked after very well by the family, who were very kind to me, I have never believed in the way they treat blind people here. I may not be able to see but I regard myself as no different to anyone else. Why should I be separated from the rest of society?'

He thrived educationally at the school, which had been established in 1837 as an 'asylum for the indigent blind' on the strength of a £20,000 donation from the will of Thomas Henshaw, an Oldham businessman. Today it has 360 members of staff, augmented by more than 200 volunteers. Together they support individuals, families and their carers.

The headmaster at the time proved to be an influential ally for Hershel, who fought against the Blind Society's insistence that he move to an institution in Worcester, which catered for more educationally advanced pupils. His intelligence was never an issue; they wanted him to broaden his studies, with the intention of becoming a lawyer:

The Society, and the Jewish refugee committee, helped the survivors, but they wanted them to become assimilated, become Anglicized, or become part of a Jewish community that is not necessarily religious. Instinctively, I was against that, so I was always at odds with them.

I am an individualist by nature. I don't necessarily follow what is around me. Being *frum* [devoutly religious] is very important to me but even today, when I go to *davening* [prayer] every morning I still have my personal ideas. I never thought of surrendering my way of life in any way.

To tell the truth, I was perhaps too young to fully analyse it, but, looking back, I think I had the right attitude. If I had thought we shouldn't be Jewish, and given up our faith, I wouldn't have survived the camps. So many Jewish leaders have come through that process, creating schools and conditions in which our people can thrive.

The camps insulated Hershel against intimidation. When you have come so close to death that it is possible to smell and taste it, instructions from institutions, however well-meaning they may be, are placed into perspective. The Blind Society had an inkling of what was to come when he refused to use a white cane 'because white is a sign of surrender. We don't surrender to hardship. We figure out a way to adapt.'

Hershel's defiance is convincing, because it is so well articulated. 'Basically,' he says, 'my principle is not to be afraid, and to be independent in every possible way. People may want to help, to their own way of thinking, but they are no better than anyone else. I like to follow my own way.'

He refused to transfer to Worcester because, once again, he felt it would threaten his identity, as a Jew. 'They thought it would be best for my future. When I said no, they told me, "But you will go." I told them: "I have survived the concentration camps, and I will survive you. I will not go." '

Recognizing the futility of such an impasse, the headmaster

of Henshaws intervened, telling the authorities to leave Hershel alone, to forge his own path. This eventually involved his move, against the wishes of the Blind Society, to a yeshiva, a theological college that was originally established in Staines, but moved across Surrey to Egham. It was there that his spiritual and physical needs were met. He often slept in the open and sourced locally grown vegetables. He insists: 'It was there that I was cured.'

He made a living, ironically as a telephone operator for the Blind Society, but became frustrated. Though he had successfully resisted their pressure to conform, on some subliminal level their original suggestion, that he work towards a legal career, had taken hold.

He took private lessons in Kensington, and passed his preliminary legal examinations, only to have further practical problems in finding a firm of solicitors to which he could be articled. It was hard to find an organization that met his devotional priorities by allowing him to observe all Jewish holidays and to leave early on Friday afternoons in winter, so he could be prepared when Shabbat began at sunset.

He was comfortable living in the Hasidic community in Stamford Hill, in the London Borough of Hackney, and fate took a hand when his future wife Daphne Woolf approached him at a talk for blind people, and offered to help his studies twice a week, as a reader. She was born in England; her mother, whose family was from Lithuania, was killed in the Blitz in Stoke Newington. In a twist of fate, her father's family came from Germany. Though she did not speak Yiddish, her relationship with Hershel flourished.

He had matches suggested to him as part of the culture of arranged marriages, and being blind, the proposals would be what the matchmaker believed 'befitted' a visually impaired person. But Hershel turned them all down. At one point, his landlady said to him, 'What do you think, an actress will marry you?' but he persevered in finding someone he wanted.

'It was a love match,' Hershel recalls, with a warmth tinged by wistfulness. He and Daphne were engaged within two months, and married in Tottenham Library on 8 March 1955. Once again, he turned the negativity of others into positivity: 'They asked me, "How will you support your wife?" I answered that with a wife and family I would have more incentive to succeed.'

Though not from a particularly Orthodox background, Daphne embraced her husband's Hasidic way of life and community. They had four children. By that time, he was reaping the benefits of a spell in the United States, set up through contacts provided by friends from the Staines yeshiva, who also gave him financial support. He returned to Britain 'with a new sense of adventure' and unashamed ambition. His American cousin said that when he was in the USA Hershel would joke that he would end up as the Lord Mayor of London.

Hershel took on Yuri Kurtis as an apprentice in his property business. Yuri was a Budapest-born child survivor of three concentration camps and like many of his generation he struggled to find a job. Understandably, Hershel made a deep impression on him: 'Everyone thought that he didn't know what he was doing,' he recalled. 'He would go into a property, tap the walls and jump up and down on the floorboards, and know what he was dealing with. People thought he was crazy. They underestimated him.'

Hershel's acute sense of smell also enabled him to assess the quality of houses he inspected; he was attuned to any sign of damp. He would also spread his feet to feel if the floor was level. Naturally self-reliant, he depended on his ability to detect the good and bad in people, often by concentrating on their tone of voice.

He had a firm sense of perspective; rather than business, conversations in the family home centred on faith, the Bible, history and communal, national and international politics. That perspective has been painfully acquired, but it remains potent, since it sketches the parameters of Hershel's life:

> The main problem is everyone feels they have no limits. In your good moments you think you can conquer the world, to go to the sun and the moon. In your bad moments, you become very down if you do not have a basic understanding of how you live your life.
>
> Some people succeed in having plenty of money, but they are afraid they will lose it, or someone will take it away from them. My advice is to accept whatever happens to you. You need to have inner peace. Don't look for more. Don't envy others.

Hershel believes in the principle of *tzedakah*, a Hebrew word that translates as 'righteousness' or 'justice' but is more commonly used to refer to the concept of charity, a central tenet of Judaism. It feeds into a moral obligation to help the weak, the poor and the needy. Individuals are encouraged to share their resources with those in need, even though those resources may be meagre.

Chaim Schwimmer described how Hershel put that principle into profound practice in Auschwitz-Birkenau, by giving away his food ration card to enable another boy to survive the Yom Kippur selection. The Nazis, searching for escapees, demanded the card as proof that the holder could not have been in the holding block.

'I can still see this boy before my eyes, because I was so close to him. He was from Irshava in the old Czechoslovakia, small, and very young. I remember like it was today. Hershy gave him his ticket. He said, "I'm not concerned because they won't take me as I am tall enough to pass selection." That's how the boy remained alive.'

Tragically, the boy failed to survive a small selection several days later. Despite that, the gesture, in guaranteeing him at least a temporary reprieve, is a measure of Hershel as a man. Typically, he only confirmed the story to his family when it was mentioned by his cousin.

The family unit is the cornerstone of his life. It has not been easy; Hershel brought up his children by himself when Daphne passed away on 13 April 1978. He cooked meals, had the assistance of a cleaner, and with his children managed to run the home.

His determination to reunite his family included a BBC interview and a sustained lobbying campaign. He and Daphne, who is mentioned in the papers of the Labour leader Hugh Gaitskell in relation to a proposed visit to the USSR in January 1963, made representations to senior politicians like Gaitskell and Harold Wilson to help persuade the Soviet authorities to allow Hershel's father and elder brother Berish to leave Ukraine to join them in England.

Hershel visited the USSR twice to state his case, and even offered to buy their freedom. Berish initially refused to leave his father, but once his father passed away and the Soviets softened their stance in the aftermath of the Six Day War, his freedom was secured in 1972 with the help of the British Embassy in Moscow. After spending some time in England, Berish decided to emigrate to Israel, where he settled in Bnai Brak, a hub of Hasidic Judaism on the central Mediterranean coastal plain.

Yisroel, Hershel's other surviving brother, toyed with the idea of moving to Canada, but quietly lived out his life in London until his death in 2018, aged eighty-nine. Intensely religious, he married soon after the war and worked in the rag trade from the 1950s. Hershel was by far the most gregarious of the siblings.

His sons, David and Abraham, have graphic recollections of family holidays in Suffolk, which reminded their father of the family's former mill, in the countryside outside Munkacs. Hershel would defy his blindness on the country lanes by riding down to the village on the front seat of a tandem. It was the job of the boy on the back to tell him whether any cars were coming, from left or right, when they reached an intersection.

Hershel also had a single-seater bicycle that he happily rode solo, and once he leapt from a boat, to swim in the sea, before making his way back to the beach. He loved offshore swimming in resorts as far apart as Bournemouth and Eilat, in Israel. Perhaps his greatest stunt was reserved annually, for Simchat Torah, where, well into middle age, he would dance in the synagogue before performing a headstand on a central table, next to the one that held the Torah. This was a celebration of his miraculous escape, in an environment that meant so much to him. Simchat Torah is also Hershel's Hebrew birthday and he always says that he was born twice on this day.

His joie de vivre was contagious, but with his moral courage, steadfast faith and resolute nature, he also had much in common with Yaakov Yosef Weiss, another prominent member of the fifty-one. They were not especially close, but they met several times before Yaakov's death in 2013.

By his own admission, Yaakov drifted, both spiritually and geographically, in the immediate aftermath of his liberation from Gunskirchen. He gravitated initially towards the Austrian city of Linz, midway between Vienna and Salzburg, but described himself as 'being out for the count' for four or five months while he took time to come to terms with the fact that long-awaited freedom was, of itself, no panacea.

'There was no real organization after liberation, so everybody did whatever they fancied,' Yaakov explained:

The main thing, because we were all hungry, was food. We simply did not have enough of it. For weeks and weeks we went from house to house, trying to get some.

You had to look after yourself. We banged on doors, and very often the householders did not want to give us anything. That's when we would find an American soldier. He would come with his gun, bang on the door, and order them to bring out whatever food they had. We were desperate.

We had no clothes – I had one shirt, a pair of sandals, and some pants – so being free felt such a let-down. In the camp I could not imagine that, when it was all over, there would still be people quarrelling, fighting for a piece of bread or a scrap of food. I thought the Messiah would come to save us.

To use his illuminating phrase, Yaakov's faith was 'not an unbroken chain'. His disillusion led to a dilution of his identity as a practising Jew. He had lost his affinity with the tenets and traditions of the religious community that had shaped his personality and philosophy before and during his incarceration.

Portentously, the turning point came on Simchat Torah in 1945, the first anniversary of his reprieve from the gas chamber. He was wandering the streets with a couple of companions when they were approached by a worshipper from a local synagogue. Recognizing them as Jews, he asked if they would join them in making up a *minyan*, the Jewish prayer quorum that requires ten adult males aged thirteen years or older.

They agreed to do so, and the familiarity of the rituals renewed Yaakov's sense of serenity and belonging. Enthused by a blessing for his deliverance, Yaakov proclaimed: 'This is who I am.' It was an act of simple, unsophisticated faith, a spiritual rebirth that involved the recalibration of his life.

A penny dropped, just as it had done for Eva 'Bobby' Neumann in similar circumstances as she found her philosophical bearings after the war. There was a resonance deep inside Yaakov, more visceral than philosophical. He resolved to be an upstanding member of his community, and promised to work on his faults.

'Let's not beat around the bush,' he reflected, with accustomed intensity:

There was a period of time after liberation when I had no feeling for *Yiddishkeit* [the Jewish way of life]. No feeling whatsoever. I don't really know what dragged me back. It's a long story. I had no connection, but I wasn't worried, and it didn't hurt. That puzzled me.

Why didn't I give up on my beliefs? Maybe – and this is my interpretation of it – because I was descended from great people, with great strength. I've since noticed the majority of people who kept themselves *frum* [devoutly religious] after liberation had a *zechus avos* [a Jewish term which refers to the concept of ancestors shielding their descendants].

We went through Auschwitz-Birkenau. We went through all Hell. But you can turn away from all those troubles, and start off a new life, because God will help you. My message is that your strength is nothing, your wisdom is nothing, your wealth is nothing. The main thing is to hold on, to have belief, to be a good person.

Yaakov became successful through his creativity and inventiveness, but remained wary of the dangers of excessive pride. His principles were challenged by some of his wealthier peers, who had a tendency to look down on those less fortunate than themselves.

'That's a form of pride that belittles other people,' he rationalized. 'You cannot say, "I am the one and you are nothing." It's better to say, "You are great and I am also great" than to say, "I am great and you are nothing."'

He never wavered from his belief in charity, humility and humanity.

'If a person knocks on your door and he says, "I'm starving hungry, I haven't a penny in my pocket. Can you help me?", some think, "I don't need to help you. God is there to help you." I believe I have God-given blessings and it is upon me to share them. You should put everything in his pocket, do whatever you can. Give him bread, give him food, give him money.'

Yaakov began to close the circle of his life in the summer of 2011, when he visited his home town of Szilágysomlyó, which, in modern Romania, is called Şimleu Silvaniei. It was a form of pilgrimage, during which he found the grave of his father, Naftali. To his delight, the original *matzevah*, the headstone, was still standing.

As he prayed over the grave, a respectful ritual, he thought of his childhood Rabbi, who had boarded the same train to Auschwitz-Birkenau. Yaakov revived dormant memories of long-gone summers, when, in an age of fragile innocence, he played with friends in the ruins of the sixteenth-century fort known as Báthory Castle.

He had looked, without success, for the synagogue in which he once worshipped. The Jewish community, which featured 450 families, encompassing around 2,500 people, before the war, had shrunk to only fifty or so individuals by the millennium, but was slowly expanding once again.

As he took his leave, there was a sense that Yaakov was at peace: 'It was a very pleasant environment,' he remembered. 'The town itself is still very picturesque. There's a nice river going through the centre. The air is great and the nature is absolutely fantastic. It might not have the greatest spiritual base, but it has fine, upstanding people.'

Wolf Greenwald felt similarly when he returned to his home town of Hajduhadhaz, sixty-eight years after he had been deported to Auschwitz-Birkenau. He was initially reluctant, but did so at the insistence of his children, two of whom had been educated in Manchester before the family's move to the United States.

The site of a brutal forced labour camp in 1944, Hajduhadhaz had been scoured of many of the landmarks of his childhood. His former family home, thick-walled and supposedly solid, and his first synagogue no longer stood. Yet a barely believable find brought the past flooding back.

By pure chance, Wolf came across a copy of the Mishnah, the first work of rabbinic literature dating back to the sixth century, once owned by his father. He remembered it instantly, as part of a twelve-volume set printed in Berlin. It was almost as if it was a ghostly gift.

Wolf had built a second life, based on the virtues of service. He often had a twinkle in his eye, and would toast his good fortune with whisky and the cry of 'L'chaim' ('To life'). He had the sort of large and loving family that seemed an unrealizable fantasy when he was liberated from the charnel house of Bergen-Belsen.

Memories, of stumbling around and between piles of 13,000 unburied bodies after the unchallenged arrival of British and Canadian troops, endured. Wolf was one of 60,000 emaciated survivors; he only avoided becoming one of the 28,000 who died within a month, through disease or malnutrition, by following the advice of a similarly skeletal, but streetwise, inmate:

He knew me from Auschwitz, and told me not to touch anything but potatoes cooked in water and salt. I barely ate anything for the first week. It is no exaggeration to say that if I did eat something and opened up my shirt, you would have seen the food making its way down to my stomach.

When the troops arrived on that Sunday, one of the officers popped his head out from his tank and told us to go nowhere.

He said: 'I don't know what we are going to do to help you, but we are going to do our best.' Unfortunately, they made the big mistake of dropping in thousands of packages containing heavy food. People were dying with their last meal still in their hands. Sickness was everywhere.

Wolf had suffered horrendously with typhus, and only managed to taste freedom because of the care of two Jewish orderlies, who moistened his mouth with water when the disease was at its height and he slipped in and out of consciousness. Such acts of kindness were often the difference between life and death.

The blasphemy of Bergen-Belsen was brought to a horrified world by the immediate and unprecedentedly vivid coverage from journalists, photographers and soldiers. Unlike other death camps, like Auschwitz, Sobibor and Treblinka, which had either been destroyed or evacuated, Bergen-Belsen exposed the grotesque reality of the Final Solution.

The evidence of inhumanity was intact. Eyewitnesses detailed the suffering of the victims, and the guilt of those who tormented them. The Bergen-Belsen war-crimes trial, conducted by the British, was ultimately overshadowed by the Nuremberg trials, overseen by the Americans, but the eleven worst offenders were executed.

Like several other of the fifty-one boys who emerged from the gas chamber in Auschwitz-Birkenau on Simchat Torah in 1944, Wolf Greenwald harboured one lasting regret. He felt cheated that Josef Mengele managed to evade justice. It was left to the Mossad, Israel's foreign-intelligence agency, to bring a degree of closure.

FOURTEEN

The Banality of Evil

RICARDO KLEMENT WAS A MAN of routine. Each evening, he took the same bus from his work as a department head for Mercedes-Benz to his self-built family home on Garibaldi Street in San Fernando, an industrial suburb of Buenos Aires. It was a short walk, beside an open field, from the bus stop to his front door.

Uncharacteristically, on Wednesday 11 May 1960, he was delayed, arriving half an hour later than usual. He was instantly suspicious of the Spanish-speaking stranger who sought to strike up a conversation, but before he could flee he was wrestled to the ground by three members of an eight-man Mossad snatch squad, and bundled into a car that took him to a safe house.

Operation Finale was nearing completion. The man known as Otto Eckmann when apprehended by American forces at the end of the war, Otto Henninger when he fled from a detention camp in January 1946, and Ricardo Klement when he sailed secretly from Italy to Argentina in 1950, admitted under interrogation he was Adolf Eichmann.

One of the architects of the Final Solution, initially identified through surveillance photographs by the shape of his ears, which appeared identical to those in his SS records, he gave his consent to standing trial in Israel. He was smuggled on to an El Al aircraft eleven days later, and flown to Tel Aviv.

The Mossad did not follow through on sightings of Josef Mengele in Brazil in the early 1960s, but Eichmann's capture had inescapable relevance for the Hungarian boys, since he planned and oversaw the extermination of 437,000 Hungarian Jews. His sixteen-week trial in Jerusalem, in the summer of 1961, convulsed a nation and shaped global public opinion.

Found guilty of fifteen charges relating to crimes against humanity in December of that year, he was hanged just after midnight on 1 June 1962, following an unsuccessful appeal for clemency to the Israeli President, who followed the advice of his Prime Minister, David Ben Gurion. Eichmann was cremated, and his ashes were thrown into the Mediterranean, outside Israel's territorial waters.

His trial was cathartic for Holocaust survivors who, until that moment, had been reluctant to share their stories because they feared they would not be believed. Reflections on a tragedy almost beyond human comprehension had been considered ill-mannered and inappropriate. Conventional wisdom, so often a contradiction in terms, decreed that ghosts should not be disturbed.

Accumulated evidence changed the attitudes of an emerging generation of Israelis who, until they processed the searing testimony of 112 witnesses during Eichmann's prosecution, found the Holocaust too fresh, too traumatic, too raw, almost too holy. It lifted the lid on the Nazis' industrialization of death, and the systemic, historically based persecution of an entire race. It was a collective national outpouring of pain, which helped also to counter the impression that millions of Jews had meekly surrendered to their fate.

Another pivotal element to greater understanding, Steven Spielberg's 1993 film *Schindler's List*, completed the process of social change. The Holocaust became an essential element of Jewish identity, an integral educational experience for the young, who visited death camps in Poland in great numbers to indelibly affirm the horrors of what had occurred there.

It continues to echo down the generations. The phrase 'the Banality of Evil', coined by Hannah Arendt in her 1963 book *Eichmann in Jerusalem*, has come to define the concept that purportedly normal human beings can be so emotionally desensitized they can do unspeakably evil things.

Eichmann's dispassionate defence that he was only following orders, since he was bound by an oath of loyalty to Hitler, contrasted with the febrile mood he created. Attendees lunged at him as he sat behind bulletproof glass. Hundreds sent death threats. Israel's Attorney General Gideon Hausner, who acted as chief prosecutor and was often in tears during proceedings, received around 10,000 letters, largely from survivors stating their case.

Our boys, now grown men, had their most significant day in that air-conditioned courtroom on Wednesday, 7 June 1961, through the trial's youngest witness, Yosef Zalman Kleinman. After surviving successive selections, he had escaped Auschwitz with his brother Solomon by creeping into a work detail destined for Kaufering, a sub-camp of Dachau.

Courtroom photographs from Session Number 68 depict Kleinman as a relatively tall, thin-faced man, with receding hair combed across a high forehead. He is wearing a lightweight summer suit, with the collar of a white shirt draped across its lapels. He had no time to prepare his testimony, since, as the first alternate witness, he only took the stand hurriedly, when the day's supposed star, the journalist Yechiel Dinur, fainted during his attempt to answer Hausner's first question.

Presiding judge Moshe Landau tempered Hausner's characteristic impatience by stressing that Kleinman could take as much time as he needed to share his experiences of Auschwitz-Birkenau. Kleinman concentrated on what he termed 'an unknown chapter in Holocaust history', the trials and tribulations of 'our unprecedented group' of Hungarian boys.

Unlike Nachum Hoch, who drilled down into descriptions of the gas chamber, from which he was released with the fifty other boys, when he gave evidence the following day, Kleinman focused on the scale and inhumanity of the selections overseen by Mengele. In particular, he electrified a global audience with his vivid extended summary of the football-pitch selection on Yom Kippur.

He had a powerful sense of recall and explained:

I saw more than the others because I was curious by nature. Everyone was busy surviving and they had neither time nor patience to be busy with anything else. But I believed that I would survive and the day would come that I would convey what I had seen.

I remember when we were in a transit camp in Italy. We sat there for hours, telling stories of our miracles and our salvation. We were young boys and each one felt that Hashem [God] saved him, and lifted him out of the inferno. That was the feeling. Hope and gratitude. That's what I've passed on.

That sense of mission consumed him when he settled in the nascent state of Israel after being interned in Cyprus. Kleinman was dispirited for several years, when he petitioned successive newspapers, who were not interested in the story of the Hungarian boys. But his zeal returned in 1960, when he heard that Yad Vashem was proactively interviewing survivors.

Although Kleinman was originally treated with indifference by a young female clerk at the fabled Holocaust memorial centre in

Jerusalem, a more senior figure, who quickly realized the unique nature of his contribution, chased after him as he left, and asked him to return to the office. 'Tell us all,' he implored him. 'We haven't heard this story yet.'

Kleinman was subsequently recommended to Eichmann's prosecutors by a family friend, the journalist Eli Rosenheim, who was convinced of the authenticity of his backstory by Yosef's brother Solomon. Rosenheim subsequently covered the trial for several news agencies as part of a 750-strong global media presence; newsreel footage of the day's events was flown to the United States each night.

Approached, once more, for his perspective by Yad Vashem in 1996, Kleinman concluded: 'In my opinion the trial was a great thing. It saw to it that all the world would know what had happened to us during the Holocaust. Without this trial, many things would never have become known, and history would have passed quietly over the whole matter.'

He created a furniture business with his brother but, in old age, Kleinman continued to be driven by the need to bear witness. He spoke to schools and military training groups because 'I experienced so many miracles. I had so much to tell.' He was in his mid-seventies when he involved his entire family in publishing the autobiographical book *Chilatzta Nafshi Mimaves* ('You Saved My Soul From Death').

His sixteen grandchildren were assigned individual inspirational aspects of his life to dwell upon, and to promote in the wider philosophical interests of acknowledging the spiritual significance of his salvation. He refused to wallow in self-pity, apportion blame, or indulge in excessive anger. In the words of his son Meir, interviewed before his father's death, aged ninety-one, in May 2021, 'his stories are of strength, not of misery'.

They retained their emotional power. Yosef spoke movingly

about his family's arrival in Auschwitz, humanizing their ordeal through memories of his father, who was dehydrated and disbelieving. Sensing his distress, Yosef found a small cup, discarded by the passenger of a previous train, and gathered rainwater so he could at least moisten his father's lips. It was his last act of fealty to the man who gave him life.

He cherished the contents of the backpack he carried with him during his extended attempt to immigrate to Israel. They included his striped cap and other items of prison clothing from Auschwitz-Birkenau, and the expensive shirt he was given by an American soldier soon after liberation. The GI had found that shirt in a wealthy man's house, along with the orange that Yosef craved.

Freedom pushed him into a vacuum of uncertainty. When Kleinman decided to head south, through Europe, on what he described as 'an enormous train with two large locomotives pulling it', he found that his sense of loss contrasted with the joy of others, whose new lives had firmer foundations.

'At every train station, Italians would alight from the train, returning to homes they hadn't seen in years,' he recalled. 'All the townspeople waited for this train with refreshments, here and there even a welcoming orchestra. Every station, people would get off, but for us Jews, no one was waiting for us. For me it was a twinge in my heart. It was a clear picture that we had no one.'

The subconscious impact of his survival was never far from the surface. He told his family he had 'wasted all my bravery in Auschwitz'. He did not allow Meir to ride a bicycle because he was fearful of accidents. He prevented his three children from getting driving licences for a similar reason.

'Still, we feel privileged to be part of his legacy,' reflected Kleinman's daughter, Tova Strassberg, in a 2011 interview for *Mishpacha*, a weekly magazine aimed at the Haredi community in Israel. 'He imbued us with rock-solid faith that Hashem [God] can pull you out of the blackest places.'

The lattice work of history bound him to apparent strangers. Some thirty years after the war he met, by chance, the boy who had helped him move a heavy wooden barrel into the kitchen at Auschwitz. Yosef had hidden in the barrel that night before sneaking into the Kaufering work detail, and had never forgotten his fleeting friend's act of selflessness.

Similarly, he retained a graphic mental image of the knowing look he received from the kapo who recognized he should not have been in the line waiting to leave. 'How did you manage to get here?' the kapo murmured. Yosef threw himself on his mercy, and, against all expectation, was told 'take your life'. Everyone in the cattle car was given a full loaf of bread, a sign they were about to embark on a long journey, away from the clutches of Mengele.

Speaking to Naftali, my collaborator, towards the end of his life, in August 2020, it was clear Yosef Kleinman understood the nature of his calling, and the impact of his legacy:

> I appear in many places, but I always end my story by saying, 'I will not die, because you can pass on to future generations that you have heard of Auschwitz, first hand.'

Mordechai Eldar was another survivor to be influenced by the Eichmann effect: 'Until the trial I couldn't hear about the Holocaust. I didn't want to hear about it. I can understand the scepticism of others because they weren't in our situation, and that is part of war in any case, but I won't forget that we were laughed at. The veterans are the heroes.'

He started to relate his Holocaust experiences in the 1980s, and prepared a pamphlet outlining his ordeal for his closest family members, including his aunts, uncles and cousins. This developed into a book, published in 2002. His one regret is that his brother Judah passed away before he could read it.

They had reunited in Holland in 1946: 'I walked in the door and there he was. We hugged and kissed and I told him about his two sisters, who had survived. He took me to his apartment, a beautiful place, and he hosted me for a day. He had worked as a slave labourer in a road-paving factory, and had been looking for us in lists of survivors.'

Throughout it all something was missing. He found himself craving the validation of relationships with the remnants of the group of boys who walked out of the gas chamber with him. He was, in effect, searching for a surrogate family and the comfort of a shared truth.

He met Mordechai Linder, a little-known member of the fifty-one, shortly before his death in Israel in 2011, by which time he had already struck up a firm friendship with Dugo Leitner. Unlike Nachum Hoch, who took time to respond when Mordechai tracked him down, Dugo was typically unrestrained in his enthusiasm.

Their first meeting was therapeutic, but uniquely intense: 'Dugo said "I'm coming to meet you on Friday, but I don't know exactly where you live, so I will wait outside for you." When I opened the door and saw him, my legs gave way. I was so excited I collapsed. He had to support me.'

The bond was instant. Years melted away in a moment and, from then on, they made a point of speaking at length every Friday. Even the silences that sometimes punctuated their conversations felt meaningful, since each understood the emotional power of an unspoken word.

Mordechai Eldar settled in Herzliya, an affluent city to the north of Tel Aviv, but during the holidays he would take Dugo and his daughter Zehava Leitner Kor, who has written a book about her father, aimed at the young adult market, to Megiddo, a kibbutz located in the Jezreel Valley in northern Israel.

Mordechai's plea for personal contact, recycled in a 2016 'Seeking Kin' column that led to a link to Hershel Herskovic, Chaim Schwimmer and Wolf Greenwald, was another element of his search for closure. He had once again returned to his home town, Campulung La Tisa, to piece together the jigsaw of his early life, but found perspective painful.

He was confronted by what could have been, had he stayed after the war, when he visited a Hungarian-speaking school friend, from the third grade: 'I saw how poor he was. The Jews were poorer than they were before the war. I took out a 100 Euro bill and gave it to him. He hugged and kissed me and told me "now I can go to the dentist".'

The greatest casualty of Mordechai's time in the death camps was his faith. He rejects the notion that the greatest gift a divine entity has given the world is humanity's gift of choice. He is unconvinced by the logic that in order to have the right to do good, human beings also must have the option to do heinous things:

You are either saying God does everything, or He does nothing. There's no proof, no justice. I'd rather say He doesn't exist and not call Him a murderer all the time, since to my mind He is the biggest killer. Fifty million people died because of one man, Hitler. Could He not have prevented it?

People talk about a merciful God. They may be saying such things from the heart, out of faith, but they may be hypocrites, just saying it so that people think they are a very nice person. Hitler was sure God had chosen the German people. He planned to eliminate all the Slavs after the Jews, leaving only as many as he needed to be slaves.

Who gave him that idea? God? Tell me how many righteous

people, those who believed, and lived devout lives, were killed. Millions. Why were they punished in that way? Why didn't He kill all the bad guys? Why didn't He kill Mengele? Why didn't He kill Hitler? If He is a God he knew fifty million would die, because He knows what will happen tomorrow.

I'll speak my mind. I'm done with what happened. If you want to know whether I was a good boy you'd have to ask my mother, or even my sister. Unfortunately they are already dead. My brother died, too. Why am I alive? Don't tell me I am here because God saved me.

Mordechai reasoned it was only a matter of time before he was exterminated in the camps. He accepted that, at some stage, his turn would come. That he was just seconds from death, but lived to tell the tale, still seems as surreal today as it did on Simchat Torah in 1944:

Why did I survive? I still ask myself that question. Surely I am not one of the righteous ones. If anyone was righteous, it was my father. He was our king, a perfect saint. My mother was righteous as well, in the most positive way. They were murdered.

I arrived in Israel as a Zionist, a real Zionist. That was the main lesson I learned from the Holocaust. The best thing I ever did was to serve in the military. I guarded the country. I did everything for my people, and hope I have helped. I live on a pension and have to think about every expense, but I still try to donate to military charities.

What turned my heart? The country, certainly, but I saw so many friends in the military die alongside me that it really shocked me. As a commander I had to eulogize the fallen, before their parents and family. I was given details, so I knew the right things to say. I cried at funerals. I cried as a soldier, even though soldiers are not supposed to cry.

Mordechai arrived in Israel on 27 June 1948, undeterred by a warning from his sister that 'we are in a hard war'. By 1 July he was enlisted in the Alexandroni Brigade, recruit 75683 in the War of Independence. Training at the Tal Hashomer base was rudimentary, to say the least.

He arrived with his detachment on a clear night, in a truck with its lights doused. It was a Yiddish-speaking unit so he spent two days learning the basics of the language with other newly arrived immigrants from Eastern Europe. They camped on the edge of a forest, and were given a one-hour lesson in how to fire a standard-issue Czech rifle.

This tuition basically amounted to 'lie down and shoot in the direction from which they are shooting at you'. Mordechai's hands were shaking, and he feared he would not be able to reload the rifle under the stresses of combat. His first taste of action had symbolic significance, because it was the first time Holocaust survivors had been sent into battle by the new nation state.

He slept for two or three hours before he was awoken just before dawn: 'I was excited, no doubt. I was thrilled by the thought of going to war, but I was also afraid. They put us in trucks. We didn't know where we were going but we knew we were going to war. We knew people were going to die. We were met by our platoon commander. I can't remember precisely what he told us, but it was something on the lines of "welcome to the battlefield".'

That commander was Ariel Sharon, a future Israeli Prime Minister. He was then known as Arik Scheinerman, and had established a reputation as a fearsome soldier during a series of ruthless attacks on Arab settlements, supply lines, military bases and strategically important bridges.

Sharon captured the essence of his brigade's activity in his 2001 autobiography, *Warrior*: 'We had become skilled at finding our way in the darkest nights and gradually we built up the strength and endurance these kind of operations required. Under the stress of constant combat we drew closer to one another and began to operate not just as a military unit but almost as a family. We were in combat almost every day. Ambushes and battles followed each other until they all seemed to run together.'

Mordechai was to be initially engaged in the first Battle of Latrun, an unsuccessful attempt to break through enemy lines, so the besieged Jewish community of Jerusalem could be relieved. It began on 25 May and continued until 18 July, by which time five separate Israeli assaults had been repulsed by the Jordanian Arab Legion.

Latrun was geographically important, since it was close to the junction of two major highways, between Jerusalem and Tel Aviv and Gaza and Ramallah. Sharon called it a 'horrible battle'; though some estimates of casualties were as high as 2,000, he recorded that his brigade had 139 men killed.

Mordechai sustained a severe head wound on his fourth day in action, when Sharon was also shot in the groin, foot and stomach. There were no ambulances, so they walked together to an evacuation centre in a local town. Of the eight men in the truck that subsequently took them to hospital, two died before they arrived.

Latrun stayed under Jordanian control until the Six Day War in June 1967, when Mordechai saw action with the 48th Division in the Sinai Peninsula. By then he was a senior soldier. After taking six weeks to recover from his wounds, he spent six months on an officer-training course.

As Sharon moved up the ranks rapidly, ending as a general in charge of the Southern Command of the Israel Defence Forces, Mordechai became an instructor, lecturing on the principles of leadership. He identified the ideal leader in simple terms as 'one other people want to follow'.

He retired after thirty years' military service in 1978 and though his erstwhile commander climbed the greasy pole of Israeli politics, becoming Prime Minister between 2001 and 2006, he has an enduring distaste for those who shamelessly seek public office. 'How do politicians help?' he asks, caustically.

He is distinctly unimpressed by current Prime Minister Benjamin Netanyahu, suggesting, 'I get the feeling he is willing to burn the country down for his own ends.' Mordechai is comfortable with the public aspects of his status as a senior survivor, and confident in expressing trenchant opinion, yet, as he approaches his ninety-sixth birthday, there are signs of vulnerability.

He described marriage as 'the dream of my life' yet he divorced. He dotes on his grandchildren and great-grandchildren, but worries about the ill-health of his sons Uri and Ofer, who are in their sixties. He cries occasionally when he has imaginary conversations with his mother, and asks himself, 'Why am I behaving like a child?'

Ultimately, Mordechai accepts that he will be defined as a survivor, although he insists his tattoo from Auschwitz 'does not do anything for me because I see it every day in the shower'. He celebrated when Mengele drowned in 1979 after suffering a stroke while swimming off São Paulo, but maintains 'I wouldn't have let him die so easily.'

He has seen such unimaginable suffering, and endured such profound loss, that it is unsurprising his concluding message of hope has the ring of an epitaph: 'I only wish that future generations will be smart enough to maintain unity and love. Let there be peace.'

FIFTEEN

Reflections

KINGS AND QUEENS, PRIME MINISTERS and Presidents, digni-
taries and diplomats, gathered with due solemnity at Auschwitz
on 27 January 2020, to mark the seventy-fifth anniversary of
the death camp's liberation. Dugo Leitner was seated prominently among 200 Holocaust survivors, who wore blue and white
scarves to signify their prison uniforms.

The mood of the ceremony, broadcast to 250 countries, had
been set by excerpts from the hidden diaries of Załmen Grad-
owski, a Polish Jew who died during the *Sonderkommando* revolt
of 7 October 1944. He spoke from beyond the grave, even though
he had been denied the dignity of a final resting place:

> Who was prepared to believe that millions of people were being
> seized for no reason whatever and led to slaughter by multiple
> means? Who was prepared to believe that a whole people was
> being led to destruction at the diabolical will of a gang of con-
> temptible criminals?
>
> Who was prepared to believe that a whole people was to be
> exterminated to compensate for failure in a struggle for power
> and supremacy? Who was prepared to believe that a people
> would blindly obey a law leading to death and destruction?

It may be that this, these very lines I am writing, will be the only witnesses to what was my life. But I will be happy if my writings reach you, free citizen of the world. Perhaps a spark of my inner fire will ignite in you, and you will fulfill at least a part of our life's desire: you shall avenge, avenge our deaths.

Dugo's vengeance came in the form of a long life and relentless retelling of his story. He found the ceremony respectful and heartfelt, but too formal and formulaic. It lacked soul, and turned the ninety-year-old man into the rebellious nine-year-old he had once been. Defying protocol in a moment of silence, he screamed: 'Am Yisrael Chai.' Directly translated as 'The People of Israel Live', it summarized his spirit of resilience.

Within three days the world would be plunged into an unprecedented crisis, when a global public-health emergency was declared due to the emergence of the Covid-19 virus. Many survivors, vulnerable because of their age and declining health, would become victims of the pandemic. Only fifty-six were able to attend the eightieth-anniversary commemorations on 27 January 2025, during which they assembled at the so-called Death Gate at Auschwitz-Birkenau.

Their voices are being steadily silenced. According to official data, 10 per cent of Holocaust survivors in Israel passed away in the year following national Remembrance Day in April 2024. This sobering statistic included Josef Lewkowicz, a personal inspiration, who died on Boxing Day, aged ninety-eight.

Dugo Leitner was a national institution when he passed away on 27 July 2023. His annual ritual, of eating falafel on the anniversary of the start of the death march from Auschwitz-Birkenau, is still marked all around the world. It honours the memory of his mother, and of countless, nameless victims.

His sense of loss was evocative:

After the war we learned three things very quickly: almost no one wanted to hear our stories and of those that did, most did not believe what we told them. Even if someone listened with a sympathetic ear, there was no way that they could understand what they heard.

Having food to eat was a miracle. And though we didn't talk we remembered. All the time. I held close to myself the memory of those who fell by the way on the death marches. One moment marching beside me, the next moment their place taken by a puff of snow swirling in the empty space where once scuffled along a breathing Jew.

I decided to have my own memorial day for those lost Jewish souls. I fixed the date to January 18th. That would be the day, and on that day I would eat. I would eat for them and for myself until I could eat no more.

With his chiselled features, open face and firm gaze, Dugo looked the part of a military veteran, and told his war stories with relish. He quoted extensively from the Psalms to give a philosophical context to his survival, both as a concentration-camp inmate and a front-line soldier.

In Auschwitz, inspired by his father, he recited Psalm 23:

The Lord is my shepherd, I lack nothing. He makes me lie down in green pastures, he leads me beside quiet waters, he refreshes my soul. He guides me along the right paths for his name's sake. Even though I walk through the valley of the shadow of death I will fear no evil, for you are with me; your rod and your staff, they comfort me.

He recited Psalm 50 – 'And call upon me in the day of trouble: I will deliver thee, and thou shalt glorify me' – during a battle in the so-called War of Attrition in March 1970. He was in command of an outpost on the Sinai Peninsula when it was attacked by Egyptian forces determined to reclaim land lost in the Six Day War, three years earlier.

Heavily outnumbered by 'tens of dozens of terrorists', his ten-man platoon fought from behind sandbanks. Two attackers were killed when they triggered a booby-trap at the entrance, which consisted of a tripwire hidden in a crop of watermelons, but Dugo sensed his platoon was in danger of being overrun.

'It felt like that station was at the end of the world,' he remembered. The firefight was raging when a grenade, thrown over the protective earthworks, landed among them but failed to go off. Dugo took it as a sign of divine providence, and continually shouted the psalm as the enemy were repulsed. It took him back to his moment of salvation in the death camp.

'A true story,' he said:

The world is always looking for what is most convenient. It may be that what is more convenient for some is not being religious, so it was important for us to keep the faith. Judaism is in my blood. It is inside; it grows with me. I can't run away from it, and nor do I want to run away from it. It's wonderful stuff.

What is a Jew? To me, loving the land of Israel is the first thing. It is our home. I would love it if others showed us a bit more love. I love people. I have always had good friends. Ask any child around here, 'Who is Dugo?' and they will know. I say to each of them a kind word. I give them a warm smile.

That comes from my education, in a warm Jewish home. My father was a righteous man, an amazing, very, very strong man. He taught me to have simple pleasures. Have you seen my grandchildren and great-grandchildren? They're my friends. All of them. I am bewitched by them. I tell you, the young give you power.

Families are fundamental to survivors. Those destroyed during the Holocaust linger in the memory, and speak to those rebuilt, as tangible evidence of the triumph of hope and indomitability.

The emotional impact was written across Eva 'Bobby' Neumann's face when she showed off a photograph of her extended family. It was her concession to a basic contradiction. She might feel indifferent to the symbolism of the Auschwitz tattoo on her arm, and consider the death camp, in its current form, as 'a tourist attraction' that diminishes the brutal realities she experienced there, but that photograph, the sort that can be found in countless homes, meant something uniquely special:

This is quite something. These are all my children, grandchildren and great-grandchildren. When I hold this photograph in my hand I should feel something, but I cannot let it all out. The feelings are there, but they are too big, so you suppress them. I can't really explain that, but I do remember my father's love of children.

Why isn't he here? He would have had a lot of *nachas* [a Hebrew term referring to pride in the achievements of others]. I pretended he and my mother would come back, after I left Auschwitz. I looked everywhere for them, but you only kid yourself. The main thing is I wanted to please them. I wanted to be like them.

Eventually, time passes. You accept things as they are. My parents would not have wanted me to dwell on the bad things, and I am who I am because of them. You have to go forward, and if you want to go forward, you think of the nice things, the *simcha* [joy or happiness] in the family.

My father was very strict, and very loving. I still have that image in my head of him more or less begging me to survive. You need willpower to achieve anything you want to do, but were the angels watching over me? I don't know, but I did say that Hashem [God] must have had a hand in it.

When you are in that sort of situation, everybody needs somebody. If you have run out of everybody, He is always there. I never questioned that, because that belief was what we always had, and that is what we will always have. It is God's decision, what He wants to do with me. I have to accept that, and make the best of it.

Chaim Schwimmer was a no-nonsense sort, for whom faith was a fundamental part of life, rather than a spiritual embellishment. It defined who he was, how he behaved, why he remained steadfast.

He rose each morning at 5 a.m., read the Psalms, and prayed for two hours before breakfast. He then prayed for another two hours, between 10 a.m. and midday. It was only then that he felt able to prioritize his work, running a large and successful paper-products business. He worked for five hours, between 1 and 6 p.m., up until his late eighties.

'Do you think that Auschwitz is the only place you need faith?' he asked. 'Our success in life comes from God. People ask me what it means to be a survivor. If I have any message it is that you should never lose hope, no matter how bad the situation you find yourself in. I always trusted in the Shepherd. He did okay.'

Avigdor Neumann accepts the influence of a higher power 'because I was led to death and was saved. If you look, you can see the finger of God moving.' But his role, as an ambassador for Israeli Spirit, the country's largest civil-advocacy centre, is pro-active, telling and, above all, timely.

At the age of ninety-four he marked Holocaust Memorial Day in 2025 by featuring in a video alongside three children, fifteen-year-old Dafna Elyakim, twelve-year-old Eitan Yahalomi and eight-year-old Ella Elyakim, who were freed from Hamas captivity after they were taken hostage on 7 October 2023.

Their message, shared in Hebrew, English, Russian, German, Romanian, Polish and Yiddish, seeks to expose the rise of modern denialism, and its historic link to the Holocaust. It is intense and moving, because of the horrors perpetrated around the children when their homes were stormed.

Eitan's family sought refuge in the safe room of their home in Nir Oz, when the kibbutz came under sustained rocket fire. The door would not lock, so his father Ohad, a French-Israeli nature guide, stood guard in front of it with a pistol. He was wounded in a firefight, captured, and strapped on to two motorcycles with his wife Batsheva and three children.

Batsheva managed to escape with her two daughters during a chaotic journey to Gaza, but Eitan was held in a tunnel for fifty-two days until his release was negotiated during a fragile truce. Ohad was declared dead in January 2024 in a video released by a Hamas-aligned group, but his body was not returned until 27 February 2025, as part of a hostage-prisoner exchange.

He was forty-nine. During his funeral on 5 March, his widow addressed mourners, breaking down periodically. She was helped through her eulogy by relatives, who held her shoulders to prevent her collapsing: 'Sixteen years of joy and light, and the light has now gone out. How do I move forward without you? Where am I going? On October 7th you went out to protect us. This is your essence, to protect your family, where everyone is connected to each other with strong bonds of love.'

Dafna and Ella Elyakim also lost their father, who was last seen alive in a video taken on the morning of 7 October, being hustled along by Hamas fighters at gunpoint despite suffering a severe leg wound. They were being held hostage in Gaza when his body was discovered ten days later, in the ruins of their kibbutz, Nahal Oz. He was forty-six.

The courage that the three children required to take part in the campaign with Avigdor Neumann is extraordinary. The video begins with a ping of a mobile phone. They are confronted by a social-media influencer, claiming that the atrocities committed by Hamas are an invention.

The camera pans along from the children, who are understandably self-conscious, to Avigdor, who has the sleeve of his grey sweater rolled up to reveal his Auschwitz tattoo. 'They can deny it all they want,' he says, pointing to it, 'but some things cannot be erased.' The video ends on the campaign slogan: 'Never Again Is Now.'

It is sobering to realize that Dafna is two years older than Avigdor when he was transported to Auschwitz-Birkenau. After the war he left school, 'when I decided I was a genius', and was seventeen and a half when he volunteered for the Israel Defence Forces, soon after it was formed in May 1948.

'In the Holocaust we had no power to maintain ourselves,' he reasoned:

> The Germans murdered six million Jews, including a million and a half children, just because they were Jews. No other reason. But we had no organized protective force, no means, no nothing. Now we have a country, a framework.
>
> When I first wore the uniform, when I first had a rifle in my hand, it transcended everything. It is impossible to explain that we got so far in '48. There were 600,000 Jews, five tank armies and countless enemies lined up against us. We won. The state exists on a day-to-day basis, like we did in the camps.
>
> I have been through it all, physical suffering, mental suffering,

torture, death. Since Auschwitz, I have had no parents. I had no home, no one to turn to. I have been through wars. I was wounded. Yet I found the courage not to despair. We stood up, and established a country here.

On the one hand you participate, you live the grief of others, but you still live. If you live, you rejoice. That does not impair their sadness, or their memories. Your childhood passes before you all the time. You are reminded of your mum, your dad, those you have lost, but despite everything I am still here and living a normal life. I have raised a family.

To this day I do not understand why I was saved, but my fate was imposed on me. It is not in my hands. I know I'm at that age, thanks to God, where not so many people are alive. No one wants to die, but I do not have the fear of leaving. What do I believe? I believe He is holding me here because I'm telling the story of the last generation to the new generation.

History is an echo chamber that can be soothing or discordant, according to mood or timing. Hershel Herskovic's son, David, is an accomplished blogger who offers a revealing perspective on what it is like to be brought up by a survivor, and the emotional aftershocks the Holocaust continues to create:

When we were kids, and I don't think it's much different now in our communities, Holocaust education was non-existent. We knew the details from our parents and from grandparents, the few who had them, but it was all one big muddle. I knew my father had been in Auschwitz and contracted typhus later. The stories he told were of stealing food, making a complaint to Mengele, being deselected from the gas chamber.

We of course knew the six million number but the rest was a blur. Six million flies off the tongue too easily and we had no geography or context. My father spoke of the Munkacs ghetto and we knew of ghettos in the Middle Ages, so what exactly was different? We heard of Warsaw but not of Kovno or other ghettos, while Babi Yar was a foreign word.

But still we breathed the Holocaust in our blood because it was everywhere around us. The guy who saw his parents being shot. The kitchen manager in our yeshiva who would only hand out yesterday's bread. When challenged, he would retort, 'In Auschwitz we had not even this.'

The parents who wouldn't talk to their children about their experiences. The adult conversations we couldn't follow. The sobbing at Yizkor [the Jewish Memorial Service recited four times a year]. The list of murdered brothers and sisters in books and on walls.

Missing was the emotional trauma which the survivors couldn't and wouldn't speak of because it was so raw and because the world wasn't ready to listen. Missing also was our own trauma of being raised by that generation of parents, family, teachers and *shul* members These are difficult subjects with no simple or single answer.

David's father still likes to sing and dance. Hershel Herskovic drinks vodka on the Sabbath, and makes the toast '*L'chaim*' ('To life') with a tot of whisky. He tries to walk regularly 'because otherwise my bones will dry up'. He refuses to succumb to sadness 'because when I'm unhappy I feel those enemies who wanted to kill me would be very pleased'. He is slowing down, but he is at peace:

What's the point of being unhappy? I don't gain anything from it. Basically I know this is not going to last. I'm going to disappear so I don't take life so seriously in that aspect. I've lived,

I've done this and that, and I try to learn from my own contemplation. I see what goes on in the world.

I mean, I can see from my flesh that God has created me. I can move my fingers. I can talk. I can hear. I can think. But when a person gets old, they get weaker. Why has God made us that way? I can't answer that question. We need more energy when we are old, but He takes it away and gives it to others.

We live in a mysterious world which no one really understands. I have my sad days but I am not sad because of what is happening in the world around me, because I can't do anything about it. I can't contribute to it, and I can't dismiss it, so why should I be sad about it?

My faith has not been shaken. Human existence is an enigma in any case. People who have everything in life have nothing in the end, because life vanishes. No one knows what the next day brings. Remember that after this life there will be another life. God is the be all and end all. He lifts us up to elevated levels.

Ultimately, the fifty-one boys who walked out of that gas chamber on Simchat Torah, 1944, are punctuation marks in a story with innumerable twists and turns. To prove the point, the last of countless interviews conducted for this book, in late May 2025, threw up an intriguing probability, and a very human form of redemption.

Lifshe Silver, at home in Montreal, spoke passionately about her search for information about her late father. Suddenly, from a fleeting, strangely heroic figure in our story, Toivie Gruen, or Tobias Green, as he would be known when he made a new life in Canada, became flesh and blood, a man of principle and boldness.

Lifshe was fifteen when he died, of a massive heart attack, in 1986. He was a loving, ultra-protective father, who would guide his children down a playground slide, rather than allowing them to descend freely, to guard against injury. He never spoke of his remarkable defiance of Josef Mengele, which allowed him to live through the football-pitch selection in Auschwitz-Birkenau.

He was twelve at the time, and would only grow tall during adolescence. In later life, he was typically reticent about the scar on his forehead, which the family believed was a result of a wartime misadventure. Logically, Lifshe reasoned, it linked to him headbutting the piece of wood Mengele had attached to the goalframe, in a desperate attempt to survive.

She contacted Naftali after seeing a still image in his documentary on Josef Lewkowicz. It depicted a boy being stretchered into an ambulance after liberation from an unnamed death camp. Filthy, emaciated and scarred, he looked much older than Toivie would have been at the time, but it bore a striking resemblance to him.

He was one of the last children to be deported by the Hungarian authorities to Auschwitz-Birkenau, as one of 7,800 Jews herded into a makeshift ghetto in the Bungăr forest, an ancient plantation of beech trees on the edge of Dej, which had been under Romanian control until 1940.

Conditions were horrific; deportees were beaten, tortured and starved. Though no passenger details have survived, it is highly likely that Toivie was in one of two freight trains, which left on 6 and 8 June 1944. Around 7,000 of those transported from the forest were exterminated on arrival at Auschwitz.

Toivie's mother and four of his five siblings were among those taken immediately to the gas chamber. His father, a respected figure in his community due to his role as a shochet, a ritual slaughterer of cattle and poultry, survived the initial selection, but was killed when he became too weak to work.

Tragically, Toivie's surviving sister, who worked in the kitchens at Auschwitz, died when the Third Reich was collapsing. She was taken from the camp, as part of a consignment of women hurriedly incarcerated in a convoy of prison ships. Three, the ocean liner SS *Cap Arcona*, and its support vessels, *Deutschland* and *Thielbek*, were sunk in the western Baltic Sea in May 1945. More than 7,000 were killed, one of the largest maritime losses of life in the war.

Toivie lived on his wits. One of the few things he shared with his son Yaakov before he passed away was his inherent mistrust of the Nazis. On the death march from Auschwitz, he urged those around him not to believe the promises of the SS, that they were being taken to comfortable barracks, where they would be fed, showered and clothed.

He was one of around seventy-five inmates who took the risk of refusing to follow them. Remarkably, they were not murdered on the spot; instead they were left to fend for themselves. Those who took the blandishments of the SS at face value were never seen again.

Toivie was in hospital for six months at the end of the war, recovering his strength. He was moved to a Displaced Persons camp, and then joined Yeshiva Meor Hagolah, a rabbinical college established in Rome by a Lithuanian Rabbi, Ephraim Oshry, for Orthodox boys from Czechoslovakia, Hungary, Lithuania, Poland and Romania.

In October 1951 he sailed, tourist class, from Italy to Halifax, Nova Scotia, as part of an orphans' resettlement programme sponsored by the Canadian government. He ensured that several of his first cousins, all women similarly bereaved, were able to accompany him, in making a fresh start.

He put down roots in Montreal, learned English, changed his name, and put himself through college, obtaining a Master's degree in finance before setting himself up as a financial adviser. In 1966 he married Martha Winter, whose father Moshe had been taken from a labour camp to Auschwitz.

His last act, while he waited for his cattle car to be linked up, was to scribble a note to his wife, which he threw on to the tracks. Against all odds, she received it, and eventually moved with her family to New York, after communist officials in post-war Budapest were bribed to issue exit visas.

Toivie, meanwhile, added a layer to his strict Hasidic religious traditions, by also becoming a fervent Zionist, donating an ambulance to Israel. 'We shouldn't have to run,' he told his children, in a rare moment of candour. 'It means so much that we, as Jews, should have our own country.'

His daughter Lifshe chuckled as she admitted she shares his habit of eating leftover food. Such abhorrence of waste, common among Holocaust survivors, was a direct result of the privations he suffered as a boy.

'Though we were too young to get too many answers, Auschwitz was in his blood,' she explained. 'He had such resilience. Whenever life had negative connotations he would remind us of the advantages we were born with. No matter what happened, he moved on with a smile. He was grateful. Nothing could be worse than Auschwitz.'

Toivie got to know Josef Lewkowicz, but he suffered from a heart condition; the response to his death provided several clues about his character. Several ultra-orthodox Jews from the Hasidic community in Williamsburg, Brooklyn, travelled to Montreal to pay their respects to the family during *shiva*, the seven-day mourning period that follows burial.

They revealed they knew Toivie from Auschwitz, and described him as a wily, courageous and caring boy, who smuggled cigarettes and exchanged them for food, which he shared with those around him. He was remembered for his big smile and his constant entreaty that 'We must never give up. We have to fight back.'

Though not conclusive, his funeral provided compelling

evidence that he was, in fact, one of the fifty-one boys released from the gas chamber. Lifshe remembers the Rabbi talking, during the service, about her father being reprieved; Toivie's cousin related that he would give thanks, every Simchat Torah, for the miracle of his survival.

When Lifshe tracked the Rabbi down, more than a decade later, his memory had dimmed due to dementia, but she, too, is convinced that her father was saved in uniquely dramatic circumstances. 'Pain makes you feel alive,' he once told her, as he recovered from a broken leg.

Toivie used his pain as a motivation, to take his second chance of life. He, and fifty others, were given a form of immortality. On that rainy October day in 1944, they became forever young.

AFTERWORD

The Things We Carry

By Naftali Schiff

THIS BOOK BEGAN WITH A mystery. How could it be that fifty-one teenage boys, young Hungarian Jews who were stripped naked and marched into the gas chambers of Auschwitz-Birkenau on Simchat Torah, October 1944, walked out alive? How could such a miracle occur in a place designed for death, where mercy was banished, and where so few stories ended in anything but silence? We have followed these boys through their narrow escape, their survival, and the lives they rebuilt with courage and faith. We have heard their voices, fragile and fierce, echoing across the years.

Now, as we bring this story to a close, I would like to share with you what this journey has come to mean to me. This is so much more than a historical account, it is a personal mission. During the years of research that led up to the writing of this book, these boys became my teachers, my fathers, my brothers, my constant and conscious reminders. The weight of their story is something I carry with me every day, quite literally.

My pockets are always too full, not with coins or keys, but with small, unassuming objects. Some stones, a few tags, even a small game. To anyone else, they might look like trinkets, but to me they are sacred cargo. Memory, mission, identity, all compressed into palm-sized weight. Each object tugs at my conscience. They whisper to me when the world is too noisy. Don't forget, don't drift, and don't lose sight of what's really important.

Little stones I picked up from Auschwitz-Birkenau. I hesitated at first. Was it right to disturb the ground of that sacred, blood-soaked place? But something deeper compelled me to take a reminder from the end of the railway tracks. Stones that bear witness, stones that felt the screams of separation and uncertainty, absorbed the smoke bellowing out of the crematoria. I carry them with me – not just for myself, but also for those who can no longer.

There are other stones too, from Be'eri and Kfar Aza, two kibbutzim in southern Israel where Jewish families lived ordinary lives with extraordinary hope, until 7 October 2023, when evil once again reared its ugly head on the same Jewish date – Simchat Torah – where a festive day was transformed into a day of pain, suffering and mourning. The symbolism is crushing. And so the stones sit together in my pocket. Cries of Jewish pain, torment and incredulity across time and space. Palpable reminders that history is not behind us, it is still unfolding as our story is still being written and that as a believing Jew, I maintain that the author of our story is using His guiding hand every step of the way. I simply cannot accept that our history or destiny is random.

That is why I feel so connected to the account of the fifty-one boys because what happened on Simchat Torah in 1944 defies human comprehension. The boys had already been marked for death. The Zyklon B was prepared. The crematorium was primed. The doors had begun to close. Their final moments on this earth, just minutes away.

At the very last moment they were pulled out – from death to life.

Fifty-one Jewish boys, aged thirteen to seventeen, were marched to unload potatoes, to a surreal dance of Simchat Torah in Auschwitz, instead of being murdered. No explanation was given. Perhaps it was confusion. Perhaps coincidence. Perhaps compassion from an unlikely German. But every survivor I spoke to over two decades would tell you it was something else. It was a *neis*, a miracle.

They had been written off, literally. Their names crossed out in ledgers. Their block marked '*gestorben*' – 'dead'. But they were not dead. They became the only known group of Jews to walk out of a Nazi gas chamber alive.

Dugo Leitner later recalled thinking, 'We do not die . . . yet.' It was a terrifying pause, not a deliverance, not a celebration. Just a fragile moment suspended between horror and survival.

The war was not over. Their suffering had not ended. These boys, skeletal, shoeless, starved, still had to survive the next months – the selections, the beatings, the death marches. One would go blind. Some would bury their friends. Some would never speak of it again. But all of them carried something profound: a stubborn refusal to give up.

The Jewish people have been called *am k'shei oref*, a stiff-necked nation. It was not necessarily a compliment. But perhaps it was always a necessity. Only a stiff-necked people could continue to believe in God after Auschwitz. Only a people this impossibly stubborn could see their loved ones consumed by fire and yet survive to raise families, build schools, dance again with a Torah scroll.

Only a stiff-necked people could transform pain into purpose.

This book is not just history. It is Torah – not in the literal sense of the Five Books of Moses, but in the deeper Jewish sense of living wisdom and moral instruction. A Torah not written in ink, but in agony. A Torah of tears, defiance and unimaginable dignity.

I have sat with these men, the boys who survived. Some blind, some fragile, some sharp as ever. I have held their hands, heard their voices tremble, seen them pause mid-sentence as memory overwhelmed language.

As a human, a parent, a teacher, a Rabbi, in seeking out to interview Holocaust survivors I searched for the human authenticity that textbooks cannot impart, that AI cannot generate. And what did I learn?

That human resilience is not a theory. It is a heartbeat. That *Emunah* [faith] does not mean that we always have the answers, it means refusing to surrender to the questions and remaining faithful even in the darkest of times. That even in Auschwitz, even in the gas chamber, the Jewish soul could flicker defiantly against the winds of death.

Even in their silence, these men are my greatest teachers.

Beside the stones are other things that I always carry with me. A silver cigarette case that my grandfather received when he was honourably discharged from the British Army after World War I. A Jew in uniform, fighting for a country that never quite knew if it wanted him.

There's my father's army dog tag. Stamped into the material: 'Schiff – Jew'. No euphemism. Just clarity.

There's my own diskit, my Israeli army ID. A badge of a Jew proudly serving the sovereign State of Israel, standing on Jewish soil, defending our future.

A hostage tag, for those still captive. A small Tehillim, a Book of Psalms to pray for them and those who are fighting for their freedom, and for decency and goodness to prevail all over.

And, believe it or not, a few tiddlywinks. A child's idle game, tucked in with all this weight. A perhaps not so light-hearted reminder that we are not here merely to play tiddlywinks, that life is not child's play, that ensuring a worthy future is not a game.

These are my personal *simanim*, my cues. They are not relics. They are road signs. They remind me each day, what will you do with this story? What will you carry forward?

Too often we treat history as a museum. Dusty, tragic, respectfully distant. But Judaism has never been about nostalgia, it is about transmission and a sacred responsibility to learn the lessons of the past in order to inform the future.

These fifty-one boys did not ask to be remembered. But from my conversations with them, it's clear to me that they want us to share their burden, to carry their pain, and at the same time draw strength from courage. Rather than being dismissible, we can choose to be inspired by their questions, their will to live, and their uncomplicated faith.

This book records the historical details, the names, the faces, the dates and the locations.

But that is not enough.

Their story only lives if it moves us to act, to teach, to build, to love, to fight against hatred, to hold our faith with integrity, to raise children who know who they are, who care about others.

If we remember, we survive. If we carry forward, we thrive.

That this happened on Simchat Torah, the day we complete the yearly cycle of Torah reading, the day we dance with the Torah, is no accident. The Nazis knew the Jewish calendar. They selected our sacred days on purpose. Playing God, Mengele selected innocents to live or die by the cynical flick of his wrist and finger. They tried to turn our joy into our destruction. But what they didn't realize, what they could never grasp, is that Simchat Torah, whilst marking the end, also signals a new beginning each year; that the dancing circle of Simchat Torah can never be curtailed, its inner light never extinguished. Because we do not dance with the Torah only in joy. We dance even in darkness.

These boys, saved on Simchat Torah, became our living Torah scrolls. Worn, battered, but holy. Their lives were scrolls. Their survival, a sanctification of God's name.

And today, when I see their grandchildren, great-grandchildren, dancing with the Torah, I realize the Nazis lost far more than a war. They lost the battle for meaning.

So what do we do now?

We carry forward.

We teach. We remember. We resist the world's forgetfulness and moral laziness. We speak the names of the boys. We tell their story not as a relic, but as a mirror. Who would I have been? Would I have stood up? Would I have shared my meagre food rations? Would I have helped smuggle a cousin into the potato line?

We ask not only what happened to them. We ask what they would want from us.

Would they want us to recite memorial prayers or light a solitary candle and then go back to business as usual?

Or would they want us to live lives of purpose, of spiritual depth, of courage?

Would they want us to remember how they survived? Or to continue what they lived for?

This book began as a search. I didn't set out to write it. I stumbled into it, whispered from the lips of a survivor who wasn't sure if anyone cared anymore.

But over the years, I found them, one by one. And each time, I felt I was meeting not a ghost, but a guardian.

They weren't just telling me what happened.

They were asking me, pleading with me, not to let it end with them.

So here I am.

Here we are.

And here you are, Jew and Gentile alike, holding this, our story, in your hands.

It is no longer theirs.

It is now yours.

Because our story must go on.

So yes, my pockets are full.

Full of stones and stories. Of faith and fear. Of memory and mission.

But so is my heart.

And I know exactly why I carry these things.

Not because our story ended.

But because it must go on.

So now our story is in your hands. Not just to be read, but to be held, carried and lived. These boys were not just saved from death, they were entrusted with life, with legacy, with the fire of Jewish continuity; with the passion to build a better world. And now, that trust has passed to us.

We are the next chapter. Let us carry it with courage. Let us honour it with action. Let us build a world that justifies their survival. Because their story is no longer theirs alone. It is our story; it is their legacy and it is our inheritance. It is our duty to ensure it never, ever fades.

Acknowledgements

The families of the boys who became husbands, fathers, grand-fathers and great-grandfathers, and pressed on to build homes, communities and lives despite the unimaginable trauma they carried with them, in many cases until their dying day, are part of this miracle.

The relatives owe their existence to the survival of the fifty-one, and we thank them for giving us an insight into the personalities and experiences of their closest kin. In particular, we owe a debt of gratitude to David Herskovic, Hershel's son, and Lifshe Silver, Toivie Gruen's daughter. We hope we have succeeded in our overarching aim, of doing justice to the indomitability of those survivors who have shared their lives with us, despite the pain inherent in doing so.

We are conscious of living in an age of denial and disinformation. In that context, we wish to amplify our respect and admiration for those outlets which articulate and authenticate the eternal truths of the Holocaust. We are thankful for the corroborative contributions of Yad Vashem, the World Holocaust Remembrance Centre in Jerusalem, and the United States Holocaust Memorial Museum in Washington.

We have drawn on the historical and educational resources of the Auschwitz-Birkenau Memorial and Museum in Poland. Its social-media channels are inspirational, in providing constant reality checks, through the publication of photographs and case studies of those who were murdered in the camp.

Other outlets, such as the World Jewish Congress, JewishGen, Steven Spielberg's Survivors of the Shoah Visual History Foundation and the Testimony Theatre in Israel, proved invaluable. We are in the debt of the Jewish Telegraphic Agency, whose 'Seeking Kin' article by Hillel Kuttler helped lead us to Mordechai Eldar, the second living survivor of the fifty-one.

Our research has involved a range of modern media sources. They are too numerous to mention individually, but *Mishpacha* magazine and Ehud Neor's blog in *The Times of Israel* proved especially informative. Closer to home, we are indebted to filmmaker Jonathan Kalmus, whose meticulous attention to detail and cataloguing of survivor testimony has been of fundamental importance to the project.

Several of the characters within this book published their own books. Historian Esther Farbstein's *The Forgotten Memoirs*, augmented by an illuminating interview with Naftali in Israel, contributed immensely to our work. Her voluminous knowledge and research gave us confidence we were on the right trail.

The dedication of Tzvi Sperber, Naftali's co-founder and partner in JRoots, to passing on the legacy of survivors through journeys to the camps and sites in Poland knows no boundaries. We have been helped enormously by Debra Sobel, Ari Kayser and the JF media team, and by the diligence of Laura Crespi and Sorana Howard.

Educators of the stature of Rabbi Raphy Garson, Zak Jeffay and Rabbi Jonny Roodyn, Naftali's daily study partner, have enabled us to double-check the facts and context of our story. Their wisdom, and conscientious application of their knowledge of the subject, has been greatly appreciated.

We are equally fortunate in having Henry Vines as our empathetic and far-sighted editor and publisher. We thank him and his team at Transworld, which includes Richard Mason, Viv

Thompson, Phil Lord, Cat Hillerton and KC Onuorah, for sharing and supporting our vision for this project.

Rory Scarfe, our perceptive literary representative, who acts as Managing Director, Client Management, at The Blair Partnership, has been an invaluable source of advice. We thank Neil Blair for his personal encouragement and unswerving commitment to ensuring the legacy of survivors of the Holocaust is passed on to future generations.

A project of this scale and intensity is an immersive procedure, so it is appropriate that we end this section by paying tribute to our families. Michael would be lost without his wife Lynn, who has become used to his thousand-yard stare during the writing process. Naftali's wife Elena has heard the accounts of survivors so many times, yet continues to stand by his determination to share them with everyone he meets.

Our grandchildren are blessings, as are our children, who have become used to the rhythms and motivations of our lives. They understand that what we do is beyond vocational, whether that is Michael writing in the early hours or survivors attending Schiff family weddings over the last twenty-five years. We are privileged to touch history.

Michael Calvin and Naftali Schiff, June 2025

Picture Acknowledgements

Every effort has been made to contact copyright holders. Any who have not been acknowledged here are invited to get in touch with the publishers.

page 1: Courtesy of Eva 'Bobby' Neumann, top left; courtesy of Zehava (Leitner) Kor, top right; Isaac Schwimmer/Jewish Telegraphic Agency, bottom left; courtesy of the family of Yaakov Yosef Weiss, bottom right.

page 2: Ghetto Fighters' House Museum Archive.

page 3: Yad Vashem, top, bottom; Galerie Bilderwelt/Getty Images, middle.

page 4: Courtesy of Eva 'Bobby' Neumann, top; David Clapp/Getty Images, middle; Bundesarchiv Federal Archives, bottom.

page 5: United States Holocaust Memorial Museum, top; CBD/Alamy, middle; Yad Vashem, bottom left, bottom right.

page 6: United States Holocaust Memorial Museum, top; Institute of National Remembrance, middle left; Victor Lochon/Getty Images, middle right; Sueddeutsche Zeitung/Alamy, bottom.

page 7: Bundesarchiv Federal Archives, top; Mark Chrzanowski/United States Holocaust Memorial Museum, middle; The National WWII Museum, bottom.

page 8: Courtesy of Naftali Schiff.

ABOUT THE AUTHORS

Michael Calvin is an award-winning writer and *Sunday Times* bestselling author, whose books have been hailed for their insight and influence. He has collaborated with such celebrated sportsmen as Sir Alastair Cook, Dylan Hartley and Gareth Thomas, and is the only writer to win the British Sports Book of the Year award in successive years. Most recently, and in a wider context, he has collaborated on critically acclaimed autobiographies of Toby Gutteridge, a quadriplegic former Special Forces soldier, and of Josef Lewkowicz, a Holocaust survivor and Nazi hunter.

Rabbi Naftali Schiff is a leading social entrepreneur and innovator who has conceived and built numerous successful educational organizations working to ensure vibrant Jewish futures. He is also a globally renowned collator of the testimonies of Holocaust survivors and a documentary film maker.

He has personally interviewed over two hundred Holocaust survivors to ensure their testimonies, legacy and values are preserved for future generations. An indefatigable font of creativity, Naftali is committed to constantly identifying new pathways and vehicles in order to inspire today's younger generation.